## PERSONAL INFORMATION

Coach Name: _____

Email Address: _____

## SCHOOL INFORMATION

School: _____

School Address: _____

School Phone Number: _____

Room Number: _____

# simply INSTRUCTIONAL COACHING planner

## Nicole S. Turner

Solution Tree | Press  a division of Solution Tree

555 North Morton Street
Bloomington, IN 47404
800.733.6786 (toll free) / 812.336.7700
FAX: 812.336.7790

email: info@SolutionTree.com
SolutionTree.com

Visit **go.SolutionTree.com/instruction** to download the free reproducibles in this book.

Printed in the United States of America

ISBN: 978-1-960574-01-5

**Solution Tree**
Jeffrey C. Jones, CEO
Edmund M. Ackerman, President

**Solution Tree Press**
*President and Publisher:* Douglas M. Rife
*Associate Publishers:* Todd Brakke and Kendra Slayton
*Editorial Director:* Laurel Hecker
*Art Director:* Rian Anderson
*Copy Chief:* Jessi Finn
*Senior Production Editor:* Laurel Hecker
*Proofreader:* Jessi Finn
*Text Designer:* Abigail Bowen
*Cover Designer:* Rian Anderson
*Acquisitions Editor:* Hilary Goff
*Assistant Acquisitions Editor:* Elijah Oates
*Content Development Specialist:* Amy Rubenstein
*Associate Editor:* Sarah Ludwig
*Editorial Assistant:* Anne Marie Watkins

# Hey, hey, coaches!

One of the biggest struggles in life is not having enough time in a day. This holds true when you are an instructional coach. I'm sure you know the feeling of coming to work in the morning ready to conquer the world but then getting lost in the shuffle and becoming unproductive because you can't remember what it was you were supposed to be doing and how long you thought it would take. When I first became an instructional coach, I was all over the place—trying to get things done, trying not to forget to complete something, and trying to keep up with email and meetings. My schedule consisted of a mess of sticky notes on my desk and scrolling through my in-box to make sure I hadn't missed anything. I was so busy with everything that I hadn't taken the time to sit down and create a proper schedule, and I know this negatively impacted the efficiency of my work.

It became clear that I needed to create a system to manage my time more effectively. My system involved dedicating a day each week to planning, mapping out each moment of the day, and making sure I included time to work and meet with others. When I was in the classroom, I did my lesson plans on Sunday afternoons. When I became a coach, I thought those days were over, but I soon figured out that I had traded lesson planning for weekly schedule planning on Sunday afternoons.

Staying organized is an important part of any job, but especially coaching. Being disorganized wastes time and resources, and instructional coaches do not have time for lower productivity. You wear so many hats and are pulled in so many directions during the day. Staying organized is the best way to ensure you can do everything on your to-do list in a timely manner.

Being organized boosts productivity in many ways (Sexton, 2016). First, when everything has a designated space and you know exactly where to find it (both physical items and things written down within an organizational planner system), it saves time that might otherwise be wasted searching. Second, it helps cut down on stress by freeing up mental space and energy that might be wasted trying to sort through chaos. Third, organization allows people to be more creative. Cluttered, disorganized spaces hinder creativity whereas clean and clear spaces open the channels to creativity in the brain. Fourth, it helps you meet your deadlines. Productivity strategies put you, as an instructional coach, in a perfect position for accomplishing all your daily tasks while providing support to teachers.

In my book *Simply Instructional Coaching* (Turner, 2023), I recommend utilizing a planner like this one to help you organize your time. I designed this companion planner as an all-in-one tool where you can plan and track every key aspect of your coaching role. In this resource, you'll find tools to support your most essential coaching tasks and calendar pages to prep, schedule, and reflect on your days, weeks, and months. The goal is to get organized and be reflective in your practice so you can be the most impactful coach possible! Happy coaching, y'all!

— Nicole S. Turner

Sexton, C. (2016, March 15). *7 reasons why being organized boosts productivity*. The Productivity Experts. Accessed at https://theproductivityexperts.com/7-reasons-why-being-organized-boosts-productivity on July 21, 2022.

Turner, N. S. (2023). *Simply instructional coaching: Questions asked and answered from the field*. Bloomington, IN: Solution Tree Press.

# How to Use the *Coaching Tools*

## Professional Development Tracker & Log
page 6

In this planner, I have created a space for you to document all of the professional development courses or seminars you attend throughout the school year. This comes in handy if you need to produce hours for your license, or if your principal needs to know whether you have already attended professional development on a specific topic. You can also use this to jot down all the professional development topics you have presented. This information helps when planning topics for future professional development sessions or identifying follow-up sessions.

## Resources I Want & Resources I Need
page 8

Many times throughout the year, you may find yourself sitting in a professional development seminar or a meeting when someone talks about a new product or resource that you want to purchase. If you're anything like me, you jot the information down on a scrap of paper but never look back at it. Months later, that resource pops back up in your head, but you don't remember what it's called. This section of the planner is the perfect solution. Write down the resource when a teacher or presenter talks about it. Review the page often, do research on the products or resources, and go from there. This page will also give you, at a glance, an answer when your family asks, "What do you want for a gift?"

## Teacher Needs
page 9

Teachers may stop you in the hallway to ask if you can send them something quickly, if you have a specific resource, or if they can schedule a meeting with you. Having a place to jot down those notes so you don't forget is crucial. Use this page to track your own impromptu teacher communications. Teachers will stop and ask you for things more often than you could ever imagine!

## Teacher Birthdays and Gift Ideas
page 10

When I was a teacher, I used to put all my students' names on a birthday poster in my classroom. Each month, we celebrated students' birthdays, and I provided each student with a pencil or pen, a birthday certificate, and a treat. Now that I coach teachers, it's no different. I record each teacher's birthday and make sure to provide the teacher with a cute handwritten note and something special from me. At the beginning of each month, I review the birthday list, create the gift bags, and get ready to celebrate! Depending on how busy the month will be, I pass out the bags on the day of each person's birthday or to everyone during the first week of the month. Use this part of the planner to track your teachers' birthdays and come up with creative but simple ways to celebrate them.

## Track Your Testing
page 12

Testing is a part of all educators' vocabulary. No matter your personal opinions on testing or what type of school you work in, it is one thing all educators have in common. Beginning of the year, middle of the year, end of the year, district test, Northwest Evaluation Association (NWEA), state test, monthly test—you name it. As an instructional coach, you will sometimes have to organize and administer testing. To keep up with the dates of the testing windows, use this section to track testing, from grades to teachers to schedule development.  Use this to stay abreast of what's happening when you create your weekly schedules.

## Professional Coaching Goals
page 14

Setting goals helps you stay focused and work on improvement. Just like you encourage your teachers to do, set goals for yourself and keep track so you will know when you've met them. I recommend using SMART goals (Conzemius & O'Neill, 2014), which means that your goals are strategic and specific, measurable, attainable, results oriented, and time bound.

Visit **go.SolutionTree.com/instruction** to download free reproducible versions of key coaching tools.

Educators often set goals at the beginning of the year with great intentions, but throughout the year, their actions have nothing to do with the overall goal. You can set large goals for the year, along with several smaller goals that will serve as benchmarks to keep you on track. Set professional development goals for yourself and goals that align with your school's improvement goals. Each term, design the steps it takes to get to your goal. Each week, complete tasks that move you toward your goal, reflect on if you are on the right track, and adjust as needed.

### The First 8 Weeks
page 16

Your first sixty days of coaching will set the stage for the year. Use this guide to help you establish your role and create a strong foundation of coaching. Set yourself up for success and hit the ground running!

### 12 Months of Monthly Focus
page 18

Using a focus or theme for each month of the year can help you stay engaged and bring energy to your work. I've suggested twelve monthly focus areas that align with educators' needs throughout the flow of the school year. Record these themes or your own at the top of each month's calendar page.

### Closing Out the Year
page 19

When it's time to close out the year, you get a sense of accomplishment. I've provided a sample checklist of things you can do to wrap up the year. I have also included a column for you to create your own.

### Project Planner & Project Tracker
page 20

Coaches take the lead on many special projects and events at school. Whether it's a data review, a testing session, a literacy night, or another project, you'll need to set a clear purpose and objectives, delegate tasks to other committee members, create an action plan, and track progress. Use these tools to ensure your projects stay on track and run smoothly from start to finish.

### Coaching Cycle Tracking Sheet
page 28

Coaching cycles are the core of coaches' work. The Plan-Act-Reflect (PAR) cycle helps you complete cycles and work strategically with teachers. While you'll keep coaching documents and official forms in separate files, utilize this section of the planner to briefly track your cycles with teachers. This gives you a quick reflection and allows you to give your administrator enough information to know exactly whom you are working with and what your focus is, but not all the deep details. Coaches walk a thin line between keeping a teacher's trust and revealing too much to administrators. If your principal asks for a coaching report, you can easily comply without breaking confidentiality by submitting this form.

### Snapshot Forms
page 40

Visiting a teacher's classroom to see them in action is a central part of every coaching cycle. While some coaches call these visits *observations*, I find that teachers negatively associate that word with formal evaluations, so I refer to them as *snapshots*. The purpose of a snapshot is to assess the teacher's needs or see how they are implementing a new strategy so you can give feedback. In addition to focused snapshots within coaching cycles, try to conduct baseline snapshots for each teacher once per quarter. These snapshot forms guide you to align your coaching with my Simple Core 4™ pillars of teaching practice: (1) organization, (2) management and culture, (3) content, and (4) instructional execution. You'll conduct PAR cycles with teachers who are working on management and culture or instructional execution and have coaching conversations with those improving organization or content.

Conzemius, A. E., & O'Neill, J. (2014). *The handbook for SMART school teams: Revitalizing best practices for collaboration* (2nd ed.). Bloomington, IN: Solution Tree Press.

# Professional Development
## Tracker & Log

| DATE | TOPIC & PRESENTER | REFLECTION |
|------|-------------------|------------|
|      |                   |            |
|      |                   |            |
|      |                   |            |
|      |                   |            |
|      |                   |            |
|      |                   |            |
|      |                   |            |
|      |                   |            |
|      |                   |            |

# Professional Development
## Tracker & Log

| DATE | TOPIC & PRESENTER | REFLECTION |
|------|-------------------|------------|
|      |                   |            |
|      |                   |            |
|      |                   |            |
|      |                   |            |
|      |                   |            |
|      |                   |            |
|      |                   |            |
|      |                   |            |
|      |                   |            |

# Resources I *Want*

# Resources I *Need*

# Teacher Needs

| DATE | TEACHER NEED | ✓ |
|------|--------------|---|
|      |              |   |
|      |              |   |
|      |              |   |
|      |              |   |
|      |              |   |
|      |              |   |
|      |              |   |
|      |              |   |
|      |              |   |
|      |              |   |
|      |              |   |
|      |              |   |
|      |              |   |
|      |              |   |
|      |              |   |
|      |              |   |
|      |              |   |

# Teacher Birthdays and
## *Gift Ideas*

| July | August |
|------|--------|
| **November** | **December** |
| **March** | **April** |

# Teacher Birthdays and
## *Gift Ideas*

| September | October |
|-----------|---------|
| **January** | **February** |
| **May** | **June** |

# Track Your
## *Testing*

| July | August | September | October |
|---|---|---|---|
| | | | |
| **November** | **December** | **January** | **February** |
| | | | |
| **March** | **April** | **May** | **June** |
| | | | |

# Testing Prep Notes
## What I Need for Testing

# Professional Coaching Goals

## Term 1

Goal:

| Did I meet the goal?     YES     NO<br>Evidence | Reflection |
|---|---|
| | |

## Term 2

Goal:

| Did I meet the goal?     YES     NO<br>Evidence | Reflection |
|---|---|
| | |

# Professional Coaching Goals

## Term 3    Goal:

| Did I meet the goal?    YES    NO  Evidence | Reflection |
|---|---|
| | |

## Term 4    Goal:

| Did I meet the goal?    YES    NO  Evidence | Reflection |
|---|---|
| | |

15

# The First 8 Weeks

Weeks (Week 1 is the week before students arrive.)

**Set up a meeting with your administration.** Establish your coaching role. Seek administration's vision for the role and discuss their expectations for it.

**Set up your space.** Visit your space and map it out.

**Review teachers' previous data.** Pay attention to teachers who will need your assistance and look at what they've previously done. Prep for the arrival of new teachers.

**Decide on a coaching tracking system** (binder or digital).

**Set up the weekly schedule framework.** Review the building schedule and previous notes from meeting with administration. Create a schedule of the things that never change.

**Send out a welcome email to teachers.** Introduce yourself to teachers. Let them know what you offer. Set up one-on-one time to meet with the individual teachers you'll coach.

**Plan your one-on-one meetings.** Map out what your first meetings will look like. Create a way for teachers to sign up. Develop the agenda for the meetings.

**Visit each classroom first thing in the morning.** Say hello and focus on building relationships.

**Make a quick visit to each classroom.** Complete five-minute positive feedback snapshots to get a feel for classroom climates and culture. Remember, this is not a baseline snapshot. Do not take a computer or snapshot rubric. Leave a positive comment after each visit.

**Offer assistance to teachers.** Create time to provide support to teachers—anything for which they might need an extra hand. Start to build their trust so they know you are there.

**Follow up on your schedule for one-on-one meetings.** Double-check to make sure all teachers signed up for their one-on-one time with you.

**Set your coaching goals for yourself.** Review last year's goals, reference notes from your conversations with your administrator, and write out your overarching goals. Create three goals and write them in your planner.

| Task | 1 | 2 | 3 | 4 | 5 | 6 | 7 | 8 |
|---|---|---|---|---|---|---|---|---|
| Set up a meeting with your administration | X | | | | | | | |
| Set up your space | X | | | | | | | |
| Review teachers' previous data | X | | | | | | | |
| Decide on a coaching tracking system | X | | | | | | | |
| Set up the weekly schedule framework | X | | | | | | | |
| Send out a welcome email to teachers | X | | | | | | | |
| Plan your one-on-one meetings | X | | | | | | | |
| Visit each classroom first thing in the morning | | X | X | X | X | X | X | X |
| Make a quick visit to each classroom | | X | | | | | | |
| Offer assistance to teachers | | X | | | | | | |
| Follow up on your schedule for one-on-one meetings | | X | X | | | | | |
| Set your coaching goals for yourself | | X | | | | | | |

# The First 8 Weeks

Weeks (Week 1 is the week before students arrive.)

**Revisit the testing schedule for the year.** Identify weeks without testing conflicts to schedule coaching cycles. You will conduct coaching in one- to three-week cycles based on teachers' tiers.

**Schedule and conduct all baseline snapshots.** Based on your teacher load, create a schedule of twenty-minute time slots to conduct baseline snapshots. Use the Simple Core 4 forms to collect evidence to inform which area you will work with the teacher on.

**Tier your teachers for support.** Use the data collected in your baseline snapshots to identify which pillars you think teachers need to work on and place them in tiers according to intensity of need.

**Do collaborative team planning.** If you are responsible for collaborative teams in your building, start to map out the agenda format and set meeting times and topics.

**Host your one-on-one meetings.** Enjoy spending time one-on-one with each teacher. During each meeting, make sure you stick to the agenda and complete your questionnaire.

**Review baseline student data.** By this time, the majority of beginning-of-the-year assessments are complete. Build time in your schedule this week to review where students are struggling. These data will come in handy when you create your teacher focus plans.

**Create focused support plans for each teacher.** Create a customized support plan for each teacher you coach. Discuss the Simple Core 4 pillars with the teacher to identify where to begin. Review evidence for each component to collaboratively decide your focus.

**Begin coaching cycles and coaching conversations.** You will start coaching cycles for the pillar of management and culture or instructional execution and coaching conversations for organization or content. Set goals and begin the work.

| Task | 1 | 2 | 3 | 4 | 5 | 6 | 7 | 8 |
|---|---|---|---|---|---|---|---|---|
| Revisit the testing schedule for the year | | | X | | | | | |
| Schedule and conduct all baseline snapshots | | | X | X | X | X | X | |
| Tier your teachers for support | | | X | X | X | X | X | |
| Do collaborative team planning | | | X | | | | | |
| Host your one-on-one meetings | | | | X | | | | |
| Review baseline student data | | | | X | X | | | |
| Create focused support plans for each teacher | | | | | | X | X | |
| Begin coaching cycles and coaching conversations | | | | | | | | X |

# 12 Months of *Monthly Focus*

**July**
Reflection and planning can be done in small parts. Think about things you want to implement next school year and write the ideas down. Enjoy your summer and spend time with family. Rest and rejuvenate for the upcoming year. It's coming soon!

**August**
Spend time with teachers—especially new teachers. Assist them with establishing successful and positive classrooms. Discuss the curriculum expectations and what it takes to build relationships with students and families.

**September**
Establish coaching norms with teachers. Host one-on-one meetings with teachers and start to build relationships. Also, complete baseline snapshots of teachers and begin to work with teachers who are struggling with behavior management.

**October**
Beginning-of-the-year testing is complete. Have your teachers set specific and attainable goals? If not, support teachers in setting goals for student improvement. If they have already done this, spend time with teachers mapping out plans to attain their goals.

**November**
Use data as an instructional tool. Work with teachers to differentiate instruction based on student needs from formative assessments.

**December**
You are halfway there. Spend time reflecting and redirecting your coaching style. Send out a midyear coaching survey to teachers and ask for honest feedback. Analyze the responses and identify opportunities to improve your coaching.

**January**
Meet with teachers one-on-one. Have teachers examine previous lesson plans. Ensure that the lesson plans include rigorous activities and higher-order thinking questions. If they don't, spend time creating a lesson plan together. Find exemplary plans for guidance and create a process for teachers to double-check that their plans are effective.

**February**
Have you hosted a meeting with teachers to touch base? Consider holding another round of relationship-building meetings. Also, now is a great time to do a data dive to get the pulse of how prepping for testing is going.

**March**
Has your coaching provided opportunities for teachers to grow? Set up opportunities for teachers to benefit from peer snapshots and collaborative planning. Host a few comparative analysis sessions using evidence of practice.

**April**
Sometimes teachers need a sounding board to talk to or a shoulder to cry on. Be that for them. This is the time of year when staff morale is low. Choose a day to visit each teacher and leave a positive note and a sweet treat to show that they are appreciated.

**May**
Set up one-on-one meetings with teachers to reflect on their beginning-of-the-year goals. Create a document to guide teachers through a self-reflection. Have each teacher identify their successes from this year and opportunities for the next year. Have each teacher set personal goals for the summer for relaxing and resting.

**June**
The end of the year is a great time for reflection. Send out an end-of-the-year survey to teachers. Analyze the results. Reflect on your three goals from this school year. Which goals did you meet and what successes did you experience? What would you like to continue next school year? What opportunities are there for improvement?

# Closing Out the Year

## General To-Do

- ☐ Administer end-of-the-year surveys to teachers
- ☐ Schedule end-of-the-year meetings to close out any outstanding tasks or conversations with administrators
- ☐ Plan end-of-the-year meetings
- ☐ Administer end-of-the-year awards or some kind of positive recognition to teachers
- ☐ Turn in materials from the teachers
- ☐ Turn in orders
- ☐ Organize files
- ☐ Organize space so it is ready for a fresh start in the fall
- ☐ Finalize plans for any summer professional development trainings
- ☐
- ☐
- ☐
- ☐

## My Plan

# Project *Planner*

Project Title:

Project Due Date:

## Description
*Describe the project.*

## Purpose of the Project
*What is the focus of the project and how does it tie to the vision of the school?*

## Committee Members
*Who will help implement the project, and what are their roles?*

## Goals and Objectives
*What will define the success of the project?*

1.

2.

3.

4.

## Overview of Action Plan
*Define key steps and key people.*

## Notes
*Identify any next steps for the following month.*

# Project *Tracker*

Project Title:

Project Due Date:

| Key Deliverables | Benchmarks | |
|---|---|---|
| | | |
| **Weekly Tasks & Action Plan** *Identify your top three weekly priorities.* | **Person Responsible** | **Date Complete** |
| **Week 1** | | |
| **Week 2** | | |
| **Week 3** | | |
| **Week 4** | | |
| **Week 5** | | |

# Project *Planner*

Project Title:

Project Due Date:

## Description
*Describe the project.*

## Purpose of the Project
*What is the focus of the project and how does it tie to the vision of the school?*

## Committee Members
*Who will help implement the project, and what are their roles?*

## Goals and Objectives
*What will define the success of the project?*

1.

2.

3.

4.

## Overview of Action Plan
*Define key steps and key people.*

## Notes
*Identify any next steps for the following month.*

# Project *Tracker*

Project Title:

Project Due Date:

| Key Deliverables | | Benchmarks | |
|---|---|---|---|
| **Weekly Tasks & Action Plan** *Identify your top three weekly priorities.* | | **Person Responsible** | **Date Complete** |
| **Week 1** | | | |
| **Week 2** | | | |
| **Week 3** | | | |
| **Week 4** | | | |
| **Week 5** | | | |

# Project *Planner*

Project Title:

Project Due Date:

### Description
*Describe the project.*

### Purpose of the Project
*What is the focus of the project and how does it tie to the vision of the school?*

### Committee Members
*Who will help implement the project, and what are their roles?*

### Goals and Objectives
*What will define the success of the project?*

1.

2.

3.

4.

### Overview of Action Plan
*Define key steps and key people.*

### Notes
*Identify any next steps for the following month.*

# Project *Tracker*

Project Title:

Project Due Date:

| Key Deliverables | Benchmarks | |
|---|---|---|
| **Weekly Tasks & Action Plan** *Identify your top three weekly priorities.* | **Person Responsible** | **Date Complete** |
| **Week 1** | | |
| **Week 2** | | |
| **Week 3** | | |
| **Week 4** | | |
| **Week 5** | | |

# Project *Planner*

Project Title:

Project Due Date:

## Description
*Describe the project.*

## Purpose of the Project
*What is the focus of the project and how does it tie to the vision of the school?*

## Committee Members
*Who will help implement the project, and what are their roles?*

## Goals and Objectives
*What will define the success of the project?*

1.

2.

3.

4.

## Overview of Action Plan
*Define key steps and key people.*

## Notes
*Identify any next steps for the following month.*

# Project *Tracker*

Project Title:

Project Due Date:

| Key Deliverables | | Benchmarks | |
|---|---|---|---|
| **Weekly Tasks & Action Plan** *Identify your top three weekly priorities.* | | **Person Responsible** | **Date Complete** |
| **Week 1** | | | |
| **Week 2** | | | |
| **Week 3** | | | |
| **Week 4** | | | |
| **Week 5** | | | |

# Coaching Cycle Tracking Sheet

PAR Cycle

| Teacher: | **PLAN** (Pre-Planning and Practice) |
| --- | --- |
| Cycle Begin Date: | |
| Cycle End Date: | |
| Cycle Goal: | |
| | **ACT** (Implement and Observe) |
| | **REFLECT** (Debrief and Analyze) |

| Teacher: | **PLAN** (Pre-Planning and Practice) |
| --- | --- |
| Cycle Begin Date: | |
| Cycle End Date: | |
| Cycle Goal: | |
| | **ACT** (Implement and Observe) |
| | **REFLECT** (Debrief and Analyze) |

# Coaching Cycle Tracking Sheet

PAR Cycle

| Teacher: | **PLAN** (Pre-Planning and Practice) |
|---|---|
| Cycle Begin Date: | |
| Cycle End Date: | |
| Cycle Goal: | **ACT** (Implement and Observe) |
| | **REFLECT** (Debrief and Analyze) |

| Teacher: | **PLAN** (Pre-Planning and Practice) |
|---|---|
| Cycle Begin Date: | |
| Cycle End Date: | |
| Cycle Goal: | **ACT** (Implement and Observe) |
| | **REFLECT** (Debrief and Analyze) |

# Coaching Cycle Tracking Sheet

PAR Cycle

| | |
|---|---|
| Teacher: | **PLAN** (Pre-Planning and Practice) |
| Cycle Begin Date: | |
| Cycle End Date: | |
| Cycle Goal: | |
| | **ACT** (Implement and Observe) |
| | **REFLECT** (Debrief and Analyze) |

| | |
|---|---|
| Teacher: | **PLAN** (Pre-Planning and Practice) |
| Cycle Begin Date: | |
| Cycle End Date: | |
| Cycle Goal: | |
| | **ACT** (Implement and Observe) |
| | **REFLECT** (Debrief and Analyze) |

# Coaching Cycle Tracking Sheet

| | |
|---|---|
| Teacher: | **PLAN** (Pre-Planning and Practice) |
| Cycle Begin Date: | |
| Cycle End Date: | |
| Cycle Goal: | |
| | **ACT** (Implement and Observe) |
| | |
| | **REFLECT** (Debrief and Analyze) |

| | |
|---|---|
| Teacher: | **PLAN** (Pre-Planning and Practice) |
| Cycle Begin Date: | |
| Cycle End Date: | |
| Cycle Goal: | |
| | **ACT** (Implement and Observe) |
| | |
| | **REFLECT** (Debrief and Analyze) |

# *Coaching Cycle* Tracking Sheet

PAR Cycle

| Teacher: |
| --- |
| Cycle Begin Date: |
| Cycle End Date: |
| Cycle Goal: |

**PLAN** (Pre-Planning and Practice)

**ACT** (Implement and Observe)

**REFLECT** (Debrief and Analyze)

| Teacher: |
| --- |
| Cycle Begin Date: |
| Cycle End Date: |
| Cycle Goal: |

**PLAN** (Pre-Planning and Practice)

**ACT** (Implement and Observe)

**REFLECT** (Debrief and Analyze)

# Coaching Cycle Tracking Sheet

| Teacher: | **PLAN** (Pre-Planning and Practice) |
|---|---|
| Cycle Begin Date: | |
| Cycle End Date: | |
| Cycle Goal: | |
| | **ACT** (Implement and Observe) |
| | **REFLECT** (Debrief and Analyze) |

| Teacher: | **PLAN** (Pre-Planning and Practice) |
|---|---|
| Cycle Begin Date: | |
| Cycle End Date: | |
| Cycle Goal: | |
| | **ACT** (Implement and Observe) |
| | **REFLECT** (Debrief and Analyze) |

# Coaching Cycle Tracking Sheet

PAR Cycle

| | |
|---|---|
| Teacher: | **PLAN** (Pre-Planning and Practice) |
| Cycle Begin Date: | |
| Cycle End Date: | |
| Cycle Goal: | |
| | **ACT** (Implement and Observe) |
| | **REFLECT** (Debrief and Analyze) |

| | |
|---|---|
| Teacher: | **PLAN** (Pre-Planning and Practice) |
| Cycle Begin Date: | |
| Cycle End Date: | |
| Cycle Goal: | |
| | **ACT** (Implement and Observe) |
| | **REFLECT** (Debrief and Analyze) |

# Coaching Cycle Tracking Sheet

| | |
|---|---|
| Teacher: | **PLAN** (Pre-Planning and Practice) |
| Cycle Begin Date: | |
| Cycle End Date: | |
| Cycle Goal: | |
| | **ACT** (Implement and Observe) |
| | |
| | **REFLECT** (Debrief and Analyze) |
| | |

| | |
|---|---|
| Teacher: | **PLAN** (Pre-Planning and Practice) |
| Cycle Begin Date: | |
| Cycle End Date: | |
| Cycle Goal: | |
| | **ACT** (Implement and Observe) |
| | |
| | **REFLECT** (Debrief and Analyze) |
| | |

# Coaching Cycle Tracking Sheet

| | |
|---|---|
| Teacher: | **PLAN** (Pre-Planning and Practice) |
| Cycle Begin Date: | |
| Cycle End Date: | |
| Cycle Goal: | |
| | **ACT** (Implement and Observe) |
| | |
| | **REFLECT** (Debrief and Analyze) |

| | |
|---|---|
| Teacher: | **PLAN** (Pre-Planning and Practice) |
| Cycle Begin Date: | |
| Cycle End Date: | |
| Cycle Goal: | |
| | **ACT** (Implement and Observe) |
| | |
| | **REFLECT** (Debrief and Analyze) |

# Coaching Cycle Tracking Sheet

| | |
|---|---|
| Teacher: | **PLAN** (Pre-Planning and Practice) |
| Cycle Begin Date: | |
| Cycle End Date: | |
| Cycle Goal: | |
| | **ACT** (Implement and Observe) |
| | **REFLECT** (Debrief and Analyze) |

| | |
|---|---|
| Teacher: | **PLAN** (Pre-Planning and Practice) |
| Cycle Begin Date: | |
| Cycle End Date: | |
| Cycle Goal: | |
| | **ACT** (Implement and Observe) |
| | **REFLECT** (Debrief and Analyze) |

# Coaching Cycle Tracking Sheet

| | |
|---|---|
| Teacher: | **PLAN** (Pre-Planning and Practice) |
| Cycle Begin Date: | |
| Cycle End Date: | |
| Cycle Goal: | |
| | **ACT** (Implement and Observe) |
| | |
| | **REFLECT** (Debrief and Analyze) |

| | |
|---|---|
| Teacher: | **PLAN** (Pre-Planning and Practice) |
| Cycle Begin Date: | |
| Cycle End Date: | |
| Cycle Goal: | |
| | **ACT** (Implement and Observe) |
| | |
| | **REFLECT** (Debrief and Analyze) |

# Coaching Cycle Tracking Sheet

PAR Cycle

| Teacher: | **PLAN** (Pre-Planning and Practice) |
| Cycle Begin Date: | |
| Cycle End Date: | |
| Cycle Goal: | |
| | **ACT** (Implement and Observe) |
| | **REFLECT** (Debrief and Analyze) |

| Teacher: | **PLAN** (Pre-Planning and Practice) |
| Cycle Begin Date: | |
| Cycle End Date: | |
| Cycle Goal: | |
| | **ACT** (Implement and Observe) |
| | **REFLECT** (Debrief and Analyze) |

# Snapshot Form
## Organization

Is the room neat and organized?  YES  NO
Describe the room setting.

Are traffic patterns well planned?  YES  NO
Jot down the evidence to support your answer.

Are the classroom expectations posted and referenced?
YES  NO
Jot down the evidence to support your answer.

Are routines and structures established?  YES  NO
Jot down the evidence to support your answer.

Are there systems in place for parent communication?
YES  NO
Ask the teacher how they plan to communicate praise
and concerns to parents.

Are there grading routines in place?  YES  NO
Ask the teacher if they have a grading routine
established. Ask questions to determine if the teacher
understands the district or school grading policies and
systems (for example, A–F, no zeros, standards-based,
mastery-based, and so on).

List the areas of strength you observed.

List the areas of opportunity you observed.

What are your next steps with this teacher?

Additional Notes

# Snapshot Form
## Management & Culture

Is there a behavior management system in place and utilized?  YES   NO
List the system the teacher is using. Is this system sustainable for this teacher?

Are students engaged and on task?  YES   NO
Look for behavioral engagement and record examples.

Are students interacting effectively with peers?   YES   NO
Look for evidence that students can agree and disagree respectfully.

Are students learning by doing?  YES   NO
Record signs of active engagement such as hands-on activities and students actively completing a task versus passively sitting.

Has a positive learning environment that fosters student success been created?  YES   NO
Examples include students sharing their thoughts, taking risks, and asking questions.

Does the teacher communicate effectively with students?  YES   NO
Write down evidence of the teacher modeling calm, positive language and giving feedback in a timely manner.

List the areas of strength you observed.

List the areas of opportunity you observed.

What are your next steps with this teacher?

Additional Notes

# Snapshot Form
## *Content*

| | |
|---|---|
| Does the teacher unpack standards, create appropriate "I can" statements, and post them in the classroom? YES   NO Jot down the evidence to support your answer. | Does the teacher demonstrate effective use of curriculum maps and pacing guides in the lesson? YES   NO Jot down the evidence to support your answer. |
| Is the teacher using data to inform instruction?  YES   NO Jot down the evidence to support your answer. | Are the lesson plans and assessments aligned with content standards?  YES   NO Jot down the evidence to support your answer. |
| Does the teacher utilize time management strategies while teaching?  YES   NO Examples include having time stamps in lesson plans and setting a timer when teaching. | Does the teacher choose activities and resources that align to the standards, are engaging and hands-on, and encourage thinking?  YES   NO Record evidence of classroom materials that support learning. |

List the areas of strength you observed.

List the areas of opportunity you observed.

What are your next steps with this teacher?

Additional Notes

# Snapshot Form
## Instructional Execution

| | |
|---|---|
| Are the lesson activities connected to the learning objective? YES NO<br>Jot down the evidence to support your answer. | Do the teacher's questions include various levels of complexity? YES NO<br>Record instances of the use of Bloom's taxonomy, Depth of Knowledge, or other examples. |
| Is there evidence of impactful instructional strategies? YES NO<br>Jot down the evidence to support your answer. | Is the pacing of the delivery of the lesson appropriate? YES NO<br>Look for evidence such as the teacher speaking neither too fast nor too slow, students responding to prompts and questions, and so on. |
| Is the teacher providing feedback to students in a timely manner and utilizing appropriate wait time? YES NO<br>Jot down the evidence to support your answer. | Is there evidence of differentiation in the classroom? YES NO<br>Examples include the use of small groups and students having appropriate options in learning activities. |

List the areas of strength you observed.

List the areas of opportunity you observed.

What are your next steps with this teacher?

Additional Notes

# How to Use Your
## *Coaching Schedule*

When you are a classroom teacher, administrators expect you to create weekly lesson plans for your students. Having the planning and prep done up front ensures you are familiar with the material and ready to deliver it in a dynamic way. Most people think being a coach means no more lesson plans. Well, this is not entirely true. Each week, just like lesson planning, you must create a schedule from the time you walk in the door to the time you walk out. Your weekly plan as a coach will look different, but the focus is the same. You need to effectively plan to create change and success for your teachers. Rather than lesson planning, you will map a scheduled plan of how you are going to help the teachers you support become more effective in the classroom. Your plan must include those you work with, their goals, as well as how you intend to work toward those goals. Not only does weekly planning provide a road map for your week (both for you and for others who need to see how they fit into your schedule), it also shows that you are prepared with materials that enable you to be an efficient coach.

When I was a teacher, I knew exactly what standards I needed to teach for each subject each week; this was how I began my lesson plans. With coaching, understanding what needs to be done each week works the same way. You must know what you will be doing before you can set a schedule. There may be testing, an all-school assembly, or professional development that will affect what can get done. Before I set goals for the upcoming week, I also see what I accomplished the previous week. Did I hit my goals? If I didn't, why not? How can I get better? Did I plan too much or not enough? If I didn't complete my weekly goals, they may get pushed to the next week, but I have thought about why they were not completed and how I can ensure I will complete them the next week. I look at all factors and create a list of goals—how many teachers' classrooms I will visit, how many coaching cycles I will complete, and so on. Setting goals for the week allows me to stay on track and get things done.

When I say plan out your schedule, I mean plan it out! Include everything from morning duty to open office hours to lunch and lunch duty. I have something scheduled for each minute of the day. This helps me to stay focused, get things done, and hold others accountable for requesting my time. The more teachers I am working with in a year, the more important it is that I make a tight schedule and stick to it. Having a plan like this makes for an impactful and effective coach.

Now, I know there are things that come up unexpectedly, and in my schedule, I leave open slots to move things around a bit, mostly on Thursdays and Fridays. But those open times are also for when a teacher wants to have an unplanned meeting with me, and I just tell the teacher when I am free. In the past, my principals sometimes randomly called and asked me to meet with them. If the meeting could wait, I learned through experience to let them know exactly when I had an opening to meet. If the meeting couldn't wait, then I moved what I was currently doing into an open slot. I let my principals know up front that I have protected time in my schedule—time I use to observe a teacher during a cycle, to schedule a co-teach, or for a debrief meeting. This way, throughout the year, you will only have to give the principal a gentle reminder and schedule a meeting for an open slot.

Use the following steps to fill in your calendar each week.

1. The first time you plan your week, make a list of all recurring weekly activities. Then, insert them into your calendar each week. For example:
   - Arrival and dismissal duty
   - Lunch duty
   - Weekly coach and principal meeting
   - Grade-level meeting
   - Collaborative team meetings
   - Staff development meetings
   - Daily office hours
   **Note:** Make sure you understand what office hours mean. Your office hours as a coach include your planning period. Do not skip your office hours! While your office

hours might change, be sure to schedule your time and keep your time. You will have a lot of documentation to cover, not to mention creating and tweaking the various plans you have with each of the teachers you are coaching. Office hours are vital to maintaining a healthy work-home balance, which is vital to being an effective coach. Burnout isn't going to do you or your teachers any favors!

2. Each week (or perhaps each month if you like to plan further in advance), consult your school or building calendar and enter any special events in your schedule. Add events like staff meetings, professional development days, holidays, school assemblies, teacher workdays, conferences, or any other schoolwide activity that will consume your required classroom minutes.

3. Now it's time to fill in the open slots on your calendar for the upcoming week. Write the reason for scheduling activities in your planning template, as well as the person you are meeting with and the time (for example, *Turner—snapshot of entry procedure* or *Jackson—snapshot debrief from mathematics lesson*). This way, you will know exactly why you scheduled the time and enable you to better prepare for the activity. The whole point of your weekly schedule is for you to prepare for the week ahead so things move along as smoothly as possible. For this, you want to keep in mind the different tiers of support you establish for teachers. You will meet with some teachers weekly, some quarterly, some in a cycle, and some you will meet with individually and some in a group—you get the idea. In addition, keep in mind the teachers' various classroom schedules and make sure they

are available at the time you assign to meet with them. This step will take the most time and be the most tedious! It is also one of the most important steps you can take.

4. In step 1, you created a weekly schedule of daily office hours. Now that you have filled the rest of the schedule, you need to go back and enter what you are planning to do during those office hours. For example, imagine you are observing Turner on Tuesday at 8:45 a.m. for entry procedures, and your debrief is scheduled for Wednesday at 9:30 a.m. You have office hours on Tuesday from 2:30 to 3:30 p.m. This is when you will plan your debrief meeting, so you will put *Turner debrief prep* in your schedule. You should do this with all your snapshots, debriefs, testing schedules, data reviews, and so on.

5. The last thing you must do every week is go back through your weekly schedule and add topics for the meetings. In step 1, you entered recurring collaborative team meetings, staff development meetings, grade-level meetings, and so on. Now is the time to go through the schedule and enter what you hope to discuss at those meetings this week. Also, note if you are hosting or need to prepare materials or documents for the meetings. If you do, schedule a time to perform those tasks during your office hours. Are you sensing a theme here? Write everything down. The more detailed you are, the easier your workflow will be.

Plan every minute of your time. This enables you to be efficient. Planning is not optional! If you fail to plan, you plan to fail. You want to be as efficient as possible; you will wear many different hats every day, and you want to wear them with a smile. Planning allows you to work ahead, which helps you stay ahead of your stress.

# A goal WITHOUT A PLAN IS JUST A wish.

—Antoine de Saint-Exupéry

# Prep Your *month*

## Personal Goals

| Day | Health & Fitness | Finances | Self-Care & Growth |
|-----|------------------|----------|--------------------|
|     |                  |          |                    |
|     |                  |          |                    |
|     |                  |          |                    |
|     |                  |          |                    |
|     |                  |          |                    |
|     |                  |          |                    |

## Important Reminders

|  |  |
|--|--|
|  |  |
|  |  |
|  |  |
|  |  |
|  |  |
|  |  |
|  |  |

# Prep Your *Month*

| Main Goal | Main Focus | Wins |
|---|---|---|
| | | |

## Monthly Tasks

**Week 1**

**Week 2**

**Week 3**

**Week 4**

**Week 5**

## Must Do This Month

## Save for Next Month

# July

*"The capacity to learn is a gift; the ability to learn is a skill; the willingness to learn is a choice."* —Brian Herbert

| Sunday | Monday | Tuesday | Wednesday |
|--------|--------|---------|-----------|
|        |        |         |           |
|        |        |         |           |
|        |        |         |           |
|        |        |         |           |
|        |        |         |           |

Monthly Focus

| Thursday | Friday | Saturday |
|----------|--------|----------|
|          |        |          |
|          |        |          |
|          |        |          |
|          |        |          |
|          |        |          |

Notes

# Prep Your *Week*

## *Priorities* This Week

- 
- 
- 
- 
- 
- 
- 
- 

## Coaching Cycles

## Classroom Snapshots

## Data Meetings

## Team & PD Meetings

## Feedback Meetings

## Other

# Reflect on Your *Week*

| What goals did you accomplish this week? | What goals did you not accomplish this week? Why? |
|---|---|
| What can you do to improve next week? | Things learned and things to remember: |

## Goal & Habit Tracker

| Goal or Habit | Day 1 | Day 2 | Day 3 | Day 4 | Day 5 | Day 6 | Day 7 |
|---|---|---|---|---|---|---|---|
| | | | | | | | |
| | | | | | | | |
| | | | | | | | |
| | | | | | | | |

## Notes

**Week:**

**Notes**

| | Sunday | Monday | Tuesday |
|---|---|---|---|
| | 4:00 a.m. | 4:00 a.m. | 4:00 a.m. |
| | 4:30 | 4:30 | 4:30 |
| | 5:00 | 5:00 | 5:00 |
| | 5:30 | 5:30 | 5:30 |
| | 6:00 | 6:00 | 6:00 |
| | 6:30 | 6:30 | 6:30 |
| | 7:00 | 7:00 | 7:00 |
| | 7:30 | 7:30 | 7:30 |
| | 8:00 | 8:00 | 8:00 |
| | 8:30 | 8:30 | 8:30 |
| | 9:00 | 9:00 | 9:00 |
| | 9:30 | 9:30 | 9:30 |
| | 10:00 | 10:00 | 10:00 |
| | 10:30 | 10:30 | 10:30 |
| | 11:00 | 11:00 | 11:00 |
| | 11:30 | 11:30 | 11:30 |
| | 12:00 p.m. | 12:00 p.m. | 12:00 p.m. |
| | 12:30 | 12:30 | 12:30 |
| | 1:00 | 1:00 | 1:00 |
| | 1:30 | 1:30 | 1:30 |
| | 2:00 | 2:00 | 2:00 |
| | 2:30 | 2:30 | 2:30 |
| | 3:00 | 3:00 | 3:00 |
| | 3:30 | 3:30 | 3:30 |
| | 4:00 | 4:00 | 4:00 |
| | 4:30 | 4:30 | 4:30 |
| | 5:00 | 5:00 | 5:00 |
| | 5:30 | 5:30 | 5:30 |
| | 6:00 | 6:00 | 6:00 |
| | 6:30 | 6:30 | 6:30 |
| | 7:00 | 7:00 | 7:00 |
| | 7:30 | 7:30 | 7:30 |
| | 8:00 | 8:00 | 8:00 |
| | 8:30 | 8:30 | 8:30 |
| | 9:00 | 9:00 | 9:00 |
| | 9:30 | 9:30 | 9:30 |
| | 10:00 | 10:00 | 10:00 |

| Wednesday | Thursday | Friday | Saturday |
|---|---|---|---|
| 4:00 a.m. | 4:00 a.m. | 4:00 a.m. | 4:00 a.m. |
| 4:30 | 4:30 | 4:30 | 4:30 |
| 5:00 | 5:00 | 5:00 | 5:00 |
| 5:30 | 5:30 | 5:30 | 5:30 |
| 6:00 | 6:00 | 6:00 | 6:00 |
| 6:30 | 6:30 | 6:30 | 6:30 |
| 7:00 | 7:00 | 7:00 | 7:00 |
| 7:30 | 7:30 | 7:30 | 7:30 |
| 8:00 | 8:00 | 8:00 | 8:00 |
| 8:30 | 8:30 | 8:30 | 8:30 |
| 9:00 | 9:00 | 9:00 | 9:00 |
| 9:30 | 9:30 | 9:30 | 9:30 |
| 10:00 | 10:00 | 10:00 | 10:00 |
| 10:30 | 10:30 | 10:30 | 10:30 |
| 11:00 | 11:00 | 11:00 | 11:00 |
| 11:30 | 11:30 | 11:30 | 11:30 |
| 12:00 p.m. | 12:00 p.m. | 12:00 p.m. | 12:00 p.m. |
| 12:30 | 12:30 | 12:30 | 12:30 |
| 1:00 | 1:00 | 1:00 | 1:00 |
| 1:30 | 1:30 | 1:30 | 1:30 |
| 2:00 | 2:00 | 2:00 | 2:00 |
| 2:30 | 2:30 | 2:30 | 2:30 |
| 3:00 | 3:00 | 3:00 | 3:00 |
| 3:30 | 3:30 | 3:30 | 3:30 |
| 4:00 | 4:00 | 4:00 | 4:00 |
| 4:30 | 4:30 | 4:30 | 4:30 |
| 5:00 | 5:00 | 5:00 | 5:00 |
| 5:30 | 5:30 | 5:30 | 5:30 |
| 6:00 | 6:00 | 6:00 | 6:00 |
| 6:30 | 6:30 | 6:30 | 6:30 |
| 7:00 | 7:00 | 7:00 | 7:00 |
| 7:30 | 7:30 | 7:30 | 7:30 |
| 8:00 | 8:00 | 8:00 | 8:00 |
| 8:30 | 8:30 | 8:30 | 8:30 |
| 9:00 | 9:00 | 9:00 | 9:00 |
| 9:30 | 9:30 | 9:30 | 9:30 |
| 10:00 | 10:00 | 10:00 | 10:00 |

# Prep Your *Week*

## Priorities This Week

- 
- 
- 
- 
- 
- 
- 
- 
- 

## Coaching Cycles

## Classroom Snapshots

## Data Meetings

## Team & PD Meetings

## Feedback Meetings

## Other

# Reflect on Your *Week*

| What goals did you accomplish this week? | What goals did you not accomplish this week? Why? |
|---|---|
| What can you do to improve next week? | Things learned and things to remember: |

## Goal & Habit Tracker

| Goal or Habit | Day 1 | Day 2 | Day 3 | Day 4 | Day 5 | Day 6 | Day 7 |
|---|---|---|---|---|---|---|---|
|  |  |  |  |  |  |  |  |
|  |  |  |  |  |  |  |  |
|  |  |  |  |  |  |  |  |
|  |  |  |  |  |  |  |  |

## Notes

**Week:**

**Notes**

| Sunday | Monday | Tuesday |
|---|---|---|
| 4:00 a.m. | 4:00 a.m. | 4:00 a.m. |
| 4:30 | 4:30 | 4:30 |
| 5:00 | 5:00 | 5:00 |
| 5:30 | 5:30 | 5:30 |
| 6:00 | 6:00 | 6:00 |
| 6:30 | 6:30 | 6:30 |
| 7:00 | 7:00 | 7:00 |
| 7:30 | 7:30 | 7:30 |
| 8:00 | 8:00 | 8:00 |
| 8:30 | 8:30 | 8:30 |
| 9:00 | 9:00 | 9:00 |
| 9:30 | 9:30 | 9:30 |
| 10:00 | 10:00 | 10:00 |
| 10:30 | 10:30 | 10:30 |
| 11:00 | 11:00 | 11:00 |
| 11:30 | 11:30 | 11:30 |
| 12:00 p.m. | 12:00 p.m. | 12:00 p.m. |
| 12:30 | 12:30 | 12:30 |
| 1:00 | 1:00 | 1:00 |
| 1:30 | 1:30 | 1:30 |
| 2:00 | 2:00 | 2:00 |
| 2:30 | 2:30 | 2:30 |
| 3:00 | 3:00 | 3:00 |
| 3:30 | 3:30 | 3:30 |
| 4:00 | 4:00 | 4:00 |
| 4:30 | 4:30 | 4:30 |
| 5:00 | 5:00 | 5:00 |
| 5:30 | 5:30 | 5:30 |
| 6:00 | 6:00 | 6:00 |
| 6:30 | 6:30 | 6:30 |
| 7:00 | 7:00 | 7:00 |
| 7:30 | 7:30 | 7:30 |
| 8:00 | 8:00 | 8:00 |
| 8:30 | 8:30 | 8:30 |
| 9:00 | 9:00 | 9:00 |
| 9:30 | 9:30 | 9:30 |
| 10:00 | 10:00 | 10:00 |

| Wednesday | Thursday | Friday | Saturday |
|---|---|---|---|
| 4:00 a.m. | 4:00 a.m. | 4:00 a.m. | 4:00 a.m. |
| 4:30 | 4:30 | 4:30 | 4:30 |
| 5:00 | 5:00 | 5:00 | 5:00 |
| 5:30 | 5:30 | 5:30 | 5:30 |
| 6:00 | 6:00 | 6:00 | 6:00 |
| 6:30 | 6:30 | 6:30 | 6:30 |
| 7:00 | 7:00 | 7:00 | 7:00 |
| 7:30 | 7:30 | 7:30 | 7:30 |
| 8:00 | 8:00 | 8:00 | 8:00 |
| 8:30 | 8:30 | 8:30 | 8:30 |
| 9:00 | 9:00 | 9:00 | 9:00 |
| 9:30 | 9:30 | 9:30 | 9:30 |
| 10:00 | 10:00 | 10:00 | 10:00 |
| 10:30 | 10:30 | 10:30 | 10:30 |
| 11:00 | 11:00 | 11:00 | 11:00 |
| 11:30 | 11:30 | 11:30 | 11:30 |
| 12:00 p.m. | 12:00 p.m. | 12:00 p.m. | 12:00 p.m. |
| 12:30 | 12:30 | 12:30 | 12:30 |
| 1:00 | 1:00 | 1:00 | 1:00 |
| 1:30 | 1:30 | 1:30 | 1:30 |
| 2:00 | 2:00 | 2:00 | 2:00 |
| 2:30 | 2:30 | 2:30 | 2:30 |
| 3:00 | 3:00 | 3:00 | 3:00 |
| 3:30 | 3:30 | 3:30 | 3:30 |
| 4:00 | 4:00 | 4:00 | 4:00 |
| 4:30 | 4:30 | 4:30 | 4:30 |
| 5:00 | 5:00 | 5:00 | 5:00 |
| 5:30 | 5:30 | 5:30 | 5:30 |
| 6:00 | 6:00 | 6:00 | 6:00 |
| 6:30 | 6:30 | 6:30 | 6:30 |
| 7:00 | 7:00 | 7:00 | 7:00 |
| 7:30 | 7:30 | 7:30 | 7:30 |
| 8:00 | 8:00 | 8:00 | 8:00 |
| 8:30 | 8:30 | 8:30 | 8:30 |
| 9:00 | 9:00 | 9:00 | 9:00 |
| 9:30 | 9:30 | 9:30 | 9:30 |
| 10:00 | 10:00 | 10:00 | 10:00 |

# Prep Your *Week*

## Priorities This Week

- 
- 
- 
- 
- 
- 
- 
- 
- 

## Coaching Cycles

## Classroom Snapshots

## Data Meetings

## Team & PD Meetings

## Feedback Meetings

## Other

# Reflect on Your *Week*

| What goals did you accomplish this week? | What goals did you not accomplish this week? Why? |
|---|---|
| What can you do to improve next week? | Things learned and things to remember: |

## Goal & Habit Tracker

| Goal or Habit | Day 1 | Day 2 | Day 3 | Day 4 | Day 5 | Day 6 | Day 7 |
|---|---|---|---|---|---|---|---|
| | | | | | | | |
| | | | | | | | |
| | | | | | | | |
| | | | | | | | |

## Notes

Week:

Notes ⟍

| | Sunday | Monday | Tuesday |
|---|---|---|---|
| | 4:00 a.m. | 4:00 a.m. | 4:00 a.m. |
| | 4:30 | 4:30 | 4:30 |
| | 5:00 | 5:00 | 5:00 |
| | 5:30 | 5:30 | 5:30 |
| | 6:00 | 6:00 | 6:00 |
| | 6:30 | 6:30 | 6:30 |
| | 7:00 | 7:00 | 7:00 |
| | 7:30 | 7:30 | 7:30 |
| | 8:00 | 8:00 | 8:00 |
| | 8:30 | 8:30 | 8:30 |
| | 9:00 | 9:00 | 9:00 |
| | 9:30 | 9:30 | 9:30 |
| | 10:00 | 10:00 | 10:00 |
| | 10:30 | 10:30 | 10:30 |
| | 11:00 | 11:00 | 11:00 |
| | 11:30 | 11:30 | 11:30 |
| | 12:00 p.m. | 12:00 p.m. | 12:00 p.m. |
| | 12:30 | 12:30 | 12:30 |
| | 1:00 | 1:00 | 1:00 |
| | 1:30 | 1:30 | 1:30 |
| | 2:00 | 2:00 | 2:00 |
| | 2:30 | 2:30 | 2:30 |
| | 3:00 | 3:00 | 3:00 |
| | 3:30 | 3:30 | 3:30 |
| | 4:00 | 4:00 | 4:00 |
| | 4:30 | 4:30 | 4:30 |
| | 5:00 | 5:00 | 5:00 |
| | 5:30 | 5:30 | 5:30 |
| | 6:00 | 6:00 | 6:00 |
| | 6:30 | 6:30 | 6:30 |
| | 7:00 | 7:00 | 7:00 |
| | 7:30 | 7:30 | 7:30 |
| | 8:00 | 8:00 | 8:00 |
| | 8:30 | 8:30 | 8:30 |
| | 9:00 | 9:00 | 9:00 |
| | 9:30 | 9:30 | 9:30 |
| | 10:00 | 10:00 | 10:00 |

| Wednesday | Thursday | Friday | Saturday |
|---|---|---|---|
| 4:00 a.m. | 4:00 a.m. | 4:00 a.m. | 4:00 a.m. |
| 4:30 | 4:30 | 4:30 | 4:30 |
| 5:00 | 5:00 | 5:00 | 5:00 |
| 5:30 | 5:30 | 5:30 | 5:30 |
| 6:00 | 6:00 | 6:00 | 6:00 |
| 6:30 | 6:30 | 6:30 | 6:30 |
| 7:00 | 7:00 | 7:00 | 7:00 |
| 7:30 | 7:30 | 7:30 | 7:30 |
| 8:00 | 8:00 | 8:00 | 8:00 |
| 8:30 | 8:30 | 8:30 | 8:30 |
| 9:00 | 9:00 | 9:00 | 9:00 |
| 9:30 | 9:30 | 9:30 | 9:30 |
| 10:00 | 10:00 | 10:00 | 10:00 |
| 10:30 | 10:30 | 10:30 | 10:30 |
| 11:00 | 11:00 | 11:00 | 11:00 |
| 11:30 | 11:30 | 11:30 | 11:30 |
| 12:00 p.m. | 12:00 p.m. | 12:00 p.m. | 12:00 p.m. |
| 12:30 | 12:30 | 12:30 | 12:30 |
| 1:00 | 1:00 | 1:00 | 1:00 |
| 1:30 | 1:30 | 1:30 | 1:30 |
| 2:00 | 2:00 | 2:00 | 2:00 |
| 2:30 | 2:30 | 2:30 | 2:30 |
| 3:00 | 3:00 | 3:00 | 3:00 |
| 3:30 | 3:30 | 3:30 | 3:30 |
| 4:00 | 4:00 | 4:00 | 4:00 |
| 4:30 | 4:30 | 4:30 | 4:30 |
| 5:00 | 5:00 | 5:00 | 5:00 |
| 5:30 | 5:30 | 5:30 | 5:30 |
| 6:00 | 6:00 | 6:00 | 6:00 |
| 6:30 | 6:30 | 6:30 | 6:30 |
| 7:00 | 7:00 | 7:00 | 7:00 |
| 7:30 | 7:30 | 7:30 | 7:30 |
| 8:00 | 8:00 | 8:00 | 8:00 |
| 8:30 | 8:30 | 8:30 | 8:30 |
| 9:00 | 9:00 | 9:00 | 9:00 |
| 9:30 | 9:30 | 9:30 | 9:30 |
| 10:00 | 10:00 | 10:00 | 10:00 |

# Prep Your *Week*

## Priorities This Week

- 
- 
- 
- 
- 
- 
- 
- 
- 

## Coaching Cycles

## Classroom Snapshots

## Data Meetings

## Team & PD Meetings

## Feedback Meetings

## Other

# Reflect on Your *Week*

| What goals did you accomplish this week? | What goals did you not accomplish this week? Why? |
|---|---|
| | |
| **What can you do to improve next week?** | **Things learned and things to remember:** |
| | |

## Goal & Habit Tracker

| Goal or Habit | Day 1 | Day 2 | Day 3 | Day 4 | Day 5 | Day 6 | Day 7 |
|---|---|---|---|---|---|---|---|
| | | | | | | | |
| | | | | | | | |
| | | | | | | | |
| | | | | | | | |

## Notes

Notes

| | Sunday | Monday | Tuesday |
|---|---|---|---|
| | 4:00 a.m. | 4:00 a.m. | 4:00 a.m. |
| | 4:30 | 4:30 | 4:30 |
| | 5:00 | 5:00 | 5:00 |
| | 5:30 | 5:30 | 5:30 |
| | 6:00 | 6:00 | 6:00 |
| | 6:30 | 6:30 | 6:30 |
| | 7:00 | 7:00 | 7:00 |
| | 7:30 | 7:30 | 7:30 |
| | 8:00 | 8:00 | 8:00 |
| | 8:30 | 8:30 | 8:30 |
| | 9:00 | 9:00 | 9:00 |
| | 9:30 | 9:30 | 9:30 |
| | 10:00 | 10:00 | 10:00 |
| | 10:30 | 10:30 | 10:30 |
| | 11:00 | 11:00 | 11:00 |
| | 11:30 | 11:30 | 11:30 |
| | 12:00 p.m. | 12:00 p.m. | 12:00 p.m. |
| | 12:30 | 12:30 | 12:30 |
| | 1:00 | 1:00 | 1:00 |
| | 1:30 | 1:30 | 1:30 |
| | 2:00 | 2:00 | 2:00 |
| | 2:30 | 2:30 | 2:30 |
| | 3:00 | 3:00 | 3:00 |
| | 3:30 | 3:30 | 3:30 |
| | 4:00 | 4:00 | 4:00 |
| | 4:30 | 4:30 | 4:30 |
| | 5:00 | 5:00 | 5:00 |
| | 5:30 | 5:30 | 5:30 |
| | 6:00 | 6:00 | 6:00 |
| | 6:30 | 6:30 | 6:30 |
| | 7:00 | 7:00 | 7:00 |
| | 7:30 | 7:30 | 7:30 |
| | 8:00 | 8:00 | 8:00 |
| | 8:30 | 8:30 | 8:30 |
| | 9:00 | 9:00 | 9:00 |
| | 9:30 | 9:30 | 9:30 |
| | 10:00 | 10:00 | 10:00 |

| Wednesday | Thursday | Friday | Saturday |
|---|---|---|---|
| 4:00 a.m. | 4:00 a.m. | 4:00 a.m. | 4:00 a.m. |
| 4:30 | 4:30 | 4:30 | 4:30 |
| 5:00 | 5:00 | 5:00 | 5:00 |
| 5:30 | 5:30 | 5:30 | 5:30 |
| 6:00 | 6:00 | 6:00 | 6:00 |
| 6:30 | 6:30 | 6:30 | 6:30 |
| 7:00 | 7:00 | 7:00 | 7:00 |
| 7:30 | 7:30 | 7:30 | 7:30 |
| 8:00 | 8:00 | 8:00 | 8:00 |
| 8:30 | 8:30 | 8:30 | 8:30 |
| 9:00 | 9:00 | 9:00 | 9:00 |
| 9:30 | 9:30 | 9:30 | 9:30 |
| 10:00 | 10:00 | 10:00 | 10:00 |
| 10:30 | 10:30 | 10:30 | 10:30 |
| 11:00 | 11:00 | 11:00 | 11:00 |
| 11:30 | 11:30 | 11:30 | 11:30 |
| 12:00 p.m. | 12:00 p.m. | 12:00 p.m. | 12:00 p.m. |
| 12:30 | 12:30 | 12:30 | 12:30 |
| 1:00 | 1:00 | 1:00 | 1:00 |
| 1:30 | 1:30 | 1:30 | 1:30 |
| 2:00 | 2:00 | 2:00 | 2:00 |
| 2:30 | 2:30 | 2:30 | 2:30 |
| 3:00 | 3:00 | 3:00 | 3:00 |
| 3:30 | 3:30 | 3:30 | 3:30 |
| 4:00 | 4:00 | 4:00 | 4:00 |
| 4:30 | 4:30 | 4:30 | 4:30 |
| 5:00 | 5:00 | 5:00 | 5:00 |
| 5:30 | 5:30 | 5:30 | 5:30 |
| 6:00 | 6:00 | 6:00 | 6:00 |
| 6:30 | 6:30 | 6:30 | 6:30 |
| 7:00 | 7:00 | 7:00 | 7:00 |
| 7:30 | 7:30 | 7:30 | 7:30 |
| 8:00 | 8:00 | 8:00 | 8:00 |
| 8:30 | 8:30 | 8:30 | 8:30 |
| 9:00 | 9:00 | 9:00 | 9:00 |
| 9:30 | 9:30 | 9:30 | 9:30 |
| 10:00 | 10:00 | 10:00 | 10:00 |

# Prep Your *Week*

## *Priorities* This Week

- 
- 
- 
- 
- 
- 
- 
- 
- 

## Coaching Cycles

## Classroom Snapshots

## Data Meetings

## Team & PD Meetings

## Feedback Meetings

## Other

# Reflect on Your *Week*

| | |
|---|---|
| What goals did you accomplish this week? | What goals did you not accomplish this week? Why? |
| What can you do to improve next week? | Things learned and things to remember: |

## Goal & Habit Tracker

| Goal or Habit | Day 1 | Day 2 | Day 3 | Day 4 | Day 5 | Day 6 | Day 7 |
|---|---|---|---|---|---|---|---|
| | | | | | | | |
| | | | | | | | |
| | | | | | | | |
| | | | | | | | |

## Notes

Week:

Notes

| Sunday | Monday | Tuesday |
|---|---|---|
| 4:00 a.m. | 4:00 a.m. | 4:00 a.m. |
| 4:30 | 4:30 | 4:30 |
| 5:00 | 5:00 | 5:00 |
| 5:30 | 5:30 | 5:30 |
| 6:00 | 6:00 | 6:00 |
| 6:30 | 6:30 | 6:30 |
| 7:00 | 7:00 | 7:00 |
| 7:30 | 7:30 | 7:30 |
| 8:00 | 8:00 | 8:00 |
| 8:30 | 8:30 | 8:30 |
| 9:00 | 9:00 | 9:00 |
| 9:30 | 9:30 | 9:30 |
| 10:00 | 10:00 | 10:00 |
| 10:30 | 10:30 | 10:30 |
| 11:00 | 11:00 | 11:00 |
| 11:30 | 11:30 | 11:30 |
| 12:00 p.m. | 12:00 p.m. | 12:00 p.m. |
| 12:30 | 12:30 | 12:30 |
| 1:00 | 1:00 | 1:00 |
| 1:30 | 1:30 | 1:30 |
| 2:00 | 2:00 | 2:00 |
| 2:30 | 2:30 | 2:30 |
| 3:00 | 3:00 | 3:00 |
| 3:30 | 3:30 | 3:30 |
| 4:00 | 4:00 | 4:00 |
| 4:30 | 4:30 | 4:30 |
| 5:00 | 5:00 | 5:00 |
| 5:30 | 5:30 | 5:30 |
| 6:00 | 6:00 | 6:00 |
| 6:30 | 6:30 | 6:30 |
| 7:00 | 7:00 | 7:00 |
| 7:30 | 7:30 | 7:30 |
| 8:00 | 8:00 | 8:00 |
| 8:30 | 8:30 | 8:30 |
| 9:00 | 9:00 | 9:00 |
| 9:30 | 9:30 | 9:30 |
| 10:00 | 10:00 | 10:00 |

| Wednesday | Thursday | Friday | Saturday |
|---|---|---|---|
| 4:00 a.m. | 4:00 a.m. | 4:00 a.m. | 4:00 a.m. |
| 4:30 | 4:30 | 4:30 | 4:30 |
| 5:00 | 5:00 | 5:00 | 5:00 |
| 5:30 | 5:30 | 5:30 | 5:30 |
| 6:00 | 6:00 | 6:00 | 6:00 |
| 6:30 | 6:30 | 6:30 | 6:30 |
| 7:00 | 7:00 | 7:00 | 7:00 |
| 7:30 | 7:30 | 7:30 | 7:30 |
| 8:00 | 8:00 | 8:00 | 8:00 |
| 8:30 | 8:30 | 8:30 | 8:30 |
| 9:00 | 9:00 | 9:00 | 9:00 |
| 9:30 | 9:30 | 9:30 | 9:30 |
| 10:00 | 10:00 | 10:00 | 10:00 |
| 10:30 | 10:30 | 10:30 | 10:30 |
| 11:00 | 11:00 | 11:00 | 11:00 |
| 11:30 | 11:30 | 11:30 | 11:30 |
| 12:00 p.m. | 12:00 p.m. | 12:00 p.m. | 12:00 p.m. |
| 12:30 | 12:30 | 12:30 | 12:30 |
| 1:00 | 1:00 | 1:00 | 1:00 |
| 1:30 | 1:30 | 1:30 | 1:30 |
| 2:00 | 2:00 | 2:00 | 2:00 |
| 2:30 | 2:30 | 2:30 | 2:30 |
| 3:00 | 3:00 | 3:00 | 3:00 |
| 3:30 | 3:30 | 3:30 | 3:30 |
| 4:00 | 4:00 | 4:00 | 4:00 |
| 4:30 | 4:30 | 4:30 | 4:30 |
| 5:00 | 5:00 | 5:00 | 5:00 |
| 5:30 | 5:30 | 5:30 | 5:30 |
| 6:00 | 6:00 | 6:00 | 6:00 |
| 6:30 | 6:30 | 6:30 | 6:30 |
| 7:00 | 7:00 | 7:00 | 7:00 |
| 7:30 | 7:30 | 7:30 | 7:30 |
| 8:00 | 8:00 | 8:00 | 8:00 |
| 8:30 | 8:30 | 8:30 | 8:30 |
| 9:00 | 9:00 | 9:00 | 9:00 |
| 9:30 | 9:30 | 9:30 | 9:30 |
| 10:00 | 10:00 | 10:00 | 10:00 |

# IF YOU DON'T KNOW WHERE YOU ARE GOING, you'll end up someplace else.

—Yogi Berra

# Prep Your *Month*

| Personal Goals | | | |
|---|---|---|---|
| Day | Health & Fitness | Finances | Self-Care & Growth |
| | | | |
| | | | |
| | | | |
| | | | |
| | | | |
| | | | |

| Important Reminders | |
|---|---|
| | |
| | |
| | |
| | |
| | |
| | |
| | |

# Prep Your *Month*

| Main Goal | Main Focus | Wins |
|---|---|---|
| | | |

## Monthly Tasks

Week 1

Week 2

Week 3

Week 4

Week 5

## Must Do This Month

## Save for Next Month

# August

"People rarely *succeed* unless they have *fun* in what they are doing." —Dale Carnegie

| Sunday | Monday | Tuesday | Wednesday |
|--------|--------|---------|-----------|
|        |        |         |           |
|        |        |         |           |
|        |        |         |           |
|        |        |         |           |
|        |        |         |           |

Monthly Focus

| Thursday | Friday | Saturday |
|----------|--------|----------|
|          |        |          |
|          |        |          |
|          |        |          |
|          |        |          |
|          |        |          |

Notes

# Prep Your *Week*

## Priorities This Week

- 
- 
- 
- 
- 
- 
- 
- 
- 

## Coaching Cycles

## Classroom Snapshots

## Data Meetings

## Team & PD Meetings

## Feedback Meetings

## Other

# Reflect on Your *Week*

| What goals did you accomplish this week? | What goals did you not accomplish this week? Why? |
|---|---|
| What can you do to improve next week? | Things learned and things to remember: |

## Goal & Habit Tracker

| Goal or Habit | Day 1 | Day 2 | Day 3 | Day 4 | Day 5 | Day 6 | Day 7 |
|---|---|---|---|---|---|---|---|
| | | | | | | | |
| | | | | | | | |
| | | | | | | | |
| | | | | | | | |

## Notes

Notes ↘

| | Sunday | Monday | Tuesday |
|---|---|---|---|
| | 4:00 a.m. | 4:00 a.m. | 4:00 a.m. |
| | 4:30 | 4:30 | 4:30 |
| | 5:00 | 5:00 | 5:00 |
| | 5:30 | 5:30 | 5:30 |
| | 6:00 | 6:00 | 6:00 |
| | 6:30 | 6:30 | 6:30 |
| | 7:00 | 7:00 | 7:00 |
| | 7:30 | 7:30 | 7:30 |
| | 8:00 | 8:00 | 8:00 |
| | 8:30 | 8:30 | 8:30 |
| | 9:00 | 9:00 | 9:00 |
| | 9:30 | 9:30 | 9:30 |
| | 10:00 | 10:00 | 10:00 |
| | 10:30 | 10:30 | 10:30 |
| | 11:00 | 11:00 | 11:00 |
| | 11:30 | 11:30 | 11:30 |
| | 12:00 p.m. | 12:00 p.m. | 12:00 p.m. |
| | 12:30 | 12:30 | 12:30 |
| | 1:00 | 1:00 | 1:00 |
| | 1:30 | 1:30 | 1:30 |
| | 2:00 | 2:00 | 2:00 |
| | 2:30 | 2:30 | 2:30 |
| | 3:00 | 3:00 | 3:00 |
| | 3:30 | 3:30 | 3:30 |
| | 4:00 | 4:00 | 4:00 |
| | 4:30 | 4:30 | 4:30 |
| | 5:00 | 5:00 | 5:00 |
| | 5:30 | 5:30 | 5:30 |
| | 6:00 | 6:00 | 6:00 |
| | 6:30 | 6:30 | 6:30 |
| | 7:00 | 7:00 | 7:00 |
| | 7:30 | 7:30 | 7:30 |
| | 8:00 | 8:00 | 8:00 |
| | 8:30 | 8:30 | 8:30 |
| | 9:00 | 9:00 | 9:00 |
| | 9:30 | 9:30 | 9:30 |
| | 10:00 | 10:00 | 10:00 |

| Wednesday | Thursday | Friday | Saturday |
|---|---|---|---|
| 4:00 a.m. | 4:00 a.m. | 4:00 a.m. | 4:00 a.m. |
| 4:30 | 4:30 | 4:30 | 4:30 |
| 5:00 | 5:00 | 5:00 | 5:00 |
| 5:30 | 5:30 | 5:30 | 5:30 |
| 6:00 | 6:00 | 6:00 | 6:00 |
| 6:30 | 6:30 | 6:30 | 6:30 |
| 7:00 | 7:00 | 7:00 | 7:00 |
| 7:30 | 7:30 | 7:30 | 7:30 |
| 8:00 | 8:00 | 8:00 | 8:00 |
| 8:30 | 8:30 | 8:30 | 8:30 |
| 9:00 | 9:00 | 9:00 | 9:00 |
| 9:30 | 9:30 | 9:30 | 9:30 |
| 10:00 | 10:00 | 10:00 | 10:00 |
| 10:30 | 10:30 | 10:30 | 10:30 |
| 11:00 | 11:00 | 11:00 | 11:00 |
| 11:30 | 11:30 | 11:30 | 11:30 |
| 12:00 p.m. | 12:00 p.m. | 12:00 p.m. | 12:00 p.m. |
| 12:30 | 12:30 | 12:30 | 12:30 |
| 1:00 | 1:00 | 1:00 | 1:00 |
| 1:30 | 1:30 | 1:30 | 1:30 |
| 2:00 | 2:00 | 2:00 | 2:00 |
| 2:30 | 2:30 | 2:30 | 2:30 |
| 3:00 | 3:00 | 3:00 | 3:00 |
| 3:30 | 3:30 | 3:30 | 3:30 |
| 4:00 | 4:00 | 4:00 | 4:00 |
| 4:30 | 4:30 | 4:30 | 4:30 |
| 5:00 | 5:00 | 5:00 | 5:00 |
| 5:30 | 5:30 | 5:30 | 5:30 |
| 6:00 | 6:00 | 6:00 | 6:00 |
| 6:30 | 6:30 | 6:30 | 6:30 |
| 7:00 | 7:00 | 7:00 | 7:00 |
| 7:30 | 7:30 | 7:30 | 7:30 |
| 8:00 | 8:00 | 8:00 | 8:00 |
| 8:30 | 8:30 | 8:30 | 8:30 |
| 9:00 | 9:00 | 9:00 | 9:00 |
| 9:30 | 9:30 | 9:30 | 9:30 |
| 10:00 | 10:00 | 10:00 | 10:00 |

# Prep Your *Week*

## *Priorities* This Week

- 
- 
- 
- 
- 
- 
- 
- 

## Coaching Cycles

## Classroom Snapshots

## Data Meetings

## Team & PD Meetings

## Feedback Meetings

## Other

# Reflect on Your *Week*

| What goals did you accomplish this week? | What goals did you not accomplish this week? Why? |
|---|---|
| | |
| **What can you do to improve next week?** | **Things learned and things to remember:** |
| | |

## Goal & Habit Tracker

| Goal or Habit | Day 1 | Day 2 | Day 3 | Day 4 | Day 5 | Day 6 | Day 7 |
|---|---|---|---|---|---|---|---|
| | | | | | | | |
| | | | | | | | |
| | | | | | | | |
| | | | | | | | |

## Notes

Week:

Notes ➘

| Sunday | Monday | Tuesday |
|--------|--------|---------|
| 4:00 a.m. | 4:00 a.m. | 4:00 a.m. |
| 4:30 | 4:30 | 4:30 |
| 5:00 | 5:00 | 5:00 |
| 5:30 | 5:30 | 5:30 |
| 6:00 | 6:00 | 6:00 |
| 6:30 | 6:30 | 6:30 |
| 7:00 | 7:00 | 7:00 |
| 7:30 | 7:30 | 7:30 |
| 8:00 | 8:00 | 8:00 |
| 8:30 | 8:30 | 8:30 |
| 9:00 | 9:00 | 9:00 |
| 9:30 | 9:30 | 9:30 |
| 10:00 | 10:00 | 10:00 |
| 10:30 | 10:30 | 10:30 |
| 11:00 | 11:00 | 11:00 |
| 11:30 | 11:30 | 11:30 |
| 12:00 p.m. | 12:00 p.m. | 12:00 p.m. |
| 12:30 | 12:30 | 12:30 |
| 1:00 | 1:00 | 1:00 |
| 1:30 | 1:30 | 1:30 |
| 2:00 | 2:00 | 2:00 |
| 2:30 | 2:30 | 2:30 |
| 3:00 | 3:00 | 3:00 |
| 3:30 | 3:30 | 3:30 |
| 4:00 | 4:00 | 4:00 |
| 4:30 | 4:30 | 4:30 |
| 5:00 | 5:00 | 5:00 |
| 5:30 | 5:30 | 5:30 |
| 6:00 | 6:00 | 6:00 |
| 6:30 | 6:30 | 6:30 |
| 7:00 | 7:00 | 7:00 |
| 7:30 | 7:30 | 7:30 |
| 8:00 | 8:00 | 8:00 |
| 8:30 | 8:30 | 8:30 |
| 9:00 | 9:00 | 9:00 |
| 9:30 | 9:30 | 9:30 |
| 10:00 | 10:00 | 10:00 |

| Wednesday | Thursday | Friday | Saturday |
|---|---|---|---|
| 4:00 a.m. | 4:00 a.m. | 4:00 a.m. | 4:00 a.m. |
| 4:30 | 4:30 | 4:30 | 4:30 |
| 5:00 | 5:00 | 5:00 | 5:00 |
| 5:30 | 5:30 | 5:30 | 5:30 |
| 6:00 | 6:00 | 6:00 | 6:00 |
| 6:30 | 6:30 | 6:30 | 6:30 |
| 7:00 | 7:00 | 7:00 | 7:00 |
| 7:30 | 7:30 | 7:30 | 7:30 |
| 8:00 | 8:00 | 8:00 | 8:00 |
| 8:30 | 8:30 | 8:30 | 8:30 |
| 9:00 | 9:00 | 9:00 | 9:00 |
| 9:30 | 9:30 | 9:30 | 9:30 |
| 10:00 | 10:00 | 10:00 | 10:00 |
| 10:30 | 10:30 | 10:30 | 10:30 |
| 11:00 | 11:00 | 11:00 | 11:00 |
| 11:30 | 11:30 | 11:30 | 11:30 |
| 12:00 p.m. | 12:00 p.m. | 12:00 p.m. | 12:00 p.m. |
| 12:30 | 12:30 | 12:30 | 12:30 |
| 1:00 | 1:00 | 1:00 | 1:00 |
| 1:30 | 1:30 | 1:30 | 1:30 |
| 2:00 | 2:00 | 2:00 | 2:00 |
| 2:30 | 2:30 | 2:30 | 2:30 |
| 3:00 | 3:00 | 3:00 | 3:00 |
| 3:30 | 3:30 | 3:30 | 3:30 |
| 4:00 | 4:00 | 4:00 | 4:00 |
| 4:30 | 4:30 | 4:30 | 4:30 |
| 5:00 | 5:00 | 5:00 | 5:00 |
| 5:30 | 5:30 | 5:30 | 5:30 |
| 6:00 | 6:00 | 6:00 | 6:00 |
| 6:30 | 6:30 | 6:30 | 6:30 |
| 7:00 | 7:00 | 7:00 | 7:00 |
| 7:30 | 7:30 | 7:30 | 7:30 |
| 8:00 | 8:00 | 8:00 | 8:00 |
| 8:30 | 8:30 | 8:30 | 8:30 |
| 9:00 | 9:00 | 9:00 | 9:00 |
| 9:30 | 9:30 | 9:30 | 9:30 |
| 10:00 | 10:00 | 10:00 | 10:00 |

# Prep Your *Week*

## *Priorities* This Week

- 
- 
- 
- 
- 
- 
- 
- 
- 

## Coaching Cycles

## Classroom Snapshots

## Data Meetings

## Team & PD Meetings

## Feedback Meetings

## Other

# Reflect on Your *Week*

| What goals did you accomplish this week? | What goals did you not accomplish this week? Why? |
|---|---|
| What can you do to improve next week? | Things learned and things to remember: |

## Goal & Habit Tracker

| Goal or Habit | Day 1 | Day 2 | Day 3 | Day 4 | Day 5 | Day 6 | Day 7 |
|---|---|---|---|---|---|---|---|
| | | | | | | | |
| | | | | | | | |
| | | | | | | | |
| | | | | | | | |

## Notes

**Week:**

**Notes**

| Sunday | Monday | Tuesday |
|---|---|---|
| 4:00 a.m. | 4:00 a.m. | 4:00 a.m. |
| 4:30 | 4:30 | 4:30 |
| 5:00 | 5:00 | 5:00 |
| 5:30 | 5:30 | 5:30 |
| 6:00 | 6:00 | 6:00 |
| 6:30 | 6:30 | 6:30 |
| 7:00 | 7:00 | 7:00 |
| 7:30 | 7:30 | 7:30 |
| 8:00 | 8:00 | 8:00 |
| 8:30 | 8:30 | 8:30 |
| 9:00 | 9:00 | 9:00 |
| 9:30 | 9:30 | 9:30 |
| 10:00 | 10:00 | 10:00 |
| 10:30 | 10:30 | 10:30 |
| 11:00 | 11:00 | 11:00 |
| 11:30 | 11:30 | 11:30 |
| 12:00 p.m. | 12:00 p.m. | 12:00 p.m. |
| 12:30 | 12:30 | 12:30 |
| 1:00 | 1:00 | 1:00 |
| 1:30 | 1:30 | 1:30 |
| 2:00 | 2:00 | 2:00 |
| 2:30 | 2:30 | 2:30 |
| 3:00 | 3:00 | 3:00 |
| 3:30 | 3:30 | 3:30 |
| 4:00 | 4:00 | 4:00 |
| 4:30 | 4:30 | 4:30 |
| 5:00 | 5:00 | 5:00 |
| 5:30 | 5:30 | 5:30 |
| 6:00 | 6:00 | 6:00 |
| 6:30 | 6:30 | 6:30 |
| 7:00 | 7:00 | 7:00 |
| 7:30 | 7:30 | 7:30 |
| 8:00 | 8:00 | 8:00 |
| 8:30 | 8:30 | 8:30 |
| 9:00 | 9:00 | 9:00 |
| 9:30 | 9:30 | 9:30 |
| 10:00 | 10:00 | 10:00 |

| Wednesday | Thursday | Friday | Saturday |
|---|---|---|---|
| 4:00 a.m. | 4:00 a.m. | 4:00 a.m. | 4:00 a.m. |
| 4:30 | 4:30 | 4:30 | 4:30 |
| 5:00 | 5:00 | 5:00 | 5:00 |
| 5:30 | 5:30 | 5:30 | 5:30 |
| 6:00 | 6:00 | 6:00 | 6:00 |
| 6:30 | 6:30 | 6:30 | 6:30 |
| 7:00 | 7:00 | 7:00 | 7:00 |
| 7:30 | 7:30 | 7:30 | 7:30 |
| 8:00 | 8:00 | 8:00 | 8:00 |
| 8:30 | 8:30 | 8:30 | 8:30 |
| 9:00 | 9:00 | 9:00 | 9:00 |
| 9:30 | 9:30 | 9:30 | 9:30 |
| 10:00 | 10:00 | 10:00 | 10:00 |
| 10:30 | 10:30 | 10:30 | 10:30 |
| 11:00 | 11:00 | 11:00 | 11:00 |
| 11:30 | 11:30 | 11:30 | 11:30 |
| 12:00 p.m. | 12:00 p.m. | 12:00 p.m. | 12:00 p.m. |
| 12:30 | 12:30 | 12:30 | 12:30 |
| 1:00 | 1:00 | 1:00 | 1:00 |
| 1:30 | 1:30 | 1:30 | 1:30 |
| 2:00 | 2:00 | 2:00 | 2:00 |
| 2:30 | 2:30 | 2:30 | 2:30 |
| 3:00 | 3:00 | 3:00 | 3:00 |
| 3:30 | 3:30 | 3:30 | 3:30 |
| 4:00 | 4:00 | 4:00 | 4:00 |
| 4:30 | 4:30 | 4:30 | 4:30 |
| 5:00 | 5:00 | 5:00 | 5:00 |
| 5:30 | 5:30 | 5:30 | 5:30 |
| 6:00 | 6:00 | 6:00 | 6:00 |
| 6:30 | 6:30 | 6:30 | 6:30 |
| 7:00 | 7:00 | 7:00 | 7:00 |
| 7:30 | 7:30 | 7:30 | 7:30 |
| 8:00 | 8:00 | 8:00 | 8:00 |
| 8:30 | 8:30 | 8:30 | 8:30 |
| 9:00 | 9:00 | 9:00 | 9:00 |
| 9:30 | 9:30 | 9:30 | 9:30 |
| 10:00 | 10:00 | 10:00 | 10:00 |

# Prep Your *Week*

## Priorities This Week

- 
- 
- 
- 
- 
- 
- 
- 

## Coaching Cycles

## Classroom Snapshots

## Data Meetings

## Team & PD Meetings

## Feedback Meetings

## Other

# Reflect on Your *Week*

| What goals did you accomplish this week? | What goals did you not accomplish this week? Why? |
|---|---|
| **What can you do to improve next week?** | **Things learned and things to remember:** |

## Goal & Habit Tracker

| Goal or Habit | Day 1 | Day 2 | Day 3 | Day 4 | Day 5 | Day 6 | Day 7 |
|---|---|---|---|---|---|---|---|
| | | | | | | | |
| | | | | | | | |
| | | | | | | | |
| | | | | | | | |

## Notes

Week:

Notes ↗

| Sunday | Monday | Tuesday |
|---|---|---|
| 4:00 a.m. | 4:00 a.m. | 4:00 a.m. |
| 4:30 | 4:30 | 4:30 |
| 5:00 | 5:00 | 5:00 |
| 5:30 | 5:30 | 5:30 |
| 6:00 | 6:00 | 6:00 |
| 6:30 | 6:30 | 6:30 |
| 7:00 | 7:00 | 7:00 |
| 7:30 | 7:30 | 7:30 |
| 8:00 | 8:00 | 8:00 |
| 8:30 | 8:30 | 8:30 |
| 9:00 | 9:00 | 9:00 |
| 9:30 | 9:30 | 9:30 |
| 10:00 | 10:00 | 10:00 |
| 10:30 | 10:30 | 10:30 |
| 11:00 | 11:00 | 11:00 |
| 11:30 | 11:30 | 11:30 |
| 12:00 p.m. | 12:00 p.m. | 12:00 p.m. |
| 12:30 | 12:30 | 12:30 |
| 1:00 | 1:00 | 1:00 |
| 1:30 | 1:30 | 1:30 |
| 2:00 | 2:00 | 2:00 |
| 2:30 | 2:30 | 2:30 |
| 3:00 | 3:00 | 3:00 |
| 3:30 | 3:30 | 3:30 |
| 4:00 | 4:00 | 4:00 |
| 4:30 | 4:30 | 4:30 |
| 5:00 | 5:00 | 5:00 |
| 5:30 | 5:30 | 5:30 |
| 6:00 | 6:00 | 6:00 |
| 6:30 | 6:30 | 6:30 |
| 7:00 | 7:00 | 7:00 |
| 7:30 | 7:30 | 7:30 |
| 8:00 | 8:00 | 8:00 |
| 8:30 | 8:30 | 8:30 |
| 9:00 | 9:00 | 9:00 |
| 9:30 | 9:30 | 9:30 |
| 10:00 | 10:00 | 10:00 |

| Wednesday | Thursday | Friday | Saturday |
|---|---|---|---|
| 4:00 a.m. | 4:00 a.m. | 4:00 a.m. | 4:00 a.m. |
| 4:30 | 4:30 | 4:30 | 4:30 |
| 5:00 | 5:00 | 5:00 | 5:00 |
| 5:30 | 5:30 | 5:30 | 5:30 |
| 6:00 | 6:00 | 6:00 | 6:00 |
| 6:30 | 6:30 | 6:30 | 6:30 |
| 7:00 | 7:00 | 7:00 | 7:00 |
| 7:30 | 7:30 | 7:30 | 7:30 |
| 8:00 | 8:00 | 8:00 | 8:00 |
| 8:30 | 8:30 | 8:30 | 8:30 |
| 9:00 | 9:00 | 9:00 | 9:00 |
| 9:30 | 9:30 | 9:30 | 9:30 |
| 10:00 | 10:00 | 10:00 | 10:00 |
| 10:30 | 10:30 | 10:30 | 10:30 |
| 11:00 | 11:00 | 11:00 | 11:00 |
| 11:30 | 11:30 | 11:30 | 11:30 |
| 12:00 p.m. | 12:00 p.m. | 12:00 p.m. | 12:00 p.m. |
| 12:30 | 12:30 | 12:30 | 12:30 |
| 1:00 | 1:00 | 1:00 | 1:00 |
| 1:30 | 1:30 | 1:30 | 1:30 |
| 2:00 | 2:00 | 2:00 | 2:00 |
| 2:30 | 2:30 | 2:30 | 2:30 |
| 3:00 | 3:00 | 3:00 | 3:00 |
| 3:30 | 3:30 | 3:30 | 3:30 |
| 4:00 | 4:00 | 4:00 | 4:00 |
| 4:30 | 4:30 | 4:30 | 4:30 |
| 5:00 | 5:00 | 5:00 | 5:00 |
| 5:30 | 5:30 | 5:30 | 5:30 |
| 6:00 | 6:00 | 6:00 | 6:00 |
| 6:30 | 6:30 | 6:30 | 6:30 |
| 7:00 | 7:00 | 7:00 | 7:00 |
| 7:30 | 7:30 | 7:30 | 7:30 |
| 8:00 | 8:00 | 8:00 | 8:00 |
| 8:30 | 8:30 | 8:30 | 8:30 |
| 9:00 | 9:00 | 9:00 | 9:00 |
| 9:30 | 9:30 | 9:30 | 9:30 |
| 10:00 | 10:00 | 10:00 | 10:00 |

# Prep Your *Week*

## Priorities This Week

- 
- 
- 
- 
- 
- 
- 
- 
- 

## Coaching Cycles

## Classroom Snapshots

## Data Meetings

## Team & PD Meetings

## Feedback Meetings

## Other

# Reflect on Your *Week*

| What goals did you accomplish this week? | What goals did you not accomplish this week? Why? |
|---|---|
| What can you do to improve next week? | Things learned and things to remember: |

## Goal & Habit Tracker

| Goal or Habit | Day 1 | Day 2 | Day 3 | Day 4 | Day 5 | Day 6 | Day 7 |
|---|---|---|---|---|---|---|---|
|  |  |  |  |  |  |  |  |
|  |  |  |  |  |  |  |  |
|  |  |  |  |  |  |  |  |
|  |  |  |  |  |  |  |  |

## Notes

Week:

Notes

| | Sunday | Monday | Tuesday |
|---|---|---|---|
| | 4:00 a.m. | 4:00 a.m. | 4:00 a.m. |
| | 4:30 | 4:30 | 4:30 |
| | 5:00 | 5:00 | 5:00 |
| | 5:30 | 5:30 | 5:30 |
| | 6:00 | 6:00 | 6:00 |
| | 6:30 | 6:30 | 6:30 |
| | 7:00 | 7:00 | 7:00 |
| | 7:30 | 7:30 | 7:30 |
| | 8:00 | 8:00 | 8:00 |
| | 8:30 | 8:30 | 8:30 |
| | 9:00 | 9:00 | 9:00 |
| | 9:30 | 9:30 | 9:30 |
| | 10:00 | 10:00 | 10:00 |
| | 10:30 | 10:30 | 10:30 |
| | 11:00 | 11:00 | 11:00 |
| | 11:30 | 11:30 | 11:30 |
| | 12:00 p.m. | 12:00 p.m. | 12:00 p.m. |
| | 12:30 | 12:30 | 12:30 |
| | 1:00 | 1:00 | 1:00 |
| | 1:30 | 1:30 | 1:30 |
| | 2:00 | 2:00 | 2:00 |
| | 2:30 | 2:30 | 2:30 |
| | 3:00 | 3:00 | 3:00 |
| | 3:30 | 3:30 | 3:30 |
| | 4:00 | 4:00 | 4:00 |
| | 4:30 | 4:30 | 4:30 |
| | 5:00 | 5:00 | 5:00 |
| | 5:30 | 5:30 | 5:30 |
| | 6:00 | 6:00 | 6:00 |
| | 6:30 | 6:30 | 6:30 |
| | 7:00 | 7:00 | 7:00 |
| | 7:30 | 7:30 | 7:30 |
| | 8:00 | 8:00 | 8:00 |
| | 8:30 | 8:30 | 8:30 |
| | 9:00 | 9:00 | 9:00 |
| | 9:30 | 9:30 | 9:30 |
| | 10:00 | 10:00 | 10:00 |

| Wednesday | Thursday | Friday | Saturday |
|---|---|---|---|
| 4:00 a.m. | 4:00 a.m. | 4:00 a.m. | 4:00 a.m. |
| 4:30 | 4:30 | 4:30 | 4:30 |
| 5:00 | 5:00 | 5:00 | 5:00 |
| 5:30 | 5:30 | 5:30 | 5:30 |
| 6:00 | 6:00 | 6:00 | 6:00 |
| 6:30 | 6:30 | 6:30 | 6:30 |
| 7:00 | 7:00 | 7:00 | 7:00 |
| 7:30 | 7:30 | 7:30 | 7:30 |
| 8:00 | 8:00 | 8:00 | 8:00 |
| 8:30 | 8:30 | 8:30 | 8:30 |
| 9:00 | 9:00 | 9:00 | 9:00 |
| 9:30 | 9:30 | 9:30 | 9:30 |
| 10:00 | 10:00 | 10:00 | 10:00 |
| 10:30 | 10:30 | 10:30 | 10:30 |
| 11:00 | 11:00 | 11:00 | 11:00 |
| 11:30 | 11:30 | 11:30 | 11:30 |
| 12:00 p.m. | 12:00 p.m. | 12:00 p.m. | 12:00 p.m. |
| 12:30 | 12:30 | 12:30 | 12:30 |
| 1:00 | 1:00 | 1:00 | 1:00 |
| 1:30 | 1:30 | 1:30 | 1:30 |
| 2:00 | 2:00 | 2:00 | 2:00 |
| 2:30 | 2:30 | 2:30 | 2:30 |
| 3:00 | 3:00 | 3:00 | 3:00 |
| 3:30 | 3:30 | 3:30 | 3:30 |
| 4:00 | 4:00 | 4:00 | 4:00 |
| 4:30 | 4:30 | 4:30 | 4:30 |
| 5:00 | 5:00 | 5:00 | 5:00 |
| 5:30 | 5:30 | 5:30 | 5:30 |
| 6:00 | 6:00 | 6:00 | 6:00 |
| 6:30 | 6:30 | 6:30 | 6:30 |
| 7:00 | 7:00 | 7:00 | 7:00 |
| 7:30 | 7:30 | 7:30 | 7:30 |
| 8:00 | 8:00 | 8:00 | 8:00 |
| 8:30 | 8:30 | 8:30 | 8:30 |
| 9:00 | 9:00 | 9:00 | 9:00 |
| 9:30 | 9:30 | 9:30 | 9:30 |
| 10:00 | 10:00 | 10:00 | 10:00 |

# Plans ARE OF LITTLE IMPORTANCE, BUT planning is essential.

—Winston Churchill

# Prep Your *month*

## Personal Goals

| Day | Health & Fitness | Finances | Self-Care & Growth |
|-----|-----------------|----------|-------------------|
|     |                 |          |                   |
|     |                 |          |                   |
|     |                 |          |                   |
|     |                 |          |                   |
|     |                 |          |                   |
|     |                 |          |                   |

## Important Reminders

|     |     |
|-----|-----|
|     |     |
|     |     |
|     |     |
|     |     |
|     |     |
|     |     |

# Prep Your *Month*

| Main Goal | Main Focus | Wins |
|---|---|---|
| | | |

## Monthly Tasks

**Week 1**

**Week 2**

**Week 3**

**Week 4**

**Week 5**

## Must Do This Month

## Save for Next Month

# September

*"Learners need endless feedback more than they need endless teaching."* —Grant Wiggins

| Sunday | Monday | Tuesday | Wednesday |
|--------|--------|---------|-----------|
|        |        |         |           |
|        |        |         |           |
|        |        |         |           |
|        |        |         |           |
|        |        |         |           |

## Monthly Focus

| Thursday | Friday | Saturday |
|----------|--------|----------|
|          |        |          |
|          |        |          |
|          |        |          |
|          |        |          |
|          |        |          |

 Notes

SEPTEMBER

# Prep Your *Week*

## Priorities This Week

- 
- 
- 
- 
- 
- 
- 
- 

## Coaching Cycles

## Classroom Snapshots

## Data Meetings

## Team & PD Meetings

## Feedback Meetings

## Other

# Reflect on Your *Week*

| What goals did you accomplish this week? | What goals did you not accomplish this week? Why? |
|---|---|
| **What can you do to improve next week?** | **Things learned and things to remember:** |

## Goal & Habit Tracker

| Goal or Habit | Day 1 | Day 2 | Day 3 | Day 4 | Day 5 | Day 6 | Day 7 |
|---|---|---|---|---|---|---|---|
|  |  |  |  |  |  |  |  |
|  |  |  |  |  |  |  |  |
|  |  |  |  |  |  |  |  |
|  |  |  |  |  |  |  |  |

## Notes

Week:

Notes ↘

| | Sunday | Monday | Tuesday |
|---|---|---|---|
| | 4:00 a.m. | 4:00 a.m. | 4:00 a.m. |
| | 4:30 | 4:30 | 4:30 |
| | 5:00 | 5:00 | 5:00 |
| | 5:30 | 5:30 | 5:30 |
| | 6:00 | 6:00 | 6:00 |
| | 6:30 | 6:30 | 6:30 |
| | 7:00 | 7:00 | 7:00 |
| | 7:30 | 7:30 | 7:30 |
| | 8:00 | 8:00 | 8:00 |
| | 8:30 | 8:30 | 8:30 |
| | 9:00 | 9:00 | 9:00 |
| | 9:30 | 9:30 | 9:30 |
| | 10:00 | 10:00 | 10:00 |
| | 10:30 | 10:30 | 10:30 |
| | 11:00 | 11:00 | 11:00 |
| | 11:30 | 11:30 | 11:30 |
| | 12:00 p.m. | 12:00 p.m. | 12:00 p.m. |
| | 12:30 | 12:30 | 12:30 |
| | 1:00 | 1:00 | 1:00 |
| | 1:30 | 1:30 | 1:30 |
| | 2:00 | 2:00 | 2:00 |
| | 2:30 | 2:30 | 2:30 |
| | 3:00 | 3:00 | 3:00 |
| | 3:30 | 3:30 | 3:30 |
| | 4:00 | 4:00 | 4:00 |
| | 4:30 | 4:30 | 4:30 |
| | 5:00 | 5:00 | 5:00 |
| | 5:30 | 5:30 | 5:30 |
| | 6:00 | 6:00 | 6:00 |
| | 6:30 | 6:30 | 6:30 |
| | 7:00 | 7:00 | 7:00 |
| | 7:30 | 7:30 | 7:30 |
| | 8:00 | 8:00 | 8:00 |
| | 8:30 | 8:30 | 8:30 |
| | 9:00 | 9:00 | 9:00 |
| | 9:30 | 9:30 | 9:30 |
| | 10:00 | 10:00 | 10:00 |

| Wednesday | Thursday | Friday | Saturday |
|---|---|---|---|
| 4:00 a.m. | 4:00 a.m. | 4:00 a.m. | 4:00 a.m. |
| 4:30 | 4:30 | 4:30 | 4:30 |
| 5:00 | 5:00 | 5:00 | 5:00 |
| 5:30 | 5:30 | 5:30 | 5:30 |
| 6:00 | 6:00 | 6:00 | 6:00 |
| 6:30 | 6:30 | 6:30 | 6:30 |
| 7:00 | 7:00 | 7:00 | 7:00 |
| 7:30 | 7:30 | 7:30 | 7:30 |
| 8:00 | 8:00 | 8:00 | 8:00 |
| 8:30 | 8:30 | 8:30 | 8:30 |
| 9:00 | 9:00 | 9:00 | 9:00 |
| 9:30 | 9:30 | 9:30 | 9:30 |
| 10:00 | 10:00 | 10:00 | 10:00 |
| 10:30 | 10:30 | 10:30 | 10:30 |
| 11:00 | 11:00 | 11:00 | 11:00 |
| 11:30 | 11:30 | 11:30 | 11:30 |
| 12:00 p.m. | 12:00 p.m. | 12:00 p.m. | 12:00 p.m. |
| 12:30 | 12:30 | 12:30 | 12:30 |
| 1:00 | 1:00 | 1:00 | 1:00 |
| 1:30 | 1:30 | 1:30 | 1:30 |
| 2:00 | 2:00 | 2:00 | 2:00 |
| 2:30 | 2:30 | 2:30 | 2:30 |
| 3:00 | 3:00 | 3:00 | 3:00 |
| 3:30 | 3:30 | 3:30 | 3:30 |
| 4:00 | 4:00 | 4:00 | 4:00 |
| 4:30 | 4:30 | 4:30 | 4:30 |
| 5:00 | 5:00 | 5:00 | 5:00 |
| 5:30 | 5:30 | 5:30 | 5:30 |
| 6:00 | 6:00 | 6:00 | 6:00 |
| 6:30 | 6:30 | 6:30 | 6:30 |
| 7:00 | 7:00 | 7:00 | 7:00 |
| 7:30 | 7:30 | 7:30 | 7:30 |
| 8:00 | 8:00 | 8:00 | 8:00 |
| 8:30 | 8:30 | 8:30 | 8:30 |
| 9:00 | 9:00 | 9:00 | 9:00 |
| 9:30 | 9:30 | 9:30 | 9:30 |
| 10:00 | 10:00 | 10:00 | 10:00 |

# Prep Your *Week*

## Priorities This Week

- 
- 
- 
- 
- 
- 
- 
- 

## Coaching Cycles

## Classroom Snapshots

## Data Meetings

## Team & PD Meetings

## Feedback Meetings

## Other

# Reflect on Your *Week*

| What goals did you accomplish this week? | What goals did you not accomplish this week? Why? |
|---|---|
| What can you do to improve next week? | Things learned and things to remember: |

## Goal & Habit Tracker

| Goal or Habit | Day 1 | Day 2 | Day 3 | Day 4 | Day 5 | Day 6 | Day 7 |
|---|---|---|---|---|---|---|---|
|  |  |  |  |  |  |  |  |
|  |  |  |  |  |  |  |  |
|  |  |  |  |  |  |  |  |
|  |  |  |  |  |  |  |  |

## Notes

Week:

Notes

| | Sunday | Monday | Tuesday |
|---|---|---|---|
| | 4:00 a.m. | 4:00 a.m. | 4:00 a.m. |
| | 4:30 | 4:30 | 4:30 |
| | 5:00 | 5:00 | 5:00 |
| | 5:30 | 5:30 | 5:30 |
| | 6:00 | 6:00 | 6:00 |
| | 6:30 | 6:30 | 6:30 |
| | 7:00 | 7:00 | 7:00 |
| | 7:30 | 7:30 | 7:30 |
| | 8:00 | 8:00 | 8:00 |
| | 8:30 | 8:30 | 8:30 |
| | 9:00 | 9:00 | 9:00 |
| | 9:30 | 9:30 | 9:30 |
| | 10:00 | 10:00 | 10:00 |
| | 10:30 | 10:30 | 10:30 |
| | 11:00 | 11:00 | 11:00 |
| | 11:30 | 11:30 | 11:30 |
| | 12:00 p.m. | 12:00 p.m. | 12:00 p.m. |
| | 12:30 | 12:30 | 12:30 |
| | 1:00 | 1:00 | 1:00 |
| | 1:30 | 1:30 | 1:30 |
| | 2:00 | 2:00 | 2:00 |
| | 2:30 | 2:30 | 2:30 |
| | 3:00 | 3:00 | 3:00 |
| | 3:30 | 3:30 | 3:30 |
| | 4:00 | 4:00 | 4:00 |
| | 4:30 | 4:30 | 4:30 |
| | 5:00 | 5:00 | 5:00 |
| | 5:30 | 5:30 | 5:30 |
| | 6:00 | 6:00 | 6:00 |
| | 6:30 | 6:30 | 6:30 |
| | 7:00 | 7:00 | 7:00 |
| | 7:30 | 7:30 | 7:30 |
| | 8:00 | 8:00 | 8:00 |
| | 8:30 | 8:30 | 8:30 |
| | 9:00 | 9:00 | 9:00 |
| | 9:30 | 9:30 | 9:30 |
| | 10:00 | 10:00 | 10:00 |

| Wednesday | Thursday | Friday | Saturday |
|-----------|----------|--------|----------|
| 4:00 a.m. | 4:00 a.m. | 4:00 a.m. | 4:00 a.m. |
| 4:30 | 4:30 | 4:30 | 4:30 |
| 5:00 | 5:00 | 5:00 | 5:00 |
| 5:30 | 5:30 | 5:30 | 5:30 |
| 6:00 | 6:00 | 6:00 | 6:00 |
| 6:30 | 6:30 | 6:30 | 6:30 |
| 7:00 | 7:00 | 7:00 | 7:00 |
| 7:30 | 7:30 | 7:30 | 7:30 |
| 8:00 | 8:00 | 8:00 | 8:00 |
| 8:30 | 8:30 | 8:30 | 8:30 |
| 9:00 | 9:00 | 9:00 | 9:00 |
| 9:30 | 9:30 | 9:30 | 9:30 |
| 10:00 | 10:00 | 10:00 | 10:00 |
| 10:30 | 10:30 | 10:30 | 10:30 |
| 11:00 | 11:00 | 11:00 | 11:00 |
| 11:30 | 11:30 | 11:30 | 11:30 |
| 12:00 p.m. | 12:00 p.m. | 12:00 p.m. | 12:00 p.m. |
| 12:30 | 12:30 | 12:30 | 12:30 |
| 1:00 | 1:00 | 1:00 | 1:00 |
| 1:30 | 1:30 | 1:30 | 1:30 |
| 2:00 | 2:00 | 2:00 | 2:00 |
| 2:30 | 2:30 | 2:30 | 2:30 |
| 3:00 | 3:00 | 3:00 | 3:00 |
| 3:30 | 3:30 | 3:30 | 3:30 |
| 4:00 | 4:00 | 4:00 | 4:00 |
| 4:30 | 4:30 | 4:30 | 4:30 |
| 5:00 | 5:00 | 5:00 | 5:00 |
| 5:30 | 5:30 | 5:30 | 5:30 |
| 6:00 | 6:00 | 6:00 | 6:00 |
| 6:30 | 6:30 | 6:30 | 6:30 |
| 7:00 | 7:00 | 7:00 | 7:00 |
| 7:30 | 7:30 | 7:30 | 7:30 |
| 8:00 | 8:00 | 8:00 | 8:00 |
| 8:30 | 8:30 | 8:30 | 8:30 |
| 9:00 | 9:00 | 9:00 | 9:00 |
| 9:30 | 9:30 | 9:30 | 9:30 |
| 10:00 | 10:00 | 10:00 | 10:00 |

# Prep Your *Week*

## *Priorities* This Week

- 
- 
- 
- 
- 
- 
- 
- 

## Coaching Cycles

## Classroom Snapshots

## Data Meetings

## Team & PD Meetings

## Feedback Meetings

## Other

# Reflect on Your Week

| What goals did you accomplish this week? | What goals did you not accomplish this week? Why? |
|---|---|
| | |
| **What can you do to improve next week?** | **Things learned and things to remember:** |
| | |

## Goal & Habit Tracker

| Goal or Habit | Day 1 | Day 2 | Day 3 | Day 4 | Day 5 | Day 6 | Day 7 |
|---|---|---|---|---|---|---|---|
| | | | | | | | |
| | | | | | | | |
| | | | | | | | |
| | | | | | | | |

## Notes

Week:

Notes

| | Sunday | Monday | Tuesday |
|---|---|---|---|
| | 4:00 a.m. | 4:00 a.m. | 4:00 a.m. |
| | 4:30 | 4:30 | 4:30 |
| | 5:00 | 5:00 | 5:00 |
| | 5:30 | 5:30 | 5:30 |
| | 6:00 | 6:00 | 6:00 |
| | 6:30 | 6:30 | 6:30 |
| | 7:00 | 7:00 | 7:00 |
| | 7:30 | 7:30 | 7:30 |
| | 8:00 | 8:00 | 8:00 |
| | 8:30 | 8:30 | 8:30 |
| | 9:00 | 9:00 | 9:00 |
| | 9:30 | 9:30 | 9:30 |
| | 10:00 | 10:00 | 10:00 |
| | 10:30 | 10:30 | 10:30 |
| | 11:00 | 11:00 | 11:00 |
| | 11:30 | 11:30 | 11:30 |
| | 12:00 p.m. | 12:00 p.m. | 12:00 p.m. |
| | 12:30 | 12:30 | 12:30 |
| | 1:00 | 1:00 | 1:00 |
| | 1:30 | 1:30 | 1:30 |
| | 2:00 | 2:00 | 2:00 |
| | 2:30 | 2:30 | 2:30 |
| | 3:00 | 3:00 | 3:00 |
| | 3:30 | 3:30 | 3:30 |
| | 4:00 | 4:00 | 4:00 |
| | 4:30 | 4:30 | 4:30 |
| | 5:00 | 5:00 | 5:00 |
| | 5:30 | 5:30 | 5:30 |
| | 6:00 | 6:00 | 6:00 |
| | 6:30 | 6:30 | 6:30 |
| | 7:00 | 7:00 | 7:00 |
| | 7:30 | 7:30 | 7:30 |
| | 8:00 | 8:00 | 8:00 |
| | 8:30 | 8:30 | 8:30 |
| | 9:00 | 9:00 | 9:00 |
| | 9:30 | 9:30 | 9:30 |
| | 10:00 | 10:00 | 10:00 |

| Wednesday | Thursday | Friday | Saturday |
| --- | --- | --- | --- |
| 4:00 a.m. | 4:00 a.m. | 4:00 a.m. | 4:00 a.m. |
| 4:30 | 4:30 | 4:30 | 4:30 |
| 5:00 | 5:00 | 5:00 | 5:00 |
| 5:30 | 5:30 | 5:30 | 5:30 |
| 6:00 | 6:00 | 6:00 | 6:00 |
| 6:30 | 6:30 | 6:30 | 6:30 |
| 7:00 | 7:00 | 7:00 | 7:00 |
| 7:30 | 7:30 | 7:30 | 7:30 |
| 8:00 | 8:00 | 8:00 | 8:00 |
| 8:30 | 8:30 | 8:30 | 8:30 |
| 9:00 | 9:00 | 9:00 | 9:00 |
| 9:30 | 9:30 | 9:30 | 9:30 |
| 10:00 | 10:00 | 10:00 | 10:00 |
| 10:30 | 10:30 | 10:30 | 10:30 |
| 11:00 | 11:00 | 11:00 | 11:00 |
| 11:30 | 11:30 | 11:30 | 11:30 |
| 12:00 p.m. | 12:00 p.m. | 12:00 p.m. | 12:00 p.m. |
| 12:30 | 12:30 | 12:30 | 12:30 |
| 1:00 | 1:00 | 1:00 | 1:00 |
| 1:30 | 1:30 | 1:30 | 1:30 |
| 2:00 | 2:00 | 2:00 | 2:00 |
| 2:30 | 2:30 | 2:30 | 2:30 |
| 3:00 | 3:00 | 3:00 | 3:00 |
| 3:30 | 3:30 | 3:30 | 3:30 |
| 4:00 | 4:00 | 4:00 | 4:00 |
| 4:30 | 4:30 | 4:30 | 4:30 |
| 5:00 | 5:00 | 5:00 | 5:00 |
| 5:30 | 5:30 | 5:30 | 5:30 |
| 6:00 | 6:00 | 6:00 | 6:00 |
| 6:30 | 6:30 | 6:30 | 6:30 |
| 7:00 | 7:00 | 7:00 | 7:00 |
| 7:30 | 7:30 | 7:30 | 7:30 |
| 8:00 | 8:00 | 8:00 | 8:00 |
| 8:30 | 8:30 | 8:30 | 8:30 |
| 9:00 | 9:00 | 9:00 | 9:00 |
| 9:30 | 9:30 | 9:30 | 9:30 |
| 10:00 | 10:00 | 10:00 | 10:00 |

# Prep Your *Week*

## *Priorities* This Week

- 
- 
- 
- 
- 
- 
- 
- 

## Coaching Cycles

## Classroom Snapshots

## Data Meetings

## Team & PD Meetings

## Feedback Meetings

## Other

# Reflect on Your *Week*

| What goals did you accomplish this week? | What goals did you not accomplish this week? Why? |
|---|---|
| **What can you do to improve next week?** | **Things learned and things to remember:** |

## Goal & Habit Tracker

| Goal or Habit | Day 1 | Day 2 | Day 3 | Day 4 | Day 5 | Day 6 | Day 7 |
|---|---|---|---|---|---|---|---|
| | | | | | | | |
| | | | | | | | |
| | | | | | | | |
| | | | | | | | |

## Notes

Week:

Notes

| | Sunday | Monday | Tuesday |
|---|---|---|---|
| | 4:00 a.m. | 4:00 a.m. | 4:00 a.m. |
| | 4:30 | 4:30 | 4:30 |
| | 5:00 | 5:00 | 5:00 |
| | 5:30 | 5:30 | 5:30 |
| | 6:00 | 6:00 | 6:00 |
| | 6:30 | 6:30 | 6:30 |
| | 7:00 | 7:00 | 7:00 |
| | 7:30 | 7:30 | 7:30 |
| | 8:00 | 8:00 | 8:00 |
| | 8:30 | 8:30 | 8:30 |
| | 9:00 | 9:00 | 9:00 |
| | 9:30 | 9:30 | 9:30 |
| | 10:00 | 10:00 | 10:00 |
| | 10:30 | 10:30 | 10:30 |
| | 11:00 | 11:00 | 11:00 |
| | 11:30 | 11:30 | 11:30 |
| | 12:00 p.m. | 12:00 p.m. | 12:00 p.m. |
| | 12:30 | 12:30 | 12:30 |
| | 1:00 | 1:00 | 1:00 |
| | 1:30 | 1:30 | 1:30 |
| | 2:00 | 2:00 | 2:00 |
| | 2:30 | 2:30 | 2:30 |
| | 3:00 | 3:00 | 3:00 |
| | 3:30 | 3:30 | 3:30 |
| | 4:00 | 4:00 | 4:00 |
| | 4:30 | 4:30 | 4:30 |
| | 5:00 | 5:00 | 5:00 |
| | 5:30 | 5:30 | 5:30 |
| | 6:00 | 6:00 | 6:00 |
| | 6:30 | 6:30 | 6:30 |
| | 7:00 | 7:00 | 7:00 |
| | 7:30 | 7:30 | 7:30 |
| | 8:00 | 8:00 | 8:00 |
| | 8:30 | 8:30 | 8:30 |
| | 9:00 | 9:00 | 9:00 |
| | 9:30 | 9:30 | 9:30 |
| | 10:00 | 10:00 | 10:00 |

| Wednesday | Thursday | Friday | Saturday |
|---|---|---|---|
| 4:00 a.m. | 4:00 a.m. | 4:00 a.m. | 4:00 a.m. |
| 4:30 | 4:30 | 4:30 | 4:30 |
| 5:00 | 5:00 | 5:00 | 5:00 |
| 5:30 | 5:30 | 5:30 | 5:30 |
| 6:00 | 6:00 | 6:00 | 6:00 |
| 6:30 | 6:30 | 6:30 | 6:30 |
| 7:00 | 7:00 | 7:00 | 7:00 |
| 7:30 | 7:30 | 7:30 | 7:30 |
| 8:00 | 8:00 | 8:00 | 8:00 |
| 8:30 | 8:30 | 8:30 | 8:30 |
| 9:00 | 9:00 | 9:00 | 9:00 |
| 9:30 | 9:30 | 9:30 | 9:30 |
| 10:00 | 10:00 | 10:00 | 10:00 |
| 10:30 | 10:30 | 10:30 | 10:30 |
| 11:00 | 11:00 | 11:00 | 11:00 |
| 11:30 | 11:30 | 11:30 | 11:30 |
| 12:00 p.m. | 12:00 p.m. | 12:00 p.m. | 12:00 p.m. |
| 12:30 | 12:30 | 12:30 | 12:30 |
| 1:00 | 1:00 | 1:00 | 1:00 |
| 1:30 | 1:30 | 1:30 | 1:30 |
| 2:00 | 2:00 | 2:00 | 2:00 |
| 2:30 | 2:30 | 2:30 | 2:30 |
| 3:00 | 3:00 | 3:00 | 3:00 |
| 3:30 | 3:30 | 3:30 | 3:30 |
| 4:00 | 4:00 | 4:00 | 4:00 |
| 4:30 | 4:30 | 4:30 | 4:30 |
| 5:00 | 5:00 | 5:00 | 5:00 |
| 5:30 | 5:30 | 5:30 | 5:30 |
| 6:00 | 6:00 | 6:00 | 6:00 |
| 6:30 | 6:30 | 6:30 | 6:30 |
| 7:00 | 7:00 | 7:00 | 7:00 |
| 7:30 | 7:30 | 7:30 | 7:30 |
| 8:00 | 8:00 | 8:00 | 8:00 |
| 8:30 | 8:30 | 8:30 | 8:30 |
| 9:00 | 9:00 | 9:00 | 9:00 |
| 9:30 | 9:30 | 9:30 | 9:30 |
| 10:00 | 10:00 | 10:00 | 10:00 |

# Prep Your *Week*

## *Priorities* This Week

- 
- 
- 
- 
- 
- 
- 
- 

## Coaching Cycles

## Classroom Snapshots

## Data Meetings

## Team & PD Meetings

## Feedback Meetings

## Other

# Reflect on Your *Week*

| What goals did you accomplish this week? | What goals did you not accomplish this week? Why? |
|---|---|
| What can you do to improve next week? | Things learned and things to remember: |

## Goal & Habit Tracker

| Goal or Habit | Day 1 | Day 2 | Day 3 | Day 4 | Day 5 | Day 6 | Day 7 |
|---|---|---|---|---|---|---|---|
| | | | | | | | |
| | | | | | | | |
| | | | | | | | |
| | | | | | | | |

## Notes

Week:

Notes ↗

| Sunday | Monday | Tuesday |
|--------|--------|---------|
| 4:00 a.m. | 4:00 a.m. | 4:00 a.m. |
| 4:30 | 4:30 | 4:30 |
| 5:00 | 5:00 | 5:00 |
| 5:30 | 5:30 | 5:30 |
| 6:00 | 6:00 | 6:00 |
| 6:30 | 6:30 | 6:30 |
| 7:00 | 7:00 | 7:00 |
| 7:30 | 7:30 | 7:30 |
| 8:00 | 8:00 | 8:00 |
| 8:30 | 8:30 | 8:30 |
| 9:00 | 9:00 | 9:00 |
| 9:30 | 9:30 | 9:30 |
| 10:00 | 10:00 | 10:00 |
| 10:30 | 10:30 | 10:30 |
| 11:00 | 11:00 | 11:00 |
| 11:30 | 11:30 | 11:30 |
| 12:00 p.m. | 12:00 p.m. | 12:00 p.m. |
| 12:30 | 12:30 | 12:30 |
| 1:00 | 1:00 | 1:00 |
| 1:30 | 1:30 | 1:30 |
| 2:00 | 2:00 | 2:00 |
| 2:30 | 2:30 | 2:30 |
| 3:00 | 3:00 | 3:00 |
| 3:30 | 3:30 | 3:30 |
| 4:00 | 4:00 | 4:00 |
| 4:30 | 4:30 | 4:30 |
| 5:00 | 5:00 | 5:00 |
| 5:30 | 5:30 | 5:30 |
| 6:00 | 6:00 | 6:00 |
| 6:30 | 6:30 | 6:30 |
| 7:00 | 7:00 | 7:00 |
| 7:30 | 7:30 | 7:30 |
| 8:00 | 8:00 | 8:00 |
| 8:30 | 8:30 | 8:30 |
| 9:00 | 9:00 | 9:00 |
| 9:30 | 9:30 | 9:30 |
| 10:00 | 10:00 | 10:00 |

| Wednesday | Thursday | Friday | Saturday |
|---|---|---|---|
| 4:00 a.m. | 4:00 a.m. | 4:00 a.m. | 4:00 a.m. |
| 4:30 | 4:30 | 4:30 | 4:30 |
| 5:00 | 5:00 | 5:00 | 5:00 |
| 5:30 | 5:30 | 5:30 | 5:30 |
| 6:00 | 6:00 | 6:00 | 6:00 |
| 6:30 | 6:30 | 6:30 | 6:30 |
| 7:00 | 7:00 | 7:00 | 7:00 |
| 7:30 | 7:30 | 7:30 | 7:30 |
| 8:00 | 8:00 | 8:00 | 8:00 |
| 8:30 | 8:30 | 8:30 | 8:30 |
| 9:00 | 9:00 | 9:00 | 9:00 |
| 9:30 | 9:30 | 9:30 | 9:30 |
| 10:00 | 10:00 | 10:00 | 10:00 |
| 10:30 | 10:30 | 10:30 | 10:30 |
| 11:00 | 11:00 | 11:00 | 11:00 |
| 11:30 | 11:30 | 11:30 | 11:30 |
| 12:00 p.m. | 12:00 p.m. | 12:00 p.m. | 12:00 p.m. |
| 12:30 | 12:30 | 12:30 | 12:30 |
| 1:00 | 1:00 | 1:00 | 1:00 |
| 1:30 | 1:30 | 1:30 | 1:30 |
| 2:00 | 2:00 | 2:00 | 2:00 |
| 2:30 | 2:30 | 2:30 | 2:30 |
| 3:00 | 3:00 | 3:00 | 3:00 |
| 3:30 | 3:30 | 3:30 | 3:30 |
| 4:00 | 4:00 | 4:00 | 4:00 |
| 4:30 | 4:30 | 4:30 | 4:30 |
| 5:00 | 5:00 | 5:00 | 5:00 |
| 5:30 | 5:30 | 5:30 | 5:30 |
| 6:00 | 6:00 | 6:00 | 6:00 |
| 6:30 | 6:30 | 6:30 | 6:30 |
| 7:00 | 7:00 | 7:00 | 7:00 |
| 7:30 | 7:30 | 7:30 | 7:30 |
| 8:00 | 8:00 | 8:00 | 8:00 |
| 8:30 | 8:30 | 8:30 | 8:30 |
| 9:00 | 9:00 | 9:00 | 9:00 |
| 9:30 | 9:30 | 9:30 | 9:30 |
| 10:00 | 10:00 | 10:00 | 10:00 |

Planning IS
BRINGING THE FUTURE
INTO THE PRESENT
SO THAT YOU CAN
do something
about it now.

—Alan Lakein

# Prep Your *Month*

| Personal Goals | | | |
|---|---|---|---|
| Day | Health & Fitness | Finances | Self-Care & Growth |
| | | | |
| | | | |
| | | | |
| | | | |
| | | | |
| | | | |

| Important Reminders | |
|---|---|
| | |
| | |
| | |
| | |
| | |
| | |
| | |

# Prep Your *Month*

| Main Goal | Main Focus | Wins |
|---|---|---|
| | | |

## Monthly Tasks

Week 1

Week 2

Week 3

Week 4

Week 5

## Must Do This Month

## Save for Next Month

# October

*"An ounce of practice is worth more than tons of preaching."* —Gandhi

| Sunday | Monday | Tuesday | Wednesday |
|--------|--------|---------|-----------|
|        |        |         |           |
|        |        |         |           |
|        |        |         |           |
|        |        |         |           |
|        |        |         |           |

Monthly Focus

| Thursday | Friday | Saturday |
|---|---|---|
|  |  |  |
|  |  |  |
|  |  |  |
|  |  |  |
|  |  |  |

Notes

# Prep Your *Week*

## Priorities This Week

- 
- 
- 
- 
- 
- 
- 
- 
- 

## Coaching Cycles

## Classroom Snapshots

## Data Meetings

## Team & PD Meetings

## Feedback Meetings

## Other

# Reflect on Your *Week*

| What goals did you accomplish this week? | What goals did you not accomplish this week? Why? |
|---|---|
| **What can you do to improve next week?** | **Things learned and things to remember:** |

## Goal & Habit Tracker

| Goal or Habit | Day 1 | Day 2 | Day 3 | Day 4 | Day 5 | Day 6 | Day 7 |
|---|---|---|---|---|---|---|---|
| | | | | | | | |
| | | | | | | | |
| | | | | | | | |
| | | | | | | | |

## Notes

Week:

Notes ➤

| Sunday | Monday | Tuesday |
|---|---|---|
| 4:00 a.m. | 4:00 a.m. | 4:00 a.m. |
| 4:30 | 4:30 | 4:30 |
| 5:00 | 5:00 | 5:00 |
| 5:30 | 5:30 | 5:30 |
| 6:00 | 6:00 | 6:00 |
| 6:30 | 6:30 | 6:30 |
| 7:00 | 7:00 | 7:00 |
| 7:30 | 7:30 | 7:30 |
| 8:00 | 8:00 | 8:00 |
| 8:30 | 8:30 | 8:30 |
| 9:00 | 9:00 | 9:00 |
| 9:30 | 9:30 | 9:30 |
| 10:00 | 10:00 | 10:00 |
| 10:30 | 10:30 | 10:30 |
| 11:00 | 11:00 | 11:00 |
| 11:30 | 11:30 | 11:30 |
| 12:00 p.m. | 12:00 p.m. | 12:00 p.m. |
| 12:30 | 12:30 | 12:30 |
| 1:00 | 1:00 | 1:00 |
| 1:30 | 1:30 | 1:30 |
| 2:00 | 2:00 | 2:00 |
| 2:30 | 2:30 | 2:30 |
| 3:00 | 3:00 | 3:00 |
| 3:30 | 3:30 | 3:30 |
| 4:00 | 4:00 | 4:00 |
| 4:30 | 4:30 | 4:30 |
| 5:00 | 5:00 | 5:00 |
| 5:30 | 5:30 | 5:30 |
| 6:00 | 6:00 | 6:00 |
| 6:30 | 6:30 | 6:30 |
| 7:00 | 7:00 | 7:00 |
| 7:30 | 7:30 | 7:30 |
| 8:00 | 8:00 | 8:00 |
| 8:30 | 8:30 | 8:30 |
| 9:00 | 9:00 | 9:00 |
| 9:30 | 9:30 | 9:30 |
| 10:00 | 10:00 | 10:00 |

| Wednesday | Thursday | Friday | Saturday |
|---|---|---|---|
| 4:00 a.m. | 4:00 a.m. | 4:00 a.m. | 4:00 a.m. |
| 4:30 | 4:30 | 4:30 | 4:30 |
| 5:00 | 5:00 | 5:00 | 5:00 |
| 5:30 | 5:30 | 5:30 | 5:30 |
| 6:00 | 6:00 | 6:00 | 6:00 |
| 6:30 | 6:30 | 6:30 | 6:30 |
| 7:00 | 7:00 | 7:00 | 7:00 |
| 7:30 | 7:30 | 7:30 | 7:30 |
| 8:00 | 8:00 | 8:00 | 8:00 |
| 8:30 | 8:30 | 8:30 | 8:30 |
| 9:00 | 9:00 | 9:00 | 9:00 |
| 9:30 | 9:30 | 9:30 | 9:30 |
| 10:00 | 10:00 | 10:00 | 10:00 |
| 10:30 | 10:30 | 10:30 | 10:30 |
| 11:00 | 11:00 | 11:00 | 11:00 |
| 11:30 | 11:30 | 11:30 | 11:30 |
| 12:00 p.m. | 12:00 p.m. | 12:00 p.m. | 12:00 p.m. |
| 12:30 | 12:30 | 12:30 | 12:30 |
| 1:00 | 1:00 | 1:00 | 1:00 |
| 1:30 | 1:30 | 1:30 | 1:30 |
| 2:00 | 2:00 | 2:00 | 2:00 |
| 2:30 | 2:30 | 2:30 | 2:30 |
| 3:00 | 3:00 | 3:00 | 3:00 |
| 3:30 | 3:30 | 3:30 | 3:30 |
| 4:00 | 4:00 | 4:00 | 4:00 |
| 4:30 | 4:30 | 4:30 | 4:30 |
| 5:00 | 5:00 | 5:00 | 5:00 |
| 5:30 | 5:30 | 5:30 | 5:30 |
| 6:00 | 6:00 | 6:00 | 6:00 |
| 6:30 | 6:30 | 6:30 | 6:30 |
| 7:00 | 7:00 | 7:00 | 7:00 |
| 7:30 | 7:30 | 7:30 | 7:30 |
| 8:00 | 8:00 | 8:00 | 8:00 |
| 8:30 | 8:30 | 8:30 | 8:30 |
| 9:00 | 9:00 | 9:00 | 9:00 |
| 9:30 | 9:30 | 9:30 | 9:30 |
| 10:00 | 10:00 | 10:00 | 10:00 |

# Prep Your Week

## Priorities This Week

- 
- 
- 
- 
- 
- 
- 
- 
- 

## Coaching Cycles

## Classroom Snapshots

## Data Meetings

## Team & PD Meetings

## Feedback Meetings

## Other

# Reflect on Your *Week*

| What goals did you accomplish this week? | What goals did you not accomplish this week? Why? |
|---|---|
| What can you do to improve next week? | Things learned and things to remember: |

## Goal & Habit Tracker

| Goal or Habit | Day 1 | Day 2 | Day 3 | Day 4 | Day 5 | Day 6 | Day 7 |
|---|---|---|---|---|---|---|---|
|  |  |  |  |  |  |  |  |
|  |  |  |  |  |  |  |  |
|  |  |  |  |  |  |  |  |
|  |  |  |  |  |  |  |  |

## Notes

Week:

Notes

| | Sunday | Monday | Tuesday |
|---|---|---|---|
| | 4:00 a.m. | 4:00 a.m. | 4:00 a.m. |
| | 4:30 | 4:30 | 4:30 |
| | 5:00 | 5:00 | 5:00 |
| | 5:30 | 5:30 | 5:30 |
| | 6:00 | 6:00 | 6:00 |
| | 6:30 | 6:30 | 6:30 |
| | 7:00 | 7:00 | 7:00 |
| | 7:30 | 7:30 | 7:30 |
| | 8:00 | 8:00 | 8:00 |
| | 8:30 | 8:30 | 8:30 |
| | 9:00 | 9:00 | 9:00 |
| | 9:30 | 9:30 | 9:30 |
| | 10:00 | 10:00 | 10:00 |
| | 10:30 | 10:30 | 10:30 |
| | 11:00 | 11:00 | 11:00 |
| | 11:30 | 11:30 | 11:30 |
| | 12:00 p.m. | 12:00 p.m. | 12:00 p.m. |
| | 12:30 | 12:30 | 12:30 |
| | 1:00 | 1:00 | 1:00 |
| | 1:30 | 1:30 | 1:30 |
| | 2:00 | 2:00 | 2:00 |
| | 2:30 | 2:30 | 2:30 |
| | 3:00 | 3:00 | 3:00 |
| | 3:30 | 3:30 | 3:30 |
| | 4:00 | 4:00 | 4:00 |
| | 4:30 | 4:30 | 4:30 |
| | 5:00 | 5:00 | 5:00 |
| | 5:30 | 5:30 | 5:30 |
| | 6:00 | 6:00 | 6:00 |
| | 6:30 | 6:30 | 6:30 |
| | 7:00 | 7:00 | 7:00 |
| | 7:30 | 7:30 | 7:30 |
| | 8:00 | 8:00 | 8:00 |
| | 8:30 | 8:30 | 8:30 |
| | 9:00 | 9:00 | 9:00 |
| | 9:30 | 9:30 | 9:30 |
| | 10:00 | 10:00 | 10:00 |

| Wednesday | Thursday | Friday | Saturday |
|---|---|---|---|
| 4:00 a.m. | 4:00 a.m. | 4:00 a.m. | 4:00 a.m. |
| 4:30 | 4:30 | 4:30 | 4:30 |
| 5:00 | 5:00 | 5:00 | 5:00 |
| 5:30 | 5:30 | 5:30 | 5:30 |
| 6:00 | 6:00 | 6:00 | 6:00 |
| 6:30 | 6:30 | 6:30 | 6:30 |
| 7:00 | 7:00 | 7:00 | 7:00 |
| 7:30 | 7:30 | 7:30 | 7:30 |
| 8:00 | 8:00 | 8:00 | 8:00 |
| 8:30 | 8:30 | 8:30 | 8:30 |
| 9:00 | 9:00 | 9:00 | 9:00 |
| 9:30 | 9:30 | 9:30 | 9:30 |
| 10:00 | 10:00 | 10:00 | 10:00 |
| 10:30 | 10:30 | 10:30 | 10:30 |
| 11:00 | 11:00 | 11:00 | 11:00 |
| 11:30 | 11:30 | 11:30 | 11:30 |
| 12:00 p.m. | 12:00 p.m. | 12:00 p.m. | 12:00 p.m. |
| 12:30 | 12:30 | 12:30 | 12:30 |
| 1:00 | 1:00 | 1:00 | 1:00 |
| 1:30 | 1:30 | 1:30 | 1:30 |
| 2:00 | 2:00 | 2:00 | 2:00 |
| 2:30 | 2:30 | 2:30 | 2:30 |
| 3:00 | 3:00 | 3:00 | 3:00 |
| 3:30 | 3:30 | 3:30 | 3:30 |
| 4:00 | 4:00 | 4:00 | 4:00 |
| 4:30 | 4:30 | 4:30 | 4:30 |
| 5:00 | 5:00 | 5:00 | 5:00 |
| 5:30 | 5:30 | 5:30 | 5:30 |
| 6:00 | 6:00 | 6:00 | 6:00 |
| 6:30 | 6:30 | 6:30 | 6:30 |
| 7:00 | 7:00 | 7:00 | 7:00 |
| 7:30 | 7:30 | 7:30 | 7:30 |
| 8:00 | 8:00 | 8:00 | 8:00 |
| 8:30 | 8:30 | 8:30 | 8:30 |
| 9:00 | 9:00 | 9:00 | 9:00 |
| 9:30 | 9:30 | 9:30 | 9:30 |
| 10:00 | 10:00 | 10:00 | 10:00 |

# Prep Your *Week*

## Priorities This Week

- 
- 
- 
- 
- 
- 
- 
- 

## Coaching Cycles

## Classroom Snapshots

## Data Meetings

## Team & PD Meetings

## Feedback Meetings

## Other

# Reflect on Your *Week*

| What goals did you accomplish this week? | What goals did you not accomplish this week? Why? |
|---|---|
| What can you do to improve next week? | Things learned and things to remember: |

## Goal & Habit Tracker

| Goal or Habit | Day 1 | Day 2 | Day 3 | Day 4 | Day 5 | Day 6 | Day 7 |
|---|---|---|---|---|---|---|---|
| | | | | | | | |
| | | | | | | | |
| | | | | | | | |
| | | | | | | | |

## Notes

Week:

Notes ➤

| | Sunday | Monday | Tuesday |
|---|---|---|---|
| | 4:00 a.m. | 4:00 a.m. | 4:00 a.m. |
| | 4:30 | 4:30 | 4:30 |
| | 5:00 | 5:00 | 5:00 |
| | 5:30 | 5:30 | 5:30 |
| | 6:00 | 6:00 | 6:00 |
| | 6:30 | 6:30 | 6:30 |
| | 7:00 | 7:00 | 7:00 |
| | 7:30 | 7:30 | 7:30 |
| | 8:00 | 8:00 | 8:00 |
| | 8:30 | 8:30 | 8:30 |
| | 9:00 | 9:00 | 9:00 |
| | 9:30 | 9:30 | 9:30 |
| | 10:00 | 10:00 | 10:00 |
| | 10:30 | 10:30 | 10:30 |
| | 11:00 | 11:00 | 11:00 |
| | 11:30 | 11:30 | 11:30 |
| | 12:00 p.m. | 12:00 p.m. | 12:00 p.m. |
| | 12:30 | 12:30 | 12:30 |
| | 1:00 | 1:00 | 1:00 |
| | 1:30 | 1:30 | 1:30 |
| | 2:00 | 2:00 | 2:00 |
| | 2:30 | 2:30 | 2:30 |
| | 3:00 | 3:00 | 3:00 |
| | 3:30 | 3:30 | 3:30 |
| | 4:00 | 4:00 | 4:00 |
| | 4:30 | 4:30 | 4:30 |
| | 5:00 | 5:00 | 5:00 |
| | 5:30 | 5:30 | 5:30 |
| | 6:00 | 6:00 | 6:00 |
| | 6:30 | 6:30 | 6:30 |
| | 7:00 | 7:00 | 7:00 |
| | 7:30 | 7:30 | 7:30 |
| | 8:00 | 8:00 | 8:00 |
| | 8:30 | 8:30 | 8:30 |
| | 9:00 | 9:00 | 9:00 |
| | 9:30 | 9:30 | 9:30 |
| | 10:00 | 10:00 | 10:00 |

| Wednesday | Thursday | Friday | Saturday |
|---|---|---|---|
| 4:00 a.m. | 4:00 a.m. | 4:00 a.m. | 4:00 a.m. |
| 4:30 | 4:30 | 4:30 | 4:30 |
| 5:00 | 5:00 | 5:00 | 5:00 |
| 5:30 | 5:30 | 5:30 | 5:30 |
| 6:00 | 6:00 | 6:00 | 6:00 |
| 6:30 | 6:30 | 6:30 | 6:30 |
| 7:00 | 7:00 | 7:00 | 7:00 |
| 7:30 | 7:30 | 7:30 | 7:30 |
| 8:00 | 8:00 | 8:00 | 8:00 |
| 8:30 | 8:30 | 8:30 | 8:30 |
| 9:00 | 9:00 | 9:00 | 9:00 |
| 9:30 | 9:30 | 9:30 | 9:30 |
| 10:00 | 10:00 | 10:00 | 10:00 |
| 10:30 | 10:30 | 10:30 | 10:30 |
| 11:00 | 11:00 | 11:00 | 11:00 |
| 11:30 | 11:30 | 11:30 | 11:30 |
| 12:00 p.m. | 12:00 p.m. | 12:00 p.m. | 12:00 p.m. |
| 12:30 | 12:30 | 12:30 | 12:30 |
| 1:00 | 1:00 | 1:00 | 1:00 |
| 1:30 | 1:30 | 1:30 | 1:30 |
| 2:00 | 2:00 | 2:00 | 2:00 |
| 2:30 | 2:30 | 2:30 | 2:30 |
| 3:00 | 3:00 | 3:00 | 3:00 |
| 3:30 | 3:30 | 3:30 | 3:30 |
| 4:00 | 4:00 | 4:00 | 4:00 |
| 4:30 | 4:30 | 4:30 | 4:30 |
| 5:00 | 5:00 | 5:00 | 5:00 |
| 5:30 | 5:30 | 5:30 | 5:30 |
| 6:00 | 6:00 | 6:00 | 6:00 |
| 6:30 | 6:30 | 6:30 | 6:30 |
| 7:00 | 7:00 | 7:00 | 7:00 |
| 7:30 | 7:30 | 7:30 | 7:30 |
| 8:00 | 8:00 | 8:00 | 8:00 |
| 8:30 | 8:30 | 8:30 | 8:30 |
| 9:00 | 9:00 | 9:00 | 9:00 |
| 9:30 | 9:30 | 9:30 | 9:30 |
| 10:00 | 10:00 | 10:00 | 10:00 |

# Prep Your *Week*

## *Priorities* This Week

- 
- 
- 
- 
- 
- 
- 
- 

## Coaching Cycles

## Classroom Snapshots

## Data Meetings

## Team & PD Meetings

## Feedback Meetings

## Other

# Reflect on Your Week

| What goals did you accomplish this week? | What goals did you not accomplish this week? Why? |
|---|---|
| What can you do to improve next week? | Things learned and things to remember: |

## Goal & Habit Tracker

| Goal or Habit | Day 1 | Day 2 | Day 3 | Day 4 | Day 5 | Day 6 | Day 7 |
|---|---|---|---|---|---|---|---|
| | | | | | | | |
| | | | | | | | |
| | | | | | | | |
| | | | | | | | |

## Notes

Week:

Notes

| Sunday | Monday | Tuesday |
|---|---|---|
| 4:00 a.m. | 4:00 a.m. | 4:00 a.m. |
| 4:30 | 4:30 | 4:30 |
| 5:00 | 5:00 | 5:00 |
| 5:30 | 5:30 | 5:30 |
| 6:00 | 6:00 | 6:00 |
| 6:30 | 6:30 | 6:30 |
| 7:00 | 7:00 | 7:00 |
| 7:30 | 7:30 | 7:30 |
| 8:00 | 8:00 | 8:00 |
| 8:30 | 8:30 | 8:30 |
| 9:00 | 9:00 | 9:00 |
| 9:30 | 9:30 | 9:30 |
| 10:00 | 10:00 | 10:00 |
| 10:30 | 10:30 | 10:30 |
| 11:00 | 11:00 | 11:00 |
| 11:30 | 11:30 | 11:30 |
| 12:00 p.m. | 12:00 p.m. | 12:00 p.m. |
| 12:30 | 12:30 | 12:30 |
| 1:00 | 1:00 | 1:00 |
| 1:30 | 1:30 | 1:30 |
| 2:00 | 2:00 | 2:00 |
| 2:30 | 2:30 | 2:30 |
| 3:00 | 3:00 | 3:00 |
| 3:30 | 3:30 | 3:30 |
| 4:00 | 4:00 | 4:00 |
| 4:30 | 4:30 | 4:30 |
| 5:00 | 5:00 | 5:00 |
| 5:30 | 5:30 | 5:30 |
| 6:00 | 6:00 | 6:00 |
| 6:30 | 6:30 | 6:30 |
| 7:00 | 7:00 | 7:00 |
| 7:30 | 7:30 | 7:30 |
| 8:00 | 8:00 | 8:00 |
| 8:30 | 8:30 | 8:30 |
| 9:00 | 9:00 | 9:00 |
| 9:30 | 9:30 | 9:30 |
| 10:00 | 10:00 | 10:00 |

| Wednesday | Thursday | Friday | Saturday |
|---|---|---|---|
| 4:00 a.m. | 4:00 a.m. | 4:00 a.m. | 4:00 a.m. |
| 4:30 | 4:30 | 4:30 | 4:30 |
| 5:00 | 5:00 | 5:00 | 5:00 |
| 5:30 | 5:30 | 5:30 | 5:30 |
| 6:00 | 6:00 | 6:00 | 6:00 |
| 6:30 | 6:30 | 6:30 | 6:30 |
| 7:00 | 7:00 | 7:00 | 7:00 |
| 7:30 | 7:30 | 7:30 | 7:30 |
| 8:00 | 8:00 | 8:00 | 8:00 |
| 8:30 | 8:30 | 8:30 | 8:30 |
| 9:00 | 9:00 | 9:00 | 9:00 |
| 9:30 | 9:30 | 9:30 | 9:30 |
| 10:00 | 10:00 | 10:00 | 10:00 |
| 10:30 | 10:30 | 10:30 | 10:30 |
| 11:00 | 11:00 | 11:00 | 11:00 |
| 11:30 | 11:30 | 11:30 | 11:30 |
| 12:00 p.m. | 12:00 p.m. | 12:00 p.m. | 12:00 p.m. |
| 12:30 | 12:30 | 12:30 | 12:30 |
| 1:00 | 1:00 | 1:00 | 1:00 |
| 1:30 | 1:30 | 1:30 | 1:30 |
| 2:00 | 2:00 | 2:00 | 2:00 |
| 2:30 | 2:30 | 2:30 | 2:30 |
| 3:00 | 3:00 | 3:00 | 3:00 |
| 3:30 | 3:30 | 3:30 | 3:30 |
| 4:00 | 4:00 | 4:00 | 4:00 |
| 4:30 | 4:30 | 4:30 | 4:30 |
| 5:00 | 5:00 | 5:00 | 5:00 |
| 5:30 | 5:30 | 5:30 | 5:30 |
| 6:00 | 6:00 | 6:00 | 6:00 |
| 6:30 | 6:30 | 6:30 | 6:30 |
| 7:00 | 7:00 | 7:00 | 7:00 |
| 7:30 | 7:30 | 7:30 | 7:30 |
| 8:00 | 8:00 | 8:00 | 8:00 |
| 8:30 | 8:30 | 8:30 | 8:30 |
| 9:00 | 9:00 | 9:00 | 9:00 |
| 9:30 | 9:30 | 9:30 | 9:30 |
| 10:00 | 10:00 | 10:00 | 10:00 |

OCTOBER

# Prep Your *Week*

## Priorities This Week

- 
- 
- 
- 
- 
- 
- 
- 

## Coaching Cycles

## Classroom Snapshots

## Data Meetings

## Team & PD Meetings

## Feedback Meetings

## Other

# Reflect on Your *Week*

| What goals did you accomplish this week? | What goals did you not accomplish this week? Why? |
|---|---|
| What can you do to improve next week? | Things learned and things to remember: |

## Goal & Habit Tracker

| Goal or Habit | Day 1 | Day 2 | Day 3 | Day 4 | Day 5 | Day 6 | Day 7 |
|---|---|---|---|---|---|---|---|
| | | | | | | | |
| | | | | | | | |
| | | | | | | | |
| | | | | | | | |

## Notes

Week:

Notes

| | Sunday | Monday | Tuesday |
|---|---|---|---|
| | 4:00 a.m. | 4:00 a.m. | 4:00 a.m. |
| | 4:30 | 4:30 | 4:30 |
| | 5:00 | 5:00 | 5:00 |
| | 5:30 | 5:30 | 5:30 |
| | 6:00 | 6:00 | 6:00 |
| | 6:30 | 6:30 | 6:30 |
| | 7:00 | 7:00 | 7:00 |
| | 7:30 | 7:30 | 7:30 |
| | 8:00 | 8:00 | 8:00 |
| | 8:30 | 8:30 | 8:30 |
| | 9:00 | 9:00 | 9:00 |
| | 9:30 | 9:30 | 9:30 |
| | 10:00 | 10:00 | 10:00 |
| | 10:30 | 10:30 | 10:30 |
| | 11:00 | 11:00 | 11:00 |
| | 11:30 | 11:30 | 11:30 |
| | 12:00 p.m. | 12:00 p.m. | 12:00 p.m. |
| | 12:30 | 12:30 | 12:30 |
| | 1:00 | 1:00 | 1:00 |
| | 1:30 | 1:30 | 1:30 |
| | 2:00 | 2:00 | 2:00 |
| | 2:30 | 2:30 | 2:30 |
| | 3:00 | 3:00 | 3:00 |
| | 3:30 | 3:30 | 3:30 |
| | 4:00 | 4:00 | 4:00 |
| | 4:30 | 4:30 | 4:30 |
| | 5:00 | 5:00 | 5:00 |
| | 5:30 | 5:30 | 5:30 |
| | 6:00 | 6:00 | 6:00 |
| | 6:30 | 6:30 | 6:30 |
| | 7:00 | 7:00 | 7:00 |
| | 7:30 | 7:30 | 7:30 |
| | 8:00 | 8:00 | 8:00 |
| | 8:30 | 8:30 | 8:30 |
| | 9:00 | 9:00 | 9:00 |
| | 9:30 | 9:30 | 9:30 |
| | 10:00 | 10:00 | 10:00 |

| Wednesday | Thursday | Friday | Saturday |
|---|---|---|---|
| 4:00 a.m. | 4:00 a.m. | 4:00 a.m. | 4:00 a.m. |
| 4:30 | 4:30 | 4:30 | 4:30 |
| 5:00 | 5:00 | 5:00 | 5:00 |
| 5:30 | 5:30 | 5:30 | 5:30 |
| 6:00 | 6:00 | 6:00 | 6:00 |
| 6:30 | 6:30 | 6:30 | 6:30 |
| 7:00 | 7:00 | 7:00 | 7:00 |
| 7:30 | 7:30 | 7:30 | 7:30 |
| 8:00 | 8:00 | 8:00 | 8:00 |
| 8:30 | 8:30 | 8:30 | 8:30 |
| 9:00 | 9:00 | 9:00 | 9:00 |
| 9:30 | 9:30 | 9:30 | 9:30 |
| 10:00 | 10:00 | 10:00 | 10:00 |
| 10:30 | 10:30 | 10:30 | 10:30 |
| 11:00 | 11:00 | 11:00 | 11:00 |
| 11:30 | 11:30 | 11:30 | 11:30 |
| 12:00 p.m. | 12:00 p.m. | 12:00 p.m. | 12:00 p.m. |
| 12:30 | 12:30 | 12:30 | 12:30 |
| 1:00 | 1:00 | 1:00 | 1:00 |
| 1:30 | 1:30 | 1:30 | 1:30 |
| 2:00 | 2:00 | 2:00 | 2:00 |
| 2:30 | 2:30 | 2:30 | 2:30 |
| 3:00 | 3:00 | 3:00 | 3:00 |
| 3:30 | 3:30 | 3:30 | 3:30 |
| 4:00 | 4:00 | 4:00 | 4:00 |
| 4:30 | 4:30 | 4:30 | 4:30 |
| 5:00 | 5:00 | 5:00 | 5:00 |
| 5:30 | 5:30 | 5:30 | 5:30 |
| 6:00 | 6:00 | 6:00 | 6:00 |
| 6:30 | 6:30 | 6:30 | 6:30 |
| 7:00 | 7:00 | 7:00 | 7:00 |
| 7:30 | 7:30 | 7:30 | 7:30 |
| 8:00 | 8:00 | 8:00 | 8:00 |
| 8:30 | 8:30 | 8:30 | 8:30 |
| 9:00 | 9:00 | 9:00 | 9:00 |
| 9:30 | 9:30 | 9:30 | 9:30 |
| 10:00 | 10:00 | 10:00 | 10:00 |

OCTOBER

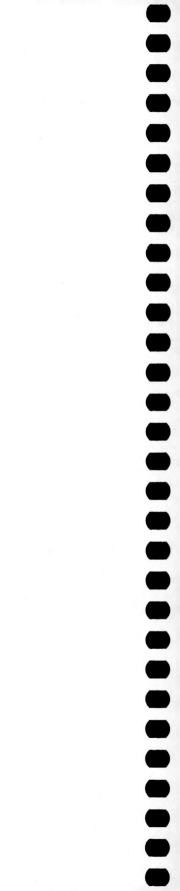

EVERY MINUTE YOU SPEND IN *planning* SAVES 10 MINUTES IN EXECUTION; THIS GIVES YOU A *1,000 percent return on energy.*

—Brian Tracy

# Prep Your *Month*

| Personal Goals | | | |
|---|---|---|---|
| Day | Health & Fitness | Finances | Self-Care & Growth |
| | | | |
| | | | |
| | | | |
| | | | |
| | | | |
| | | | |

| Important Reminders | |
|---|---|
| | |
| | |
| | |
| | |
| | |
| | |
| | |

# Prep Your *Month*

| Main Goal | Main Focus | Wins |
|---|---|---|
| | | |

## Monthly Tasks

Week 1

Week 2

Week 3

Week 4

Week 5

## Must Do This Month

## Save for Next Month

# November

*"A great coach tells you what you need to hear, not what you want to hear."* —Sagi Kalev

| Sunday | Monday | Tuesday | Wednesday |
|--------|--------|---------|-----------|
|        |        |         |           |
|        |        |         |           |
|        |        |         |           |
|        |        |         |           |
|        |        |         |           |

## Monthly Focus

| Thursday | Friday | Saturday |
|---|---|---|
|  |  |  |
|  |  |  |
|  |  |  |
|  |  |  |
|  |  |  |

Notes

# Prep Your *Week*

## Priorities This Week

- 
- 
- 
- 
- 
- 
- 
- 

## Coaching Cycles

## Classroom Snapshots

## Data Meetings

## Team & PD Meetings

## Feedback Meetings

## Other

# Reflect on Your *Week*

| What goals did you accomplish this week? | What goals did you not accomplish this week? Why? |
|---|---|
| What can you do to improve next week? | Things learned and things to remember: |

## Goal & Habit Tracker

| Goal or Habit | Day 1 | Day 2 | Day 3 | Day 4 | Day 5 | Day 6 | Day 7 |
|---|---|---|---|---|---|---|---|
| | | | | | | | |
| | | | | | | | |
| | | | | | | | |
| | | | | | | | |

## Notes

Week:

Notes ↗

| Sunday | Monday | Tuesday |
|---|---|---|
| 4:00 a.m. | 4:00 a.m. | 4:00 a.m. |
| 4:30 | 4:30 | 4:30 |
| 5:00 | 5:00 | 5:00 |
| 5:30 | 5:30 | 5:30 |
| 6:00 | 6:00 | 6:00 |
| 6:30 | 6:30 | 6:30 |
| 7:00 | 7:00 | 7:00 |
| 7:30 | 7:30 | 7:30 |
| 8:00 | 8:00 | 8:00 |
| 8:30 | 8:30 | 8:30 |
| 9:00 | 9:00 | 9:00 |
| 9:30 | 9:30 | 9:30 |
| 10:00 | 10:00 | 10:00 |
| 10:30 | 10:30 | 10:30 |
| 11:00 | 11:00 | 11:00 |
| 11:30 | 11:30 | 11:30 |
| 12:00 p.m. | 12:00 p.m. | 12:00 p.m. |
| 12:30 | 12:30 | 12:30 |
| 1:00 | 1:00 | 1:00 |
| 1:30 | 1:30 | 1:30 |
| 2:00 | 2:00 | 2:00 |
| 2:30 | 2:30 | 2:30 |
| 3:00 | 3:00 | 3:00 |
| 3:30 | 3:30 | 3:30 |
| 4:00 | 4:00 | 4:00 |
| 4:30 | 4:30 | 4:30 |
| 5:00 | 5:00 | 5:00 |
| 5:30 | 5:30 | 5:30 |
| 6:00 | 6:00 | 6:00 |
| 6:30 | 6:30 | 6:30 |
| 7:00 | 7:00 | 7:00 |
| 7:30 | 7:30 | 7:30 |
| 8:00 | 8:00 | 8:00 |
| 8:30 | 8:30 | 8:30 |
| 9:00 | 9:00 | 9:00 |
| 9:30 | 9:30 | 9:30 |
| 10:00 | 10:00 | 10:00 |

| Wednesday | Thursday | Friday | Saturday |
| --- | --- | --- | --- |
| 4:00 a.m. | 4:00 a.m. | 4:00 a.m. | 4:00 a.m. |
| 4:30 | 4:30 | 4:30 | 4:30 |
| 5:00 | 5:00 | 5:00 | 5:00 |
| 5:30 | 5:30 | 5:30 | 5:30 |
| 6:00 | 6:00 | 6:00 | 6:00 |
| 6:30 | 6:30 | 6:30 | 6:30 |
| 7:00 | 7:00 | 7:00 | 7:00 |
| 7:30 | 7:30 | 7:30 | 7:30 |
| 8:00 | 8:00 | 8:00 | 8:00 |
| 8:30 | 8:30 | 8:30 | 8:30 |
| 9:00 | 9:00 | 9:00 | 9:00 |
| 9:30 | 9:30 | 9:30 | 9:30 |
| 10:00 | 10:00 | 10:00 | 10:00 |
| 10:30 | 10:30 | 10:30 | 10:30 |
| 11:00 | 11:00 | 11:00 | 11:00 |
| 11:30 | 11:30 | 11:30 | 11:30 |
| 12:00 p.m. | 12:00 p.m. | 12:00 p.m. | 12:00 p.m. |
| 12:30 | 12:30 | 12:30 | 12:30 |
| 1:00 | 1:00 | 1:00 | 1:00 |
| 1:30 | 1:30 | 1:30 | 1:30 |
| 2:00 | 2:00 | 2:00 | 2:00 |
| 2:30 | 2:30 | 2:30 | 2:30 |
| 3:00 | 3:00 | 3:00 | 3:00 |
| 3:30 | 3:30 | 3:30 | 3:30 |
| 4:00 | 4:00 | 4:00 | 4:00 |
| 4:30 | 4:30 | 4:30 | 4:30 |
| 5:00 | 5:00 | 5:00 | 5:00 |
| 5:30 | 5:30 | 5:30 | 5:30 |
| 6:00 | 6:00 | 6:00 | 6:00 |
| 6:30 | 6:30 | 6:30 | 6:30 |
| 7:00 | 7:00 | 7:00 | 7:00 |
| 7:30 | 7:30 | 7:30 | 7:30 |
| 8:00 | 8:00 | 8:00 | 8:00 |
| 8:30 | 8:30 | 8:30 | 8:30 |
| 9:00 | 9:00 | 9:00 | 9:00 |
| 9:30 | 9:30 | 9:30 | 9:30 |
| 10:00 | 10:00 | 10:00 | 10:00 |

# Prep Your *Week*

| Priorities This Week |
| --- |
| • |
| • |
| • |
| • |
| • |
| • |
| • |
| • |

| Coaching Cycles |
| --- |
| |

| Classroom Snapshots |
| --- |
| |

| Data Meetings |
| --- |
| |

| Team & PD Meetings |
| --- |
| |

| Feedback Meetings |
| --- |
| |

| Other |
| --- |
| |

# Reflect on Your *Week*

| What goals did you accomplish this week? | What goals did you not accomplish this week? Why? |
|---|---|
| What can you do to improve next week? | Things learned and things to remember: |

## Goal & Habit Tracker

| Goal or Habit | Day 1 | Day 2 | Day 3 | Day 4 | Day 5 | Day 6 | Day 7 |
|---|---|---|---|---|---|---|---|
|  |  |  |  |  |  |  |  |
|  |  |  |  |  |  |  |  |
|  |  |  |  |  |  |  |  |
|  |  |  |  |  |  |  |  |

## Notes

**Week:**

**Notes**

| Sunday | Monday | Tuesday |
|---|---|---|
| 4:00 a.m. | 4:00 a.m. | 4:00 a.m. |
| 4:30 | 4:30 | 4:30 |
| 5:00 | 5:00 | 5:00 |
| 5:30 | 5:30 | 5:30 |
| 6:00 | 6:00 | 6:00 |
| 6:30 | 6:30 | 6:30 |
| 7:00 | 7:00 | 7:00 |
| 7:30 | 7:30 | 7:30 |
| 8:00 | 8:00 | 8:00 |
| 8:30 | 8:30 | 8:30 |
| 9:00 | 9:00 | 9:00 |
| 9:30 | 9:30 | 9:30 |
| 10:00 | 10:00 | 10:00 |
| 10:30 | 10:30 | 10:30 |
| 11:00 | 11:00 | 11:00 |
| 11:30 | 11:30 | 11:30 |
| 12:00 p.m. | 12:00 p.m. | 12:00 p.m. |
| 12:30 | 12:30 | 12:30 |
| 1:00 | 1:00 | 1:00 |
| 1:30 | 1:30 | 1:30 |
| 2:00 | 2:00 | 2:00 |
| 2:30 | 2:30 | 2:30 |
| 3:00 | 3:00 | 3:00 |
| 3:30 | 3:30 | 3:30 |
| 4:00 | 4:00 | 4:00 |
| 4:30 | 4:30 | 4:30 |
| 5:00 | 5:00 | 5:00 |
| 5:30 | 5:30 | 5:30 |
| 6:00 | 6:00 | 6:00 |
| 6:30 | 6:30 | 6:30 |
| 7:00 | 7:00 | 7:00 |
| 7:30 | 7:30 | 7:30 |
| 8:00 | 8:00 | 8:00 |
| 8:30 | 8:30 | 8:30 |
| 9:00 | 9:00 | 9:00 |
| 9:30 | 9:30 | 9:30 |
| 10:00 | 10:00 | 10:00 |

| Wednesday | Thursday | Friday | Saturday |
|---|---|---|---|
| 4:00 a.m. | 4:00 a.m. | 4:00 a.m. | 4:00 a.m. |
| 4:30 | 4:30 | 4:30 | 4:30 |
| 5:00 | 5:00 | 5:00 | 5:00 |
| 5:30 | 5:30 | 5:30 | 5:30 |
| 6:00 | 6:00 | 6:00 | 6:00 |
| 6:30 | 6:30 | 6:30 | 6:30 |
| 7:00 | 7:00 | 7:00 | 7:00 |
| 7:30 | 7:30 | 7:30 | 7:30 |
| 8:00 | 8:00 | 8:00 | 8:00 |
| 8:30 | 8:30 | 8:30 | 8:30 |
| 9:00 | 9:00 | 9:00 | 9:00 |
| 9:30 | 9:30 | 9:30 | 9:30 |
| 10:00 | 10:00 | 10:00 | 10:00 |
| 10:30 | 10:30 | 10:30 | 10:30 |
| 11:00 | 11:00 | 11:00 | 11:00 |
| 11:30 | 11:30 | 11:30 | 11:30 |
| 12:00 p.m. | 12:00 p.m. | 12:00 p.m. | 12:00 p.m. |
| 12:30 | 12:30 | 12:30 | 12:30 |
| 1:00 | 1:00 | 1:00 | 1:00 |
| 1:30 | 1:30 | 1:30 | 1:30 |
| 2:00 | 2:00 | 2:00 | 2:00 |
| 2:30 | 2:30 | 2:30 | 2:30 |
| 3:00 | 3:00 | 3:00 | 3:00 |
| 3:30 | 3:30 | 3:30 | 3:30 |
| 4:00 | 4:00 | 4:00 | 4:00 |
| 4:30 | 4:30 | 4:30 | 4:30 |
| 5:00 | 5:00 | 5:00 | 5:00 |
| 5:30 | 5:30 | 5:30 | 5:30 |
| 6:00 | 6:00 | 6:00 | 6:00 |
| 6:30 | 6:30 | 6:30 | 6:30 |
| 7:00 | 7:00 | 7:00 | 7:00 |
| 7:30 | 7:30 | 7:30 | 7:30 |
| 8:00 | 8:00 | 8:00 | 8:00 |
| 8:30 | 8:30 | 8:30 | 8:30 |
| 9:00 | 9:00 | 9:00 | 9:00 |
| 9:30 | 9:30 | 9:30 | 9:30 |
| 10:00 | 10:00 | 10:00 | 10:00 |

NOVEMBER

# Prep Your *Week*

| Priorities This Week |
| --- |
| • |
| • |
| • |
| • |
| • |
| • |
| • |
| • |
| • |

| Coaching Cycles |
| --- |
| |

| Classroom Snapshots |
| --- |
| |

| Data Meetings |
| --- |
| |

| Team & PD Meetings |
| --- |
| |

| Feedback Meetings |
| --- |
| |

| Other |
| --- |
| |

# Reflect on Your *Week*

| What goals did you accomplish this week? | What goals did you not accomplish this week? Why? |
|---|---|
| **What can you do to improve next week?** | **Things learned and things to remember:** |

## Goal & Habit Tracker

| Goal or Habit | Day 1 | Day 2 | Day 3 | Day 4 | Day 5 | Day 6 | Day 7 |
|---|---|---|---|---|---|---|---|
| | | | | | | | |
| | | | | | | | |
| | | | | | | | |
| | | | | | | | |

## Notes

Week:

Notes

| Sunday | Monday | Tuesday |
|---|---|---|
| 4:00 a.m. | 4:00 a.m. | 4:00 a.m. |
| 4:30 | 4:30 | 4:30 |
| 5:00 | 5:00 | 5:00 |
| 5:30 | 5:30 | 5:30 |
| 6:00 | 6:00 | 6:00 |
| 6:30 | 6:30 | 6:30 |
| 7:00 | 7:00 | 7:00 |
| 7:30 | 7:30 | 7:30 |
| 8:00 | 8:00 | 8:00 |
| 8:30 | 8:30 | 8:30 |
| 9:00 | 9:00 | 9:00 |
| 9:30 | 9:30 | 9:30 |
| 10:00 | 10:00 | 10:00 |
| 10:30 | 10:30 | 10:30 |
| 11:00 | 11:00 | 11:00 |
| 11:30 | 11:30 | 11:30 |
| 12:00 p.m. | 12:00 p.m. | 12:00 p.m. |
| 12:30 | 12:30 | 12:30 |
| 1:00 | 1:00 | 1:00 |
| 1:30 | 1:30 | 1:30 |
| 2:00 | 2:00 | 2:00 |
| 2:30 | 2:30 | 2:30 |
| 3:00 | 3:00 | 3:00 |
| 3:30 | 3:30 | 3:30 |
| 4:00 | 4:00 | 4:00 |
| 4:30 | 4:30 | 4:30 |
| 5:00 | 5:00 | 5:00 |
| 5:30 | 5:30 | 5:30 |
| 6:00 | 6:00 | 6:00 |
| 6:30 | 6:30 | 6:30 |
| 7:00 | 7:00 | 7:00 |
| 7:30 | 7:30 | 7:30 |
| 8:00 | 8:00 | 8:00 |
| 8:30 | 8:30 | 8:30 |
| 9:00 | 9:00 | 9:00 |
| 9:30 | 9:30 | 9:30 |
| 10:00 | 10:00 | 10:00 |

| Wednesday | Thursday | Friday | Saturday |
|---|---|---|---|
| 4:00 a.m. | 4:00 a.m. | 4:00 a.m. | 4:00 a.m. |
| 4:30 | 4:30 | 4:30 | 4:30 |
| 5:00 | 5:00 | 5:00 | 5:00 |
| 5:30 | 5:30 | 5:30 | 5:30 |
| 6:00 | 6:00 | 6:00 | 6:00 |
| 6:30 | 6:30 | 6:30 | 6:30 |
| 7:00 | 7:00 | 7:00 | 7:00 |
| 7:30 | 7:30 | 7:30 | 7:30 |
| 8:00 | 8:00 | 8:00 | 8:00 |
| 8:30 | 8:30 | 8:30 | 8:30 |
| 9:00 | 9:00 | 9:00 | 9:00 |
| 9:30 | 9:30 | 9:30 | 9:30 |
| 10:00 | 10:00 | 10:00 | 10:00 |
| 10:30 | 10:30 | 10:30 | 10:30 |
| 11:00 | 11:00 | 11:00 | 11:00 |
| 11:30 | 11:30 | 11:30 | 11:30 |
| 12:00 p.m. | 12:00 p.m. | 12:00 p.m. | 12:00 p.m. |
| 12:30 | 12:30 | 12:30 | 12:30 |
| 1:00 | 1:00 | 1:00 | 1:00 |
| 1:30 | 1:30 | 1:30 | 1:30 |
| 2:00 | 2:00 | 2:00 | 2:00 |
| 2:30 | 2:30 | 2:30 | 2:30 |
| 3:00 | 3:00 | 3:00 | 3:00 |
| 3:30 | 3:30 | 3:30 | 3:30 |
| 4:00 | 4:00 | 4:00 | 4:00 |
| 4:30 | 4:30 | 4:30 | 4:30 |
| 5:00 | 5:00 | 5:00 | 5:00 |
| 5:30 | 5:30 | 5:30 | 5:30 |
| 6:00 | 6:00 | 6:00 | 6:00 |
| 6:30 | 6:30 | 6:30 | 6:30 |
| 7:00 | 7:00 | 7:00 | 7:00 |
| 7:30 | 7:30 | 7:30 | 7:30 |
| 8:00 | 8:00 | 8:00 | 8:00 |
| 8:30 | 8:30 | 8:30 | 8:30 |
| 9:00 | 9:00 | 9:00 | 9:00 |
| 9:30 | 9:30 | 9:30 | 9:30 |
| 10:00 | 10:00 | 10:00 | 10:00 |

# Prep Your *Week*

## Priorities This Week

- 
- 
- 
- 
- 
- 
- 
- 
- 

## Coaching Cycles

## Classroom Snapshots

## Data Meetings

## Team & PD Meetings

## Feedback Meetings

## Other

# Reflect on Your *Week*

| What goals did you accomplish this week? | What goals did you not accomplish this week? Why? |
|---|---|
| | |
| **What can you do to improve next week?** | **Things learned and things to remember:** |
| | |

## Goal & Habit Tracker

| Goal or Habit | Day 1 | Day 2 | Day 3 | Day 4 | Day 5 | Day 6 | Day 7 |
|---|---|---|---|---|---|---|---|
| | | | | | | | |
| | | | | | | | |
| | | | | | | | |
| | | | | | | | |

## Notes

Week:

Notes

| | Sunday | Monday | Tuesday |
|---|---|---|---|
| | 4:00 a.m. | 4:00 a.m. | 4:00 a.m. |
| | 4:30 | 4:30 | 4:30 |
| | 5:00 | 5:00 | 5:00 |
| | 5:30 | 5:30 | 5:30 |
| | 6:00 | 6:00 | 6:00 |
| | 6:30 | 6:30 | 6:30 |
| | 7:00 | 7:00 | 7:00 |
| | 7:30 | 7:30 | 7:30 |
| | 8:00 | 8:00 | 8:00 |
| | 8:30 | 8:30 | 8:30 |
| | 9:00 | 9:00 | 9:00 |
| | 9:30 | 9:30 | 9:30 |
| | 10:00 | 10:00 | 10:00 |
| | 10:30 | 10:30 | 10:30 |
| | 11:00 | 11:00 | 11:00 |
| | 11:30 | 11:30 | 11:30 |
| | 12:00 p.m. | 12:00 p.m. | 12:00 p.m. |
| | 12:30 | 12:30 | 12:30 |
| | 1:00 | 1:00 | 1:00 |
| | 1:30 | 1:30 | 1:30 |
| | 2:00 | 2:00 | 2:00 |
| | 2:30 | 2:30 | 2:30 |
| | 3:00 | 3:00 | 3:00 |
| | 3:30 | 3:30 | 3:30 |
| | 4:00 | 4:00 | 4:00 |
| | 4:30 | 4:30 | 4:30 |
| | 5:00 | 5:00 | 5:00 |
| | 5:30 | 5:30 | 5:30 |
| | 6:00 | 6:00 | 6:00 |
| | 6:30 | 6:30 | 6:30 |
| | 7:00 | 7:00 | 7:00 |
| | 7:30 | 7:30 | 7:30 |
| | 8:00 | 8:00 | 8:00 |
| | 8:30 | 8:30 | 8:30 |
| | 9:00 | 9:00 | 9:00 |
| | 9:30 | 9:30 | 9:30 |
| | 10:00 | 10:00 | 10:00 |

| Wednesday | Thursday | Friday | Saturday |
|---|---|---|---|
| 4:00 a.m. | 4:00 a.m. | 4:00 a.m. | 4:00 a.m. |
| 4:30 | 4:30 | 4:30 | 4:30 |
| 5:00 | 5:00 | 5:00 | 5:00 |
| 5:30 | 5:30 | 5:30 | 5:30 |
| 6:00 | 6:00 | 6:00 | 6:00 |
| 6:30 | 6:30 | 6:30 | 6:30 |
| 7:00 | 7:00 | 7:00 | 7:00 |
| 7:30 | 7:30 | 7:30 | 7:30 |
| 8:00 | 8:00 | 8:00 | 8:00 |
| 8:30 | 8:30 | 8:30 | 8:30 |
| 9:00 | 9:00 | 9:00 | 9:00 |
| 9:30 | 9:30 | 9:30 | 9:30 |
| 10:00 | 10:00 | 10:00 | 10:00 |
| 10:30 | 10:30 | 10:30 | 10:30 |
| 11:00 | 11:00 | 11:00 | 11:00 |
| 11:30 | 11:30 | 11:30 | 11:30 |
| 12:00 p.m. | 12:00 p.m. | 12:00 p.m. | 12:00 p.m. |
| 12:30 | 12:30 | 12:30 | 12:30 |
| 1:00 | 1:00 | 1:00 | 1:00 |
| 1:30 | 1:30 | 1:30 | 1:30 |
| 2:00 | 2:00 | 2:00 | 2:00 |
| 2:30 | 2:30 | 2:30 | 2:30 |
| 3:00 | 3:00 | 3:00 | 3:00 |
| 3:30 | 3:30 | 3:30 | 3:30 |
| 4:00 | 4:00 | 4:00 | 4:00 |
| 4:30 | 4:30 | 4:30 | 4:30 |
| 5:00 | 5:00 | 5:00 | 5:00 |
| 5:30 | 5:30 | 5:30 | 5:30 |
| 6:00 | 6:00 | 6:00 | 6:00 |
| 6:30 | 6:30 | 6:30 | 6:30 |
| 7:00 | 7:00 | 7:00 | 7:00 |
| 7:30 | 7:30 | 7:30 | 7:30 |
| 8:00 | 8:00 | 8:00 | 8:00 |
| 8:30 | 8:30 | 8:30 | 8:30 |
| 9:00 | 9:00 | 9:00 | 9:00 |
| 9:30 | 9:30 | 9:30 | 9:30 |
| 10:00 | 10:00 | 10:00 | 10:00 |

# Prep Your *Week*

## *Priorities* This Week

- 
- 
- 
- 
- 
- 
- 
- 
- 

## Coaching Cycles

## Classroom Snapshots

## Data Meetings

## Team & PD Meetings

## Feedback Meetings

## Other

# Reflect on Your *Week*

| What goals did you accomplish this week? | What goals did you not accomplish this week? Why? |
|---|---|
| What can you do to improve next week? | Things learned and things to remember: |

## Goal & Habit Tracker

| Goal or Habit | Day 1 | Day 2 | Day 3 | Day 4 | Day 5 | Day 6 | Day 7 |
|---|---|---|---|---|---|---|---|
| | | | | | | | |
| | | | | | | | |
| | | | | | | | |
| | | | | | | | |

## Notes

**Week:**

**Notes**

| Sunday | Monday | Tuesday |
|---|---|---|
| 4:00 a.m. | 4:00 a.m. | 4:00 a.m. |
| 4:30 | 4:30 | 4:30 |
| 5:00 | 5:00 | 5:00 |
| 5:30 | 5:30 | 5:30 |
| 6:00 | 6:00 | 6:00 |
| 6:30 | 6:30 | 6:30 |
| 7:00 | 7:00 | 7:00 |
| 7:30 | 7:30 | 7:30 |
| 8:00 | 8:00 | 8:00 |
| 8:30 | 8:30 | 8:30 |
| 9:00 | 9:00 | 9:00 |
| 9:30 | 9:30 | 9:30 |
| 10:00 | 10:00 | 10:00 |
| 10:30 | 10:30 | 10:30 |
| 11:00 | 11:00 | 11:00 |
| 11:30 | 11:30 | 11:30 |
| 12:00 p.m. | 12:00 p.m. | 12:00 p.m. |
| 12:30 | 12:30 | 12:30 |
| 1:00 | 1:00 | 1:00 |
| 1:30 | 1:30 | 1:30 |
| 2:00 | 2:00 | 2:00 |
| 2:30 | 2:30 | 2:30 |
| 3:00 | 3:00 | 3:00 |
| 3:30 | 3:30 | 3:30 |
| 4:00 | 4:00 | 4:00 |
| 4:30 | 4:30 | 4:30 |
| 5:00 | 5:00 | 5:00 |
| 5:30 | 5:30 | 5:30 |
| 6:00 | 6:00 | 6:00 |
| 6:30 | 6:30 | 6:30 |
| 7:00 | 7:00 | 7:00 |
| 7:30 | 7:30 | 7:30 |
| 8:00 | 8:00 | 8:00 |
| 8:30 | 8:30 | 8:30 |
| 9:00 | 9:00 | 9:00 |
| 9:30 | 9:30 | 9:30 |
| 10:00 | 10:00 | 10:00 |

| Wednesday | Thursday | Friday | Saturday |
|---|---|---|---|
| 4:00 a.m. | 4:00 a.m. | 4:00 a.m. | 4:00 a.m. |
| 4:30 | 4:30 | 4:30 | 4:30 |
| 5:00 | 5:00 | 5:00 | 5:00 |
| 5:30 | 5:30 | 5:30 | 5:30 |
| 6:00 | 6:00 | 6:00 | 6:00 |
| 6:30 | 6:30 | 6:30 | 6:30 |
| 7:00 | 7:00 | 7:00 | 7:00 |
| 7:30 | 7:30 | 7:30 | 7:30 |
| 8:00 | 8:00 | 8:00 | 8:00 |
| 8:30 | 8:30 | 8:30 | 8:30 |
| 9:00 | 9:00 | 9:00 | 9:00 |
| 9:30 | 9:30 | 9:30 | 9:30 |
| 10:00 | 10:00 | 10:00 | 10:00 |
| 10:30 | 10:30 | 10:30 | 10:30 |
| 11:00 | 11:00 | 11:00 | 11:00 |
| 11:30 | 11:30 | 11:30 | 11:30 |
| 12:00 p.m. | 12:00 p.m. | 12:00 p.m. | 12:00 p.m. |
| 12:30 | 12:30 | 12:30 | 12:30 |
| 1:00 | 1:00 | 1:00 | 1:00 |
| 1:30 | 1:30 | 1:30 | 1:30 |
| 2:00 | 2:00 | 2:00 | 2:00 |
| 2:30 | 2:30 | 2:30 | 2:30 |
| 3:00 | 3:00 | 3:00 | 3:00 |
| 3:30 | 3:30 | 3:30 | 3:30 |
| 4:00 | 4:00 | 4:00 | 4:00 |
| 4:30 | 4:30 | 4:30 | 4:30 |
| 5:00 | 5:00 | 5:00 | 5:00 |
| 5:30 | 5:30 | 5:30 | 5:30 |
| 6:00 | 6:00 | 6:00 | 6:00 |
| 6:30 | 6:30 | 6:30 | 6:30 |
| 7:00 | 7:00 | 7:00 | 7:00 |
| 7:30 | 7:30 | 7:30 | 7:30 |
| 8:00 | 8:00 | 8:00 | 8:00 |
| 8:30 | 8:30 | 8:30 | 8:30 |
| 9:00 | 9:00 | 9:00 | 9:00 |
| 9:30 | 9:30 | 9:30 | 9:30 |
| 10:00 | 10:00 | 10:00 | 10:00 |

IT TAKES AS MUCH *energy* TO WISH AS IT DOES TO *plan.*

—Eleanor Roosevelt

# Prep Your *Month*

| Personal Goals | | | |
|---|---|---|---|
| Day | Health & Fitness | Finances | Self-Care & Growth |
| | | | |
| | | | |
| | | | |
| | | | |
| | | | |
| | | | |

| Important Reminders | |
|---|---|
| | |
| | |
| | |
| | |
| | |
| | |
| | |

# Prep Your *Month*

| Main Goal | Main Focus | Wins |
|---|---|---|
| | | |

## Monthly Tasks

**Week 1**

**Week 2**

**Week 3**

**Week 4**

**Week 5**

## Must Do This Month

## Save for Next Month

# December

| Sunday | Monday | Tuesday | Wednesday |
|--------|--------|---------|-----------|
|        |        |         |           |
|        |        |         |           |
|        |        |         |           |
|        |        |         |           |
|        |        |         |           |

Monthly Focus

| Thursday | Friday | Saturday |
|---|---|---|
|  |  |  |
|  |  |  |
|  |  |  |
|  |  |  |
|  |  |  |

Notes

# Prep Your *Week*

## *Priorities* This Week

- 
- 
- 
- 
- 
- 
- 
- 

## Coaching Cycles

## Classroom Snapshots

## Data Meetings

## Team & PD Meetings

## Feedback Meetings

## Other

# Reflect on Your *Week*

| | |
|---|---|
| **What goals did you accomplish this week?** | **What goals did you not accomplish this week? Why?** |
| **What can you do to improve next week?** | **Things learned and things to remember:** |

## Goal & Habit Tracker

| Goal or Habit | Day 1 | Day 2 | Day 3 | Day 4 | Day 5 | Day 6 | Day 7 |
|---|---|---|---|---|---|---|---|
| | | | | | | | |
| | | | | | | | |
| | | | | | | | |
| | | | | | | | |

## Notes

Week:

Notes

| | Sunday | Monday | Tuesday |
|---|---|---|---|
| | 4:00 a.m. | 4:00 a.m. | 4:00 a.m. |
| | 4:30 | 4:30 | 4:30 |
| | 5:00 | 5:00 | 5:00 |
| | 5:30 | 5:30 | 5:30 |
| | 6:00 | 6:00 | 6:00 |
| | 6:30 | 6:30 | 6:30 |
| | 7:00 | 7:00 | 7:00 |
| | 7:30 | 7:30 | 7:30 |
| | 8:00 | 8:00 | 8:00 |
| | 8:30 | 8:30 | 8:30 |
| | 9:00 | 9:00 | 9:00 |
| | 9:30 | 9:30 | 9:30 |
| | 10:00 | 10:00 | 10:00 |
| | 10:30 | 10:30 | 10:30 |
| | 11:00 | 11:00 | 11:00 |
| | 11:30 | 11:30 | 11:30 |
| | 12:00 p.m. | 12:00 p.m. | 12:00 p.m. |
| | 12:30 | 12:30 | 12:30 |
| | 1:00 | 1:00 | 1:00 |
| | 1:30 | 1:30 | 1:30 |
| | 2:00 | 2:00 | 2:00 |
| | 2:30 | 2:30 | 2:30 |
| | 3:00 | 3:00 | 3:00 |
| | 3:30 | 3:30 | 3:30 |
| | 4:00 | 4:00 | 4:00 |
| | 4:30 | 4:30 | 4:30 |
| | 5:00 | 5:00 | 5:00 |
| | 5:30 | 5:30 | 5:30 |
| | 6:00 | 6:00 | 6:00 |
| | 6:30 | 6:30 | 6:30 |
| | 7:00 | 7:00 | 7:00 |
| | 7:30 | 7:30 | 7:30 |
| | 8:00 | 8:00 | 8:00 |
| | 8:30 | 8:30 | 8:30 |
| | 9:00 | 9:00 | 9:00 |
| | 9:30 | 9:30 | 9:30 |
| | 10:00 | 10:00 | 10:00 |

| Wednesday | Thursday | Friday | Saturday |
|---|---|---|---|
| 4:00 a.m. | 4:00 a.m. | 4:00 a.m. | 4:00 a.m. |
| 4:30 | 4:30 | 4:30 | 4:30 |
| 5:00 | 5:00 | 5:00 | 5:00 |
| 5:30 | 5:30 | 5:30 | 5:30 |
| 6:00 | 6:00 | 6:00 | 6:00 |
| 6:30 | 6:30 | 6:30 | 6:30 |
| 7:00 | 7:00 | 7:00 | 7:00 |
| 7:30 | 7:30 | 7:30 | 7:30 |
| 8:00 | 8:00 | 8:00 | 8:00 |
| 8:30 | 8:30 | 8:30 | 8:30 |
| 9:00 | 9:00 | 9:00 | 9:00 |
| 9:30 | 9:30 | 9:30 | 9:30 |
| 10:00 | 10:00 | 10:00 | 10:00 |
| 10:30 | 10:30 | 10:30 | 10:30 |
| 11:00 | 11:00 | 11:00 | 11:00 |
| 11:30 | 11:30 | 11:30 | 11:30 |
| 12:00 p.m. | 12:00 p.m. | 12:00 p.m. | 12:00 p.m. |
| 12:30 | 12:30 | 12:30 | 12:30 |
| 1:00 | 1:00 | 1:00 | 1:00 |
| 1:30 | 1:30 | 1:30 | 1:30 |
| 2:00 | 2:00 | 2:00 | 2:00 |
| 2:30 | 2:30 | 2:30 | 2:30 |
| 3:00 | 3:00 | 3:00 | 3:00 |
| 3:30 | 3:30 | 3:30 | 3:30 |
| 4:00 | 4:00 | 4:00 | 4:00 |
| 4:30 | 4:30 | 4:30 | 4:30 |
| 5:00 | 5:00 | 5:00 | 5:00 |
| 5:30 | 5:30 | 5:30 | 5:30 |
| 6:00 | 6:00 | 6:00 | 6:00 |
| 6:30 | 6:30 | 6:30 | 6:30 |
| 7:00 | 7:00 | 7:00 | 7:00 |
| 7:30 | 7:30 | 7:30 | 7:30 |
| 8:00 | 8:00 | 8:00 | 8:00 |
| 8:30 | 8:30 | 8:30 | 8:30 |
| 9:00 | 9:00 | 9:00 | 9:00 |
| 9:30 | 9:30 | 9:30 | 9:30 |
| 10:00 | 10:00 | 10:00 | 10:00 |

# Prep Your *Week*

## Priorities This Week

- 
- 
- 
- 
- 
- 
- 
- 

## Coaching Cycles

## Classroom Snapshots

## Data Meetings

## Team & PD Meetings

## Feedback Meetings

## Other

# Reflect on Your Week

| What goals did you accomplish this week? | What goals did you not accomplish this week? Why? |
|---|---|
| What can you do to improve next week? | Things learned and things to remember: |

## Goal & Habit Tracker

| Goal or Habit | Day 1 | Day 2 | Day 3 | Day 4 | Day 5 | Day 6 | Day 7 |
|---|---|---|---|---|---|---|---|
| | | | | | | | |
| | | | | | | | |
| | | | | | | | |
| | | | | | | | |

## Notes

**Week:**

**Notes**

| Sunday | Monday | Tuesday |
|---|---|---|
| 4:00 a.m. | 4:00 a.m. | 4:00 a.m. |
| 4:30 | 4:30 | 4:30 |
| 5:00 | 5:00 | 5:00 |
| 5:30 | 5:30 | 5:30 |
| 6:00 | 6:00 | 6:00 |
| 6:30 | 6:30 | 6:30 |
| 7:00 | 7:00 | 7:00 |
| 7:30 | 7:30 | 7:30 |
| 8:00 | 8:00 | 8:00 |
| 8:30 | 8:30 | 8:30 |
| 9:00 | 9:00 | 9:00 |
| 9:30 | 9:30 | 9:30 |
| 10:00 | 10:00 | 10:00 |
| 10:30 | 10:30 | 10:30 |
| 11:00 | 11:00 | 11:00 |
| 11:30 | 11:30 | 11:30 |
| 12:00 p.m. | 12:00 p.m. | 12:00 p.m. |
| 12:30 | 12:30 | 12:30 |
| 1:00 | 1:00 | 1:00 |
| 1:30 | 1:30 | 1:30 |
| 2:00 | 2:00 | 2:00 |
| 2:30 | 2:30 | 2:30 |
| 3:00 | 3:00 | 3:00 |
| 3:30 | 3:30 | 3:30 |
| 4:00 | 4:00 | 4:00 |
| 4:30 | 4:30 | 4:30 |
| 5:00 | 5:00 | 5:00 |
| 5:30 | 5:30 | 5:30 |
| 6:00 | 6:00 | 6:00 |
| 6:30 | 6:30 | 6:30 |
| 7:00 | 7:00 | 7:00 |
| 7:30 | 7:30 | 7:30 |
| 8:00 | 8:00 | 8:00 |
| 8:30 | 8:30 | 8:30 |
| 9:00 | 9:00 | 9:00 |
| 9:30 | 9:30 | 9:30 |
| 10:00 | 10:00 | 10:00 |

| Wednesday | Thursday | Friday | Saturday |
|---|---|---|---|
| 4:00 a.m. | 4:00 a.m. | 4:00 a.m. | 4:00 a.m. |
| 4:30 | 4:30 | 4:30 | 4:30 |
| 5:00 | 5:00 | 5:00 | 5:00 |
| 5:30 | 5:30 | 5:30 | 5:30 |
| 6:00 | 6:00 | 6:00 | 6:00 |
| 6:30 | 6:30 | 6:30 | 6:30 |
| 7:00 | 7:00 | 7:00 | 7:00 |
| 7:30 | 7:30 | 7:30 | 7:30 |
| 8:00 | 8:00 | 8:00 | 8:00 |
| 8:30 | 8:30 | 8:30 | 8:30 |
| 9:00 | 9:00 | 9:00 | 9:00 |
| 9:30 | 9:30 | 9:30 | 9:30 |
| 10:00 | 10;00 | 10:00 | 10:00 |
| 10:30 | 10:30 | 10:30 | 10:30 |
| 11:00 | 11:00 | 11:00 | 11:00 |
| 11:30 | 11:30 | 11:30 | 11:30 |
| 12:00 p.m. | 12:00 p.m. | 12:00 p.m. | 12:00 p.m. |
| 12:30 | 12:30 | 12:30 | 12:30 |
| 1:00 | 1:00 | 1:00 | 1:00 |
| 1:30 | 1:30 | 1:30 | 1:30 |
| 2:00 | 2:00 | 2:00 | 2:00 |
| 2:30 | 2:30 | 2:30 | 2:30 |
| 3:00 | 3:00 | 3:00 | 3:00 |
| 3:30 | 3:30 | 3:30 | 3:30 |
| 4:00 | 4:00 | 4:00 | 4:00 |
| 4:30 | 4:30 | 4:30 | 4:30 |
| 5:00 | 5:00 | 5:00 | 5:00 |
| 5:30 | 5:30 | 5:30 | 5:30 |
| 6:00 | 6:00 | 6:00 | 6:00 |
| 6:30 | 6:30 | 6:30 | 6:30 |
| 7:00 | 7:00 | 7:00 | 7:00 |
| 7:30 | 7:30 | 7:30 | 7:30 |
| 8:00 | 8:00 | 8:00 | 8:00 |
| 8:30 | 8:30 | 8:30 | 8:30 |
| 9:00 | 9:00 | 9:00 | 9:00 |
| 9:30 | 9:30 | 9:30 | 9:30 |
| 10:00 | 10:00 | 10:00 | 10:00 |

DECEMBER

# Prep Your *Week*

## Priorities This Week

- 
- 
- 
- 
- 
- 
- 
- 
- 

## Coaching Cycles

## Classroom Snapshots

## Data Meetings

## Team & PD Meetings

## Feedback Meetings

## Other

# Reflect on Your *Week*

| What goals did you accomplish this week? | What goals did you not accomplish this week? Why? |
|---|---|
| What can you do to improve next week? | Things learned and things to remember: |

## Goal & Habit Tracker

| Goal or Habit | Day 1 | Day 2 | Day 3 | Day 4 | Day 5 | Day 6 | Day 7 |
|---|---|---|---|---|---|---|---|
|  |  |  |  |  |  |  |  |
|  |  |  |  |  |  |  |  |
|  |  |  |  |  |  |  |  |
|  |  |  |  |  |  |  |  |

## Notes

Week:

Notes

| | Sunday | Monday | Tuesday |
|---|---|---|---|
| | 4:00 a.m. | 4:00 a.m. | 4:00 a.m. |
| | 4:30 | 4:30 | 4:30 |
| | 5:00 | 5:00 | 5:00 |
| | 5:30 | 5:30 | 5:30 |
| | 6:00 | 6:00 | 6:00 |
| | 6:30 | 6:30 | 6:30 |
| | 7:00 | 7:00 | 7:00 |
| | 7:30 | 7:30 | 7:30 |
| | 8:00 | 8:00 | 8:00 |
| | 8:30 | 8:30 | 8:30 |
| | 9:00 | 9:00 | 9:00 |
| | 9:30 | 9:30 | 9:30 |
| | 10:00 | 10:00 | 10:00 |
| | 10:30 | 10:30 | 10:30 |
| | 11:00 | 11:00 | 11:00 |
| | 11:30 | 11:30 | 11:30 |
| | 12:00 p.m. | 12:00 p.m. | 12:00 p.m. |
| | 12:30 | 12:30 | 12:30 |
| | 1:00 | 1:00 | 1:00 |
| | 1:30 | 1:30 | 1:30 |
| | 2:00 | 2:00 | 2:00 |
| | 2:30 | 2:30 | 2:30 |
| | 3:00 | 3:00 | 3:00 |
| | 3:30 | 3:30 | 3:30 |
| | 4:00 | 4:00 | 4:00 |
| | 4:30 | 4:30 | 4:30 |
| | 5:00 | 5:00 | 5:00 |
| | 5:30 | 5:30 | 5:30 |
| | 6:00 | 6:00 | 6:00 |
| | 6:30 | 6:30 | 6:30 |
| | 7:00 | 7:00 | 7:00 |
| | 7:30 | 7:30 | 7:30 |
| | 8:00 | 8:00 | 8:00 |
| | 8:30 | 8:30 | 8:30 |
| | 9:00 | 9:00 | 9:00 |
| | 9:30 | 9:30 | 9:30 |
| | 10:00 | 10:00 | 10:00 |

| Wednesday | Thursday | Friday | Saturday |
| --- | --- | --- | --- |
| 4:00 a.m. | 4:00 a.m. | 4:00 a.m. | 4:00 a.m. |
| 4:30 | 4:30 | 4:30 | 4:30 |
| 5:00 | 5:00 | 5:00 | 5:00 |
| 5:30 | 5:30 | 5:30 | 5:30 |
| 6:00 | 6:00 | 6:00 | 6:00 |
| 6:30 | 6:30 | 6:30 | 6:30 |
| 7:00 | 7:00 | 7:00 | 7:00 |
| 7:30 | 7:30 | 7:30 | 7:30 |
| 8:00 | 8:00 | 8:00 | 8:00 |
| 8:30 | 8:30 | 8:30 | 8:30 |
| 9:00 | 9:00 | 9:00 | 9:00 |
| 9:30 | 9:30 | 9:30 | 9:30 |
| 10:00 | 10:00 | 10:00 | 10:00 |
| 10:30 | 10:30 | 10:30 | 10:30 |
| 11:00 | 11:00 | 11:00 | 11:00 |
| 11:30 | 11:30 | 11:30 | 11:30 |
| 12:00 p.m. | 12:00 p.m. | 12:00 p.m. | 12:00 p.m. |
| 12:30 | 12:30 | 12:30 | 12:30 |
| 1:00 | 1:00 | 1:00 | 1:00 |
| 1:30 | 1:30 | 1:30 | 1:30 |
| 2:00 | 2:00 | 2:00 | 2:00 |
| 2:30 | 2:30 | 2:30 | 2:30 |
| 3:00 | 3:00 | 3:00 | 3:00 |
| 3:30 | 3:30 | 3:30 | 3:30 |
| 4:00 | 4:00 | 4:00 | 4:00 |
| 4:30 | 4:30 | 4:30 | 4:30 |
| 5:00 | 5:00 | 5:00 | 5:00 |
| 5:30 | 5:30 | 5:30 | 5:30 |
| 6:00 | 6:00 | 6:00 | 6:00 |
| 6:30 | 6:30 | 6:30 | 6:30 |
| 7:00 | 7:00 | 7:00 | 7:00 |
| 7:30 | 7:30 | 7:30 | 7:30 |
| 8:00 | 8:00 | 8:00 | 8:00 |
| 8:30 | 8:30 | 8:30 | 8:30 |
| 9:00 | 9:00 | 9:00 | 9:00 |
| 9:30 | 9:30 | 9:30 | 9:30 |
| 10:00 | 10:00 | 10:00 | 10:00 |

# Prep Your *Week*

## Priorities This Week

- 
- 
- 
- 
- 
- 
- 
- 
- 

## Coaching Cycles

## Classroom Snapshots

## Data Meetings

## Team & PD Meetings

## Feedback Meetings

## Other

# Reflect on Your *Week*

| What goals did you accomplish this week? | What goals did you not accomplish this week? Why? |
|---|---|
| What can you do to improve next week? | Things learned and things to remember: |

## Goal & Habit Tracker

| Goal or Habit | Day 1 | Day 2 | Day 3 | Day 4 | Day 5 | Day 6 | Day 7 |
|---|---|---|---|---|---|---|---|
| | | | | | | | |
| | | | | | | | |
| | | | | | | | |
| | | | | | | | |

## Notes

Week:

Notes

| | Sunday | Monday | Tuesday |
|---|---|---|---|
| | 4:00 a.m. | 4:00 a.m. | 4:00 a.m. |
| | 4:30 | 4:30 | 4:30 |
| | 5:00 | 5:00 | 5:00 |
| | 5:30 | 5:30 | 5:30 |
| | 6:00 | 6:00 | 6:00 |
| | 6:30 | 6:30 | 6:30 |
| | 7:00 | 7:00 | 7:00 |
| | 7:30 | 7:30 | 7:30 |
| | 8:00 | 8:00 | 8:00 |
| | 8:30 | 8:30 | 8:30 |
| | 9:00 | 9:00 | 9:00 |
| | 9:30 | 9:30 | 9:30 |
| | 10:00 | 10:00 | 10:00 |
| | 10:30 | 10:30 | 10:30 |
| | 11:00 | 11:00 | 11:00 |
| | 11:30 | 11:30 | 11:30 |
| | 12:00 p.m. | 12:00 p.m. | 12:00 p.m. |
| | 12:30 | 12:30 | 12:30 |
| | 1:00 | 1:00 | 1:00 |
| | 1:30 | 1:30 | 1:30 |
| | 2:00 | 2:00 | 2:00 |
| | 2:30 | 2:30 | 2:30 |
| | 3:00 | 3:00 | 3:00 |
| | 3:30 | 3:30 | 3:30 |
| | 4:00 | 4:00 | 4:00 |
| | 4:30 | 4:30 | 4:30 |
| | 5:00 | 5:00 | 5:00 |
| | 5:30 | 5:30 | 5:30 |
| | 6:00 | 6:00 | 6:00 |
| | 6:30 | 6:30 | 6:30 |
| | 7:00 | 7:00 | 7:00 |
| | 7:30 | 7:30 | 7:30 |
| | 8:00 | 8:00 | 8:00 |
| | 8:30 | 8:30 | 8:30 |
| | 9:00 | 9:00 | 9:00 |
| | 9:30 | 9:30 | 9:30 |
| | 10:00 | 10:00 | 10:00 |

| Wednesday | Thursday | Friday | Saturday |
|---|---|---|---|
| 4:00 a.m. | 4:00 a.m. | 4:00 a.m. | 4:00 a.m. |
| 4:30 | 4:30 | 4:30 | 4:30 |
| 5:00 | 5:00 | 5:00 | 5:00 |
| 5:30 | 5:30 | 5:30 | 5:30 |
| 6:00 | 6:00 | 6:00 | 6:00 |
| 6:30 | 6:30 | 6:30 | 6:30 |
| 7:00 | 7:00 | 7:00 | 7:00 |
| 7:30 | 7:30 | 7:30 | 7:30 |
| 8:00 | 8:00 | 8:00 | 8:00 |
| 8:30 | 8:30 | 8:30 | 8:30 |
| 9:00 | 9:00 | 9:00 | 9:00 |
| 9:30 | 9:30 | 9:30 | 9:30 |
| 10:00 | 10:00 | 10:00 | 10:00 |
| 10:30 | 10:30 | 10:30 | 10:30 |
| 11:00 | 11:00 | 11:00 | 11:00 |
| 11:30 | 11:30 | 11:30 | 11:30 |
| 12:00 p.m. | 12:00 p.m. | 12:00 p.m. | 12:00 p.m. |
| 12:30 | 12:30 | 12:30 | 12:30 |
| 1:00 | 1:00 | 1:00 | 1:00 |
| 1:30 | 1:30 | 1:30 | 1:30 |
| 2:00 | 2:00 | 2:00 | 2:00 |
| 2:30 | 2:30 | 2:30 | 2:30 |
| 3:00 | 3:00 | 3:00 | 3:00 |
| 3:30 | 3:30 | 3:30 | 3:30 |
| 4:00 | 4:00 | 4:00 | 4:00 |
| 4:30 | 4:30 | 4:30 | 4:30 |
| 5:00 | 5:00 | 5:00 | 5:00 |
| 5:30 | 5:30 | 5:30 | 5:30 |
| 6:00 | 6:00 | 6:00 | 6:00 |
| 6:30 | 6:30 | 6:30 | 6:30 |
| 7:00 | 7:00 | 7:00 | 7:00 |
| 7:30 | 7:30 | 7:30 | 7:30 |
| 8:00 | 8:00 | 8:00 | 8:00 |
| 8:30 | 8:30 | 8:30 | 8:30 |
| 9:00 | 9:00 | 9:00 | 9:00 |
| 9:30 | 9:30 | 9:30 | 9:30 |
| 10:00 | 10:00 | 10:00 | 10:00 |

# Prep Your *Week*

## Priorities This Week

- 
- 
- 
- 
- 
- 
- 
- 
- 

## Coaching Cycles

## Classroom Snapshots

## Data Meetings

## Team & PD Meetings

## Feedback Meetings

## Other

# Reflect on Your *Week*

| What goals did you accomplish this week? | What goals did you not accomplish this week? Why? |
|---|---|
| **What can you do to improve next week?** | **Things learned and things to remember:** |

## Goal & Habit Tracker

| Goal or Habit | Day 1 | Day 2 | Day 3 | Day 4 | Day 5 | Day 6 | Day 7 |
|---|---|---|---|---|---|---|---|
|  |  |  |  |  |  |  |  |
|  |  |  |  |  |  |  |  |
|  |  |  |  |  |  |  |  |
|  |  |  |  |  |  |  |  |

## Notes

Week:

Notes

| Sunday | Monday | Tuesday |
|---|---|---|
| 4:00 a.m. | 4:00 a.m. | 4:00 a.m. |
| 4:30 | 4:30 | 4:30 |
| 5:00 | 5:00 | 5:00 |
| 5:30 | 5:30 | 5:30 |
| 6:00 | 6:00 | 6:00 |
| 6:30 | 6:30 | 6:30 |
| 7:00 | 7:00 | 7:00 |
| 7:30 | 7:30 | 7:30 |
| 8:00 | 8:00 | 8:00 |
| 8:30 | 8:30 | 8:30 |
| 9:00 | 9:00 | 9:00 |
| 9:30 | 9:30 | 9:30 |
| 10:00 | 10:00 | 10:00 |
| 10:30 | 10:30 | 10:30 |
| 11:00 | 11:00 | 11:00 |
| 11:30 | 11:30 | 11:30 |
| 12:00 p.m. | 12:00 p.m. | 12:00 p.m. |
| 12:30 | 12:30 | 12:30 |
| 1:00 | 1:00 | 1:00 |
| 1:30 | 1:30 | 1:30 |
| 2:00 | 2:00 | 2:00 |
| 2:30 | 2:30 | 2:30 |
| 3:00 | 3:00 | 3:00 |
| 3:30 | 3:30 | 3:30 |
| 4:00 | 4:00 | 4:00 |
| 4:30 | 4:30 | 4:30 |
| 5:00 | 5:00 | 5:00 |
| 5:30 | 5:30 | 5:30 |
| 6:00 | 6:00 | 6:00 |
| 6:30 | 6:30 | 6:30 |
| 7:00 | 7:00 | 7:00 |
| 7:30 | 7:30 | 7:30 |
| 8:00 | 8:00 | 8:00 |
| 8:30 | 8:30 | 8:30 |
| 9:00 | 9:00 | 9:00 |
| 9:30 | 9:30 | 9:30 |
| 10:00 | 10:00 | 10:00 |

| Wednesday | Thursday | Friday | Saturday |
|---|---|---|---|
| 4:00 a.m. | 4:00 a.m. | 4:00 a.m. | 4:00 a.m. |
| 4:30 | 4:30 | 4:30 | 4:30 |
| 5:00 | 5:00 | 5:00 | 5:00 |
| 5:30 | 5:30 | 5:30 | 5:30 |
| 6:00 | 6:00 | 6:00 | 6:00 |
| 6:30 | 6:30 | 6:30 | 6:30 |
| 7:00 | 7:00 | 7:00 | 7:00 |
| 7:30 | 7:30 | 7:30 | 7:30 |
| 8:00 | 8:00 | 8:00 | 8:00 |
| 8:30 | 8:30 | 8:30 | 8:30 |
| 9:00 | 9:00 | 9:00 | 9:00 |
| 9:30 | 9:30 | 9:30 | 9:30 |
| 10:00 | 10:00 | 10:00 | 10:00 |
| 10:30 | 10:30 | 10:30 | 10:30 |
| 11:00 | 11:00 | 11:00 | 11:00 |
| 11:30 | 11:30 | 11:30 | 11:30 |
| 12:00 p.m. | 12:00 p.m. | 12:00 p.m. | 12:00 p.m. |
| 12:30 | 12:30 | 12:30 | 12:30 |
| 1:00 | 1:00 | 1:00 | 1:00 |
| 1:30 | 1:30 | 1:30 | 1:30 |
| 2:00 | 2:00 | 2:00 | 2:00 |
| 2:30 | 2:30 | 2:30 | 2:30 |
| 3:00 | 3:00 | 3:00 | 3:00 |
| 3:30 | 3:30 | 3:30 | 3:30 |
| 4:00 | 4:00 | 4:00 | 4:00 |
| 4:30 | 4:30 | 4:30 | 4:30 |
| 5:00 | 5:00 | 5:00 | 5:00 |
| 5:30 | 5:30 | 5:30 | 5:30 |
| 6:00 | 6:00 | 6:00 | 6:00 |
| 6:30 | 6:30 | 6:30 | 6:30 |
| 7:00 | 7:00 | 7:00 | 7:00 |
| 7:30 | 7:30 | 7:30 | 7:30 |
| 8:00 | 8:00 | 8:00 | 8:00 |
| 8:30 | 8:30 | 8:30 | 8:30 |
| 9:00 | 9:00 | 9:00 | 9:00 |
| 9:30 | 9:30 | 9:30 | 9:30 |
| 10:00 | 10:00 | 10:00 | 10:00 |

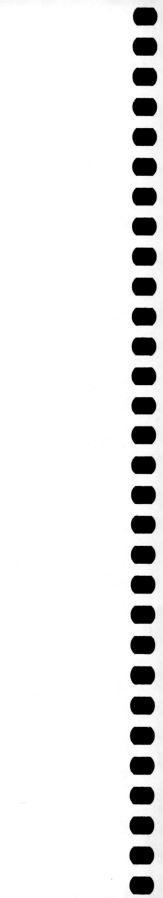

SOMEONE'S SITTING IN THE SHADE *today* BECAUSE SOMEONE PLANTED A TREE *a long time ago.*

—Warren Buffett

# Prep Your *Month*

## Personal Goals

| Day | Health & Fitness | Finances | Self-Care & Growth |
|-----|------------------|----------|--------------------|
|     |                  |          |                    |
|     |                  |          |                    |
|     |                  |          |                    |
|     |                  |          |                    |
|     |                  |          |                    |
|     |                  |          |                    |

## Important Reminders

|  |  |
|--|--|
|  |  |
|  |  |
|  |  |
|  |  |
|  |  |
|  |  |
|  |  |

# Prep Your *Month*

| Main Goal | Main Focus | Wins |
|---|---|---|
| | | |

## Monthly Tasks

**Week 1**
_____
_____
_____

**Week 2**
_____
_____
_____

**Week 3**
_____
_____
_____

**Week 4**
_____
_____
_____

**Week 5**
_____
_____
_____

### Must Do This Month

### Save for Next Month

# January

*"Do what you can, with what you have, where you are."* —Theodore Roosevelt

| Sunday | Monday | Tuesday | Wednesday |
|--------|--------|---------|-----------|
|        |        |         |           |
|        |        |         |           |
|        |        |         |           |
|        |        |         |           |
|        |        |         |           |

Monthly Focus

| Thursday | Friday | Saturday |
|----------|--------|----------|
|          |        |          |
|          |        |          |
|          |        |          |
|          |        |          |
|          |        |          |

Notes

JANUARY

# Prep Your *Week*

## Priorities This Week

- 
- 
- 
- 
- 
- 
- 
- 

## Coaching Cycles

## Classroom Snapshots

## Data Meetings

## Team & PD Meetings

## Feedback Meetings

## Other

# Reflect on Your *Week*

| | |
|---|---|
| What goals did you accomplish this week? | What goals did you not accomplish this week? Why? |
| What can you do to improve next week? | Things learned and things to remember: |

## Goal & Habit Tracker

| Goal or Habit | Day 1 | Day 2 | Day 3 | Day 4 | Day 5 | Day 6 | Day 7 |
|---|---|---|---|---|---|---|---|
| | | | | | | | |
| | | | | | | | |
| | | | | | | | |
| | | | | | | | |

## Notes

Week:

Notes ↘

| | Sunday | Monday | Tuesday |
|---|---|---|---|
| | 4:00 a.m. | 4:00 a.m. | 4:00 a.m. |
| | 4:30 | 4:30 | 4:30 |
| | 5:00 | 5:00 | 5:00 |
| | 5:30 | 5:30 | 5:30 |
| | 6:00 | 6:00 | 6:00 |
| | 6:30 | 6:30 | 6:30 |
| | 7:00 | 7:00 | 7:00 |
| | 7:30 | 7:30 | 7:30 |
| | 8:00 | 8:00 | 8:00 |
| | 8:30 | 8:30 | 8:30 |
| | 9:00 | 9:00 | 9:00 |
| | 9:30 | 9:30 | 9:30 |
| | 10:00 | 10:00 | 10:00 |
| | 10:30 | 10:30 | 10:30 |
| | 11:00 | 11:00 | 11:00 |
| | 11:30 | 11:30 | 11:30 |
| | 12:00 p.m. | 12:00 p.m. | 12:00 p.m. |
| | 12:30 | 12:30 | 12:30 |
| | 1:00 | 1:00 | 1:00 |
| | 1:30 | 1:30 | 1:30 |
| | 2:00 | 2:00 | 2:00 |
| | 2:30 | 2:30 | 2:30 |
| | 3:00 | 3:00 | 3:00 |
| | 3:30 | 3:30 | 3:30 |
| | 4:00 | 4:00 | 4:00 |
| | 4:30 | 4:30 | 4:30 |
| | 5:00 | 5:00 | 5:00 |
| | 5:30 | 5:30 | 5:30 |
| | 6:00 | 6:00 | 6:00 |
| | 6:30 | 6:30 | 6:30 |
| | 7:00 | 7:00 | 7:00 |
| | 7:30 | 7:30 | 7:30 |
| | 8:00 | 8:00 | 8:00 |
| | 8:30 | 8:30 | 8:30 |
| | 9:00 | 9:00 | 9:00 |
| | 9:30 | 9:30 | 9:30 |
| | 10:00 | 10:00 | 10:00 |

| Wednesday | Thursday | Friday | Saturday |
|---|---|---|---|
| 4:00 a.m. | 4:00 a.m. | 4:00 a.m. | 4:00 a.m. |
| 4:30 | 4:30 | 4:30 | 4:30 |
| 5:00 | 5:00 | 5:00 | 5:00 |
| 5:30 | 5:30 | 5:30 | 5:30 |
| 6:00 | 6:00 | 6:00 | 6:00 |
| 6:30 | 6:30 | 6:30 | 6:30 |
| 7:00 | 7:00 | 7:00 | 7:00 |
| 7:30 | 7:30 | 7:30 | 7:30 |
| 8:00 | 8:00 | 8:00 | 8:00 |
| 8:30 | 8:30 | 8:30 | 8:30 |
| 9:00 | 9:00 | 9:00 | 9:00 |
| 9:30 | 9:30 | 9:30 | 9:30 |
| 10:00 | 10:00 | 10:00 | 10:00 |
| 10:30 | 10:30 | 10:30 | 10:30 |
| 11:00 | 11:00 | 11:00 | 11:00 |
| 11:30 | 11:30 | 11:30 | 11:30 |
| 12:00 p.m. | 12:00 p.m. | 12:00 p.m. | 12:00 p.m. |
| 12:30 | 12:30 | 12:30 | 12:30 |
| 1:00 | 1:00 | 1:00 | 1:00 |
| 1:30 | 1:30 | 1:30 | 1:30 |
| 2:00 | 2:00 | 2:00 | 2:00 |
| 2:30 | 2:30 | 2:30 | 2:30 |
| 3:00 | 3:00 | 3:00 | 3:00 |
| 3:30 | 3:30 | 3:30 | 3:30 |
| 4:00 | 4:00 | 4:00 | 4:00 |
| 4:30 | 4:30 | 4:30 | 4:30 |
| 5:00 | 5:00 | 5:00 | 5:00 |
| 5:30 | 5:30 | 5:30 | 5:30 |
| 6:00 | 6:00 | 6:00 | 6:00 |
| 6:30 | 6:30 | 6:30 | 6:30 |
| 7:00 | 7:00 | 7:00 | 7:00 |
| 7:30 | 7:30 | 7:30 | 7:30 |
| 8:00 | 8:00 | 8:00 | 8:00 |
| 8:30 | 8:30 | 8:30 | 8:30 |
| 9:00 | 9:00 | 9:00 | 9:00 |
| 9:30 | 9:30 | 9:30 | 9:30 |
| 10:00 | 10:00 | 10:00 | 10:00 |

JANUARY

# Prep Your *Week*

## Priorities This Week

- 
- 
- 
- 
- 
- 
- 
- 

## Coaching Cycles

## Classroom Snapshots

## Data Meetings

## Team & PD Meetings

## Feedback Meetings

## Other

# Reflect on Your *Week*

| | |
|---|---|
| **What goals did you accomplish this week?** | **What goals did you not accomplish this week? Why?** |
| **What can you do to improve next week?** | **Things learned and things to remember:** |

## Goal & Habit Tracker

| Goal or Habit | Day 1 | Day 2 | Day 3 | Day 4 | Day 5 | Day 6 | Day 7 |
|---|---|---|---|---|---|---|---|
| | | | | | | | |
| | | | | | | | |
| | | | | | | | |
| | | | | | | | |

## Notes

Notes

| Sunday | Monday | Tuesday |
|--------|--------|---------|
| 4:00 a.m. | 4:00 a.m. | 4:00 a.m. |
| 4:30 | 4:30 | 4:30 |
| 5:00 | 5:00 | 5:00 |
| 5:30 | 5:30 | 5:30 |
| 6:00 | 6:00 | 6:00 |
| 6:30 | 6:30 | 6:30 |
| 7:00 | 7:00 | 7:00 |
| 7:30 | 7:30 | 7:30 |
| 8:00 | 8:00 | 8:00 |
| 8:30 | 8:30 | 8:30 |
| 9:00 | 9:00 | 9:00 |
| 9:30 | 9:30 | 9:30 |
| 10:00 | 10:00 | 10:00 |
| 10:30 | 10:30 | 10:30 |
| 11:00 | 11:00 | 11:00 |
| 11:30 | 11:30 | 11:30 |
| 12:00 p.m. | 12:00 p.m. | 12:00 p.m. |
| 12:30 | 12:30 | 12:30 |
| 1:00 | 1:00 | 1:00 |
| 1:30 | 1:30 | 1:30 |
| 2:00 | 2:00 | 2:00 |
| 2:30 | 2:30 | 2:30 |
| 3:00 | 3:00 | 3:00 |
| 3:30 | 3:30 | 3:30 |
| 4:00 | 4:00 | 4:00 |
| 4:30 | 4:30 | 4:30 |
| 5:00 | 5:00 | 5:00 |
| 5:30 | 5:30 | 5:30 |
| 6:00 | 6:00 | 6:00 |
| 6:30 | 6:30 | 6:30 |
| 7:00 | 7:00 | 7:00 |
| 7:30 | 7:30 | 7:30 |
| 8:00 | 8:00 | 8:00 |
| 8:30 | 8:30 | 8:30 |
| 9:00 | 9:00 | 9:00 |
| 9:30 | 9:30 | 9:30 |
| 10:00 | 10:00 | 10:00 |

| Wednesday | Thursday | Friday | Saturday |
|---|---|---|---|
| 4:00 a.m. | 4:00 a.m. | 4:00 a.m. | 4:00 a.m. |
| 4:30 | 4:30 | 4:30 | 4:30 |
| 5:00 | 5:00 | 5:00 | 5:00 |
| 5:30 | 5:30 | 5:30 | 5:30 |
| 6:00 | 6:00 | 6:00 | 6:00 |
| 6:30 | 6:30 | 6:30 | 6:30 |
| 7:00 | 7:00 | 7:00 | 7:00 |
| 7:30 | 7:30 | 7:30 | 7:30 |
| 8:00 | 8:00 | 8:00 | 8:00 |
| 8:30 | 8:30 | 8:30 | 8:30 |
| 9:00 | 9:00 | 9:00 | 9:00 |
| 9:30 | 9:30 | 9:30 | 9:30 |
| 10:00 | 10:00 | 10:00 | 10:00 |
| 10:30 | 10:30 | 10:30 | 10:30 |
| 11:00 | 11:00 | 11:00 | 11:00 |
| 11:30 | 11:30 | 11:30 | 11:30 |
| 12:00 p.m. | 12:00 p.m. | 12:00 p.m. | 12:00 p.m. |
| 12:30 | 12:30 | 12:30 | 12:30 |
| 1:00 | 1:00 | 1:00 | 1:00 |
| 1:30 | 1:30 | 1:30 | 1:30 |
| 2:00 | 2:00 | 2:00 | 2:00 |
| 2:30 | 2:30 | 2:30 | 2:30 |
| 3:00 | 3:00 | 3:00 | 3:00 |
| 3:30 | 3:30 | 3:30 | 3:30 |
| 4:00 | 4:00 | 4:00 | 4:00 |
| 4:30 | 4:30 | 4:30 | 4:30 |
| 5:00 | 5:00 | 5:00 | 5:00 |
| 5:30 | 5:30 | 5:30 | 5:30 |
| 6:00 | 6:00 | 6:00 | 6:00 |
| 6:30 | 6:30 | 6:30 | 6:30 |
| 7:00 | 7:00 | 7:00 | 7:00 |
| 7:30 | 7:30 | 7:30 | 7:30 |
| 8:00 | 8:00 | 8:00 | 8:00 |
| 8:30 | 8:30 | 8:30 | 8:30 |
| 9:00 | 9:00 | 9:00 | 9:00 |
| 9:30 | 9:30 | 9:30 | 9:30 |
| 10:00 | 10:00 | 10:00 | 10:00 |

JANUARY

# Prep Your *Week*

## Priorities This Week

- 
- 
- 
- 
- 
- 
- 
- 

## Coaching Cycles

## Classroom Snapshots

## Data Meetings

## Team & PD Meetings

## Feedback Meetings

## Other

# Reflect on Your *Week*

| What goals did you accomplish this week? | What goals did you not accomplish this week? Why? |
|---|---|
| What can you do to improve next week? | Things learned and things to remember: |

## Goal & Habit Tracker

| Goal or Habit | Day 1 | Day 2 | Day 3 | Day 4 | Day 5 | Day 6 | Day 7 |
|---|---|---|---|---|---|---|---|
| | | | | | | | |
| | | | | | | | |
| | | | | | | | |
| | | | | | | | |

## Notes

Week:

Notes ➔

| Sunday | Monday | Tuesday |
|---|---|---|
| 4:00 a.m. | 4:00 a.m. | 4:00 a.m. |
| 4:30 | 4:30 | 4:30 |
| 5:00 | 5:00 | 5:00 |
| 5:30 | 5:30 | 5:30 |
| 6:00 | 6:00 | 6:00 |
| 6:30 | 6:30 | 6:30 |
| 7:00 | 7:00 | 7:00 |
| 7:30 | 7:30 | 7:30 |
| 8:00 | 8:00 | 8:00 |
| 8:30 | 8:30 | 8:30 |
| 9:00 | 9:00 | 9:00 |
| 9:30 | 9:30 | 9:30 |
| 10:00 | 10:00 | 10:00 |
| 10:30 | 10:30 | 10:30 |
| 11:00 | 11:00 | 11:00 |
| 11:30 | 11:30 | 11:30 |
| 12:00 p.m. | 12:00 p.m. | 12:00 p.m. |
| 12:30 | 12:30 | 12:30 |
| 1:00 | 1:00 | 1:00 |
| 1:30 | 1:30 | 1:30 |
| 2:00 | 2:00 | 2:00 |
| 2:30 | 2:30 | 2:30 |
| 3:00 | 3:00 | 3:00 |
| 3:30 | 3:30 | 3:30 |
| 4:00 | 4:00 | 4:00 |
| 4:30 | 4:30 | 4:30 |
| 5:00 | 5:00 | 5:00 |
| 5:30 | 5:30 | 5:30 |
| 6:00 | 6:00 | 6:00 |
| 6:30 | 6:30 | 6:30 |
| 7:00 | 7:00 | 7:00 |
| 7:30 | 7:30 | 7:30 |
| 8:00 | 8:00 | 8:00 |
| 8:30 | 8:30 | 8:30 |
| 9:00 | 9:00 | 9:00 |
| 9:30 | 9:30 | 9:30 |
| 10:00 | 10:00 | 10:00 |

| Wednesday | Thursday | Friday | Saturday |
|---|---|---|---|
| 4:00 a.m. | 4:00 a.m. | 4:00 a.m. | 4:00 a.m. |
| 4:30 | 4:30 | 4:30 | 4:30 |
| 5:00 | 5:00 | 5:00 | 5:00 |
| 5:30 | 5:30 | 5:30 | 5:30 |
| 6:00 | 6:00 | 6:00 | 6:00 |
| 6:30 | 6:30 | 6:30 | 6:30 |
| 7:00 | 7:00 | 7:00 | 7:00 |
| 7:30 | 7:30 | 7:30 | 7:30 |
| 8:00 | 8:00 | 8:00 | 8:00 |
| 8:30 | 8:30 | 8:30 | 8:30 |
| 9:00 | 9:00 | 9:00 | 9:00 |
| 9:30 | 9:30 | 9:30 | 9:30 |
| 10:00 | 10:00 | 10:00 | 10:00 |
| 10:30 | 10:30 | 10:30 | 10:30 |
| 11:00 | 11:00 | 11:00 | 11:00 |
| 11:30 | 11:30 | 11:30 | 11:30 |
| 12:00 p.m. | 12:00 p.m. | 12:00 p.m. | 12:00 p.m. |
| 12:30 | 12:30 | 12:30 | 12:30 |
| 1:00 | 1:00 | 1:00 | 1:00 |
| 1:30 | 1:30 | 1:30 | 1:30 |
| 2:00 | 2:00 | 2:00 | 2:00 |
| 2:30 | 2:30 | 2:30 | 2:30 |
| 3:00 | 3:00 | 3:00 | 3:00 |
| 3:30 | 3:30 | 3:30 | 3:30 |
| 4:00 | 4:00 | 4:00 | 4:00 |
| 4:30 | 4:30 | 4:30 | 4:30 |
| 5:00 | 5:00 | 5:00 | 5:00 |
| 5:30 | 5:30 | 5:30 | 5:30 |
| 6:00 | 6:00 | 6:00 | 6:00 |
| 6:30 | 6:30 | 6:30 | 6:30 |
| 7:00 | 7:00 | 7:00 | 7:00 |
| 7:30 | 7:30 | 7:30 | 7:30 |
| 8:00 | 8:00 | 8:00 | 8:00 |
| 8:30 | 8:30 | 8:30 | 8:30 |
| 9:00 | 9:00 | 9:00 | 9:00 |
| 9:30 | 9:30 | 9:30 | 9:30 |
| 10:00 | 10:00 | 10:00 | 10:00 |

# Prep Your *Week*

## Priorities This Week

- 
- 
- 
- 
- 
- 
- 
- 

## Coaching Cycles

## Classroom Snapshots

## Data Meetings

## Team & PD Meetings

## Feedback Meetings

## Other

# Reflect on Your *Week*

| What goals did you accomplish this week? | What goals did you not accomplish this week? Why? |
|---|---|
| **What can you do to improve next week?** | **Things learned and things to remember:** |

## Goal & Habit Tracker

| Goal or Habit | Day 1 | Day 2 | Day 3 | Day 4 | Day 5 | Day 6 | Day 7 |
|---|---|---|---|---|---|---|---|
| | | | | | | | |
| | | | | | | | |
| | | | | | | | |
| | | | | | | | |

## Notes

**Week:**

**Notes**

| Sunday | Monday | Tuesday |
|---|---|---|
| 4:00 a.m. | 4:00 a.m. | 4:00 a.m. |
| 4:30 | 4:30 | 4:30 |
| 5:00 | 5:00 | 5:00 |
| 5:30 | 5:30 | 5:30 |
| 6:00 | 6:00 | 6:00 |
| 6:30 | 6:30 | 6:30 |
| 7:00 | 7:00 | 7:00 |
| 7:30 | 7:30 | 7:30 |
| 8:00 | 8:00 | 8:00 |
| 8:30 | 8:30 | 8:30 |
| 9:00 | 9:00 | 9:00 |
| 9:30 | 9:30 | 9:30 |
| 10:00 | 10:00 | 10:00 |
| 10:30 | 10:30 | 10:30 |
| 11:00 | 11:00 | 11:00 |
| 11:30 | 11:30 | 11:30 |
| 12:00 p.m. | 12:00 p.m. | 12:00 p.m. |
| 12:30 | 12:30 | 12:30 |
| 1:00 | 1:00 | 1:00 |
| 1:30 | 1:30 | 1:30 |
| 2:00 | 2:00 | 2:00 |
| 2:30 | 2:30 | 2:30 |
| 3:00 | 3:00 | 3:00 |
| 3:30 | 3:30 | 3:30 |
| 4:00 | 4:00 | 4:00 |
| 4:30 | 4:30 | 4:30 |
| 5:00 | 5:00 | 5:00 |
| 5:30 | 5:30 | 5:30 |
| 6:00 | 6:00 | 6:00 |
| 6:30 | 6:30 | 6:30 |
| 7:00 | 7:00 | 7:00 |
| 7:30 | 7:30 | 7:30 |
| 8:00 | 8:00 | 8:00 |
| 8:30 | 8:30 | 8:30 |
| 9:00 | 9:00 | 9:00 |
| 9:30 | 9:30 | 9:30 |
| 10:00 | 10:00 | 10:00 |

| Wednesday | Thursday | Friday | Saturday |
|---|---|---|---|
| 4:00 a.m. | 4:00 a.m. | 4:00 a.m. | 4:00 a.m. |
| 4:30 | 4:30 | 4:30 | 4:30 |
| 5:00 | 5:00 | 5:00 | 5:00 |
| 5:30 | 5:30 | 5:30 | 5:30 |
| 6:00 | 6:00 | 6:00 | 6:00 |
| 6:30 | 6:30 | 6:30 | 6:30 |
| 7:00 | 7:00 | 7:00 | 7:00 |
| 7:30 | 7:30 | 7:30 | 7:30 |
| 8:00 | 8:00 | 8:00 | 8:00 |
| 8:30 | 8:30 | 8:30 | 8:30 |
| 9:00 | 9:00 | 9:00 | 9:00 |
| 9:30 | 9:30 | 9:30 | 9:30 |
| 10:00 | 10:00 | 10:00 | 10:00 |
| 10:30 | 10:30 | 10:30 | 10:30 |
| 11:00 | 11:00 | 11:00 | 11:00 |
| 11:30 | 11:30 | 11:30 | 11:30 |
| 12:00 p.m. | 12:00 p.m. | 12:00 p.m. | 12:00 p.m. |
| 12:30 | 12:30 | 12:30 | 12:30 |
| 1:00 | 1:00 | 1:00 | 1:00 |
| 1:30 | 1:30 | 1:30 | 1:30 |
| 2:00 | 2:00 | 2:00 | 2:00 |
| 2:30 | 2:30 | 2:30 | 2:30 |
| 3:00 | 3:00 | 3:00 | 3:00 |
| 3:30 | 3:30 | 3:30 | 3:30 |
| 4:00 | 4:00 | 4:00 | 4:00 |
| 4:30 | 4:30 | 4:30 | 4:30 |
| 5:00 | 5:00 | 5:00 | 5:00 |
| 5:30 | 5:30 | 5:30 | 5:30 |
| 6:00 | 6:00 | 6:00 | 6:00 |
| 6:30 | 6:30 | 6:30 | 6:30 |
| 7:00 | 7:00 | 7:00 | 7:00 |
| 7:30 | 7:30 | 7:30 | 7:30 |
| 8:00 | 8:00 | 8:00 | 8:00 |
| 8:30 | 8:30 | 8:30 | 8:30 |
| 9:00 | 9:00 | 9:00 | 9:00 |
| 9:30 | 9:30 | 9:30 | 9:30 |
| 10:00 | 10:00 | 10:00 | 10:00 |

# Prep Your *Week*

## Priorities This Week

- 
- 
- 
- 
- 
- 
- 
- 

## Coaching Cycles

## Classroom Snapshots

## Data Meetings

## Team & PD Meetings

## Feedback Meetings

## Other

# Reflect on Your *Week*

| What goals did you accomplish this week? | What goals did you not accomplish this week? Why? |
|---|---|
| What can you do to improve next week? | Things learned and things to remember: |

## Goal & Habit Tracker

| Goal or Habit | Day 1 | Day 2 | Day 3 | Day 4 | Day 5 | Day 6 | Day 7 |
|---|---|---|---|---|---|---|---|
| | | | | | | | |
| | | | | | | | |
| | | | | | | | |
| | | | | | | | |

## Notes

Week:

Notes

| | Sunday | Monday | Tuesday |
|---|---|---|---|
| | 4:00 a.m. | 4:00 a.m. | 4:00 a.m. |
| | 4:30 | 4:30 | 4:30 |
| | 5:00 | 5:00 | 5:00 |
| | 5:30 | 5:30 | 5:30 |
| | 6:00 | 6:00 | 6:00 |
| | 6:30 | 6:30 | 6:30 |
| | 7:00 | 7:00 | 7:00 |
| | 7:30 | 7:30 | 7:30 |
| | 8:00 | 8:00 | 8:00 |
| | 8:30 | 8:30 | 8:30 |
| | 9:00 | 9:00 | 9:00 |
| | 9:30 | 9:30 | 9:30 |
| | 10:00 | 10:00 | 10:00 |
| | 10:30 | 10:30 | 10:30 |
| | 11:00 | 11:00 | 11:00 |
| | 11:30 | 11:30 | 11:30 |
| | 12:00 p.m. | 12:00 p.m. | 12:00 p.m. |
| | 12:30 | 12:30 | 12:30 |
| | 1:00 | 1:00 | 1:00 |
| | 1:30 | 1:30 | 1:30 |
| | 2:00 | 2:00 | 2:00 |
| | 2:30 | 2:30 | 2:30 |
| | 3:00 | 3:00 | 3:00 |
| | 3:30 | 3:30 | 3:30 |
| | 4:00 | 4:00 | 4:00 |
| | 4:30 | 4:30 | 4:30 |
| | 5:00 | 5:00 | 5:00 |
| | 5:30 | 5:30 | 5:30 |
| | 6:00 | 6:00 | 6:00 |
| | 6:30 | 6:30 | 6:30 |
| | 7:00 | 7:00 | 7:00 |
| | 7:30 | 7:30 | 7:30 |
| | 8:00 | 8:00 | 8:00 |
| | 8:30 | 8:30 | 8:30 |
| | 9:00 | 9:00 | 9:00 |
| | 9:30 | 9:30 | 9:30 |
| | 10:00 | 10:00 | 10:00 |

| Wednesday | Thursday | Friday | Saturday |
|---|---|---|---|
| 4:00 a.m. | 4:00 a.m. | 4:00 a.m. | 4:00 a.m. |
| 4:30 | 4:30 | 4:30 | 4:30 |
| 5:00 | 5:00 | 5:00 | 5:00 |
| 5:30 | 5:30 | 5:30 | 5:30 |
| 6:00 | 6:00 | 6:00 | 6:00 |
| 6:30 | 6:30 | 6:30 | 6:30 |
| 7:00 | 7:00 | 7:00 | 7:00 |
| 7:30 | 7:30 | 7:30 | 7:30 |
| 8:00 | 8:00 | 8:00 | 8:00 |
| 8:30 | 8:30 | 8:30 | 8:30 |
| 9:00 | 9:00 | 9:00 | 9:00 |
| 9:30 | 9:30 | 9:30 | 9:30 |
| 10:00 | 10:00 | 10:00 | 10:00 |
| 10:30 | 10:30 | 10:30 | 10:30 |
| 11:00 | 11:00 | 11:00 | 11:00 |
| 11:30 | 11:30 | 11:30 | 11:30 |
| 12:00 p.m. | 12:00 p.m. | 12:00 p.m. | 12:00 p.m. |
| 12:30 | 12:30 | 12:30 | 12:30 |
| 1:00 | 1:00 | 1:00 | 1:00 |
| 1:30 | 1:30 | 1:30 | 1:30 |
| 2:00 | 2:00 | 2:00 | 2:00 |
| 2:30 | 2:30 | 2:30 | 2:30 |
| 3:00 | 3:00 | 3:00 | 3:00 |
| 3:30 | 3:30 | 3:30 | 3:30 |
| 4:00 | 4:00 | 4:00 | 4:00 |
| 4:30 | 4:30 | 4:30 | 4:30 |
| 5:00 | 5:00 | 5:00 | 5:00 |
| 5:30 | 5:30 | 5:30 | 5:30 |
| 6:00 | 6:00 | 6:00 | 6:00 |
| 6:30 | 6:30 | 6:30 | 6:30 |
| 7:00 | 7:00 | 7:00 | 7:00 |
| 7:30 | 7:30 | 7:30 | 7:30 |
| 8:00 | 8:00 | 8:00 | 8:00 |
| 8:30 | 8:30 | 8:30 | 8:30 |
| 9:00 | 9:00 | 9:00 | 9:00 |
| 9:30 | 9:30 | 9:30 | 9:30 |
| 10:00 | 10:00 | 10:00 | 10:00 |

JANUARY

SETTING A *goal* IS NOT THE MAIN THING. IT IS DECIDING HOW YOU WILL GO ABOUT *achieving it* AND STAYING WITH THAT PLAN.

—Tom Landry

# Prep Your *Month*

| Personal Goals | | | |
|---|---|---|---|
| Day | Health & Fitness | Finances | Self-Care & Growth |
| | | | |
| | | | |
| | | | |
| | | | |
| | | | |
| | | | |

| Important Reminders | |
|---|---|
| | |
| | |
| | |
| | |
| | |
| | |
| | |

# Prep Your *Month*

| Main Goal | Main Focus | Wins |
|---|---|---|
| | | |

## Monthly Tasks

Week 1

Week 2

Week 3

Week 4

Week 5

## Must Do This Month

## Save for Next Month

# February

"Be somebody who *makes everybody feel like a somebody*." —Kid President

| Sunday | Monday | Tuesday | Wednesday |
|--------|--------|---------|-----------|
|        |        |         |           |
|        |        |         |           |
|        |        |         |           |
|        |        |         |           |
|        |        |         |           |

Monthly Focus

| Thursday | Friday | Saturday |
|----------|--------|----------|
|          |        |          |
|          |        |          |
|          |        |          |
|          |        |          |
|          |        |          |

Notes

# Prep Your *Week*

## *Priorities* This Week

- 
- 
- 
- 
- 
- 
- 
- 

## Coaching Cycles

## Classroom Snapshots

## Data Meetings

## Team & PD Meetings

## Feedback Meetings

## Other

# Reflect on Your *Week*

| | |
|---|---|
| **What goals did you accomplish this week?** | **What goals did you not accomplish this week? Why?** |
| **What can you do to improve next week?** | **Things learned and things to remember:** |

## Goal & Habit Tracker

| Goal or Habit | Day 1 | Day 2 | Day 3 | Day 4 | Day 5 | Day 6 | Day 7 |
|---|---|---|---|---|---|---|---|
| | | | | | | | |
| | | | | | | | |
| | | | | | | | |
| | | | | | | | |

## Notes

Week:

Notes ↗

| Sunday | Monday | Tuesday |
|---|---|---|
| 4:00 a.m. | 4:00 a.m. | 4:00 a.m. |
| 4:30 | 4:30 | 4:30 |
| 5:00 | 5:00 | 5:00 |
| 5:30 | 5:30 | 5:30 |
| 6:00 | 6:00 | 6:00 |
| 6:30 | 6:30 | 6:30 |
| 7:00 | 7:00 | 7:00 |
| 7:30 | 7:30 | 7:30 |
| 8:00 | 8:00 | 8:00 |
| 8:30 | 8:30 | 8:30 |
| 9:00 | 9:00 | 9:00 |
| 9:30 | 9:30 | 9:30 |
| 10:00 | 10:00 | 10:00 |
| 10:30 | 10:30 | 10:30 |
| 11:00 | 11:00 | 11:00 |
| 11:30 | 11:30 | 11:30 |
| 12:00 p.m. | 12:00 p.m. | 12:00 p.m. |
| 12:30 | 12:30 | 12:30 |
| 1:00 | 1:00 | 1:00 |
| 1:30 | 1:30 | 1:30 |
| 2:00 | 2:00 | 2:00 |
| 2:30 | 2:30 | 2:30 |
| 3:00 | 3:00 | 3:00 |
| 3:30 | 3:30 | 3:30 |
| 4:00 | 4:00 | 4:00 |
| 4:30 | 4:30 | 4:30 |
| 5:00 | 5:00 | 5:00 |
| 5:30 | 5:30 | 5:30 |
| 6:00 | 6:00 | 6:00 |
| 6:30 | 6:30 | 6:30 |
| 7:00 | 7:00 | 7:00 |
| 7:30 | 7:30 | 7:30 |
| 8:00 | 8:00 | 8:00 |
| 8:30 | 8:30 | 8:30 |
| 9:00 | 9:00 | 9:00 |
| 9:30 | 9:30 | 9:30 |
| 10:00 | 10:00 | 10:00 |

| Wednesday | Thursday | Friday | Saturday |
|---|---|---|---|
| 4:00 a.m. | 4:00 a.m. | 4:00 a.m. | 4:00 a.m. |
| 4:30 | 4:30 | 4:30 | 4:30 |
| 5:00 | 5:00 | 5:00 | 5:00 |
| 5:30 | 5:30 | 5:30 | 5:30 |
| 6:00 | 6:00 | 6:00 | 6:00 |
| 6:30 | 6:30 | 6:30 | 6:30 |
| 7:00 | 7:00 | 7:00 | 7:00 |
| 7:30 | 7:30 | 7:30 | 7:30 |
| 8:00 | 8:00 | 8:00 | 8:00 |
| 8:30 | 8:30 | 8:30 | 8:30 |
| 9:00 | 9:00 | 9:00 | 9:00 |
| 9:30 | 9:30 | 9:30 | 9:30 |
| 10:00 | 10:00 | 10:00 | 10:00 |
| 10:30 | 10:30 | 10:30 | 10:30 |
| 11:00 | 11:00 | 11:00 | 11:00 |
| 11:30 | 11:30 | 11:30 | 11:30 |
| 12:00 p.m. | 12:00 p.m. | 12:00 p.m. | 12:00 p.m. |
| 12:30 | 12:30 | 12:30 | 12:30 |
| 1:00 | 1:00 | 1:00 | 1:00 |
| 1:30 | 1:30 | 1:30 | 1:30 |
| 2:00 | 2:00 | 2:00 | 2:00 |
| 2:30 | 2:30 | 2:30 | 2:30 |
| 3:00 | 3:00 | 3:00 | 3:00 |
| 3:30 | 3:30 | 3:30 | 3:30 |
| 4:00 | 4:00 | 4:00 | 4:00 |
| 4:30 | 4:30 | 4:30 | 4:30 |
| 5:00 | 5:00 | 5:00 | 5:00 |
| 5:30 | 5:30 | 5:30 | 5:30 |
| 6:00 | 6:00 | 6:00 | 6:00 |
| 6:30 | 6:30 | 6:30 | 6:30 |
| 7:00 | 7:00 | 7:00 | 7:00 |
| 7:30 | 7:30 | 7:30 | 7:30 |
| 8:00 | 8:00 | 8:00 | 8:00 |
| 8:30 | 8:30 | 8:30 | 8:30 |
| 9:00 | 9:00 | 9:00 | 9:00 |
| 9:30 | 9:30 | 9:30 | 9:30 |
| 10:00 | 10:00 | 10:00 | 10:00 |

# Prep Your *Week*

## Priorities This Week

- 
- 
- 
- 
- 
- 
- 
- 

## Coaching Cycles

## Classroom Snapshots

## Data Meetings

## Team & PD Meetings

## Feedback Meetings

## Other

# Reflect on Your *Week*

| What goals did you accomplish this week? | What goals did you not accomplish this week? Why? |
|---|---|
| | |
| **What can you do to improve next week?** | **Things learned and things to remember:** |
| | |

## Goal & Habit Tracker

| Goal or Habit | Day 1 | Day 2 | Day 3 | Day 4 | Day 5 | Day 6 | Day 7 |
|---|---|---|---|---|---|---|---|
| | | | | | | | |
| | | | | | | | |
| | | | | | | | |
| | | | | | | | |

## Notes

| Sunday | Monday | Tuesday |
|---|---|---|
| 4:00 a.m. | 4:00 a.m. | 4:00 a.m. |
| 4:30 | 4:30 | 4:30 |
| 5:00 | 5:00 | 5:00 |
| 5:30 | 5:30 | 5:30 |
| 6:00 | 6:00 | 6:00 |
| 6:30 | 6:30 | 6:30 |
| 7:00 | 7:00 | 7:00 |
| 7:30 | 7:30 | 7:30 |
| 8:00 | 8:00 | 8:00 |
| 8:30 | 8:30 | 8:30 |
| 9:00 | 9:00 | 9:00 |
| 9:30 | 9:30 | 9:30 |
| 10:00 | 10:00 | 10:00 |
| 10:30 | 10:30 | 10:30 |
| 11:00 | 11:00 | 11:00 |
| 11:30 | 11:30 | 11:30 |
| 12:00 p.m. | 12:00 p.m. | 12:00 p.m. |
| 12:30 | 12:30 | 12:30 |
| 1:00 | 1:00 | 1:00 |
| 1:30 | 1:30 | 1:30 |
| 2:00 | 2:00 | 2:00 |
| 2:30 | 2:30 | 2:30 |
| 3:00 | 3:00 | 3:00 |
| 3:30 | 3:30 | 3:30 |
| 4:00 | 4:00 | 4:00 |
| 4:30 | 4:30 | 4:30 |
| 5:00 | 5:00 | 5:00 |
| 5:30 | 5:30 | 5:30 |
| 6:00 | 6:00 | 6:00 |
| 6:30 | 6:30 | 6:30 |
| 7:00 | 7:00 | 7:00 |
| 7:30 | 7:30 | 7:30 |
| 8:00 | 8:00 | 8:00 |
| 8:30 | 8:30 | 8:30 |
| 9:00 | 9:00 | 9:00 |
| 9:30 | 9:30 | 9:30 |
| 10:00 | 10:00 | 10:00 |

| Wednesday | Thursday | Friday | Saturday |
|---|---|---|---|
| 4:00 a.m. | 4:00 a.m. | 4:00 a.m. | 4:00 a.m. |
| 4:30 | 4:30 | 4:30 | 4:30 |
| 5:00 | 5:00 | 5:00 | 5:00 |
| 5:30 | 5:30 | 5:30 | 5:30 |
| 6:00 | 6:00 | 6:00 | 6:00 |
| 6:30 | 6:30 | 6:30 | 6:30 |
| 7:00 | 7:00 | 7:00 | 7:00 |
| 7:30 | 7:30 | 7:30 | 7:30 |
| 8:00 | 8:00 | 8:00 | 8:00 |
| 8:30 | 8:30 | 8:30 | 8:30 |
| 9:00 | 9:00 | 9:00 | 9:00 |
| 9:30 | 9:30 | 9:30 | 9:30 |
| 10:00 | 10:00 | 10:00 | 10:00 |
| 10:30 | 10:30 | 10:30 | 10:30 |
| 11:00 | 11:00 | 11:00 | 11:00 |
| 11:30 | 11:30 | 11:30 | 11:30 |
| 12:00 p.m. | 12:00 p.m. | 12:00 p.m. | 12:00 p.m. |
| 12:30 | 12:30 | 12:30 | 12:30 |
| 1:00 | 1:00 | 1:00 | 1:00 |
| 1:30 | 1:30 | 1:30 | 1:30 |
| 2:00 | 2:00 | 2:00 | 2:00 |
| 2:30 | 2:30 | 2:30 | 2:30 |
| 3:00 | 3:00 | 3:00 | 3:00 |
| 3:30 | 3:30 | 3:30 | 3:30 |
| 4:00 | 4:00 | 4:00 | 4:00 |
| 4:30 | 4:30 | 4:30 | 4:30 |
| 5:00 | 5:00 | 5:00 | 5:00 |
| 5:30 | 5:30 | 5:30 | 5:30 |
| 6:00 | 6:00 | 6:00 | 6:00 |
| 6:30 | 6:30 | 6:30 | 6:30 |
| 7:00 | 7:00 | 7:00 | 7:00 |
| 7:30 | 7:30 | 7:30 | 7:30 |
| 8:00 | 8:00 | 8:00 | 8:00 |
| 8:30 | 8:30 | 8:30 | 8:30 |
| 9:00 | 9:00 | 9:00 | 9:00 |
| 9:30 | 9:30 | 9:30 | 9:30 |
| 10:00 | 10:00 | 10:00 | 10:00 |

FEBRUARY

# Prep Your *Week*

## *Priorities* This Week

- 
- 
- 
- 
- 
- 
- 
- 
- 

## Coaching Cycles

## Classroom Snapshots

## Data Meetings

## Team & PD Meetings

## Feedback Meetings

## Other

# Reflect on Your Week

| What goals did you accomplish this week? | What goals did you not accomplish this week? Why? |
|---|---|
| What can you do to improve next week? | Things learned and things to remember: |

## Goal & Habit Tracker

| Goal or Habit | Day 1 | Day 2 | Day 3 | Day 4 | Day 5 | Day 6 | Day 7 |
|---|---|---|---|---|---|---|---|
| | | | | | | | |
| | | | | | | | |
| | | | | | | | |
| | | | | | | | |

## Notes

Week:

Notes

| | Sunday | Monday | Tuesday |
|---|---|---|---|
| | 4:00 a.m. | 4:00 a.m. | 4:00 a.m. |
| | 4:30 | 4:30 | 4:30 |
| | 5:00 | 5:00 | 5:00 |
| | 5:30 | 5:30 | 5:30 |
| | 6:00 | 6:00 | 6:00 |
| | 6:30 | 6:30 | 6:30 |
| | 7:00 | 7:00 | 7:00 |
| | 7:30 | 7:30 | 7:30 |
| | 8:00 | 8:00 | 8:00 |
| | 8:30 | 8:30 | 8:30 |
| | 9:00 | 9:00 | 9:00 |
| | 9:30 | 9:30 | 9:30 |
| | 10:00 | 10:00 | 10:00 |
| | 10:30 | 10:30 | 10:30 |
| | 11:00 | 11:00 | 11:00 |
| | 11:30 | 11:30 | 11:30 |
| | 12:00 p.m. | 12:00 p.m. | 12:00 p.m. |
| | 12:30 | 12:30 | 12:30 |
| | 1:00 | 1:00 | 1:00 |
| | 1:30 | 1:30 | 1:30 |
| | 2:00 | 2:00 | 2:00 |
| | 2:30 | 2:30 | 2:30 |
| | 3:00 | 3:00 | 3:00 |
| | 3:30 | 3:30 | 3:30 |
| | 4:00 | 4:00 | 4:00 |
| | 4:30 | 4:30 | 4:30 |
| | 5:00 | 5:00 | 5:00 |
| | 5:30 | 5:30 | 5:30 |
| | 6:00 | 6:00 | 6:00 |
| | 6:30 | 6:30 | 6:30 |
| | 7:00 | 7:00 | 7:00 |
| | 7:30 | 7:30 | 7:30 |
| | 8:00 | 8:00 | 8:00 |
| | 8:30 | 8:30 | 8:30 |
| | 9:00 | 9:00 | 9:00 |
| | 9:30 | 9:30 | 9:30 |
| | 10:00 | 10:00 | 10:00 |

| Wednesday | Thursday | Friday | Saturday |
|---|---|---|---|
| 4:00 a.m. | 4:00 a.m. | 4:00 a.m. | 4:00 a.m. |
| 4:30 | 4:30 | 4:30 | 4:30 |
| 5:00 | 5:00 | 5:00 | 5:00 |
| 5:30 | 5:30 | 5:30 | 5:30 |
| 6:00 | 6:00 | 6:00 | 6:00 |
| 6:30 | 6:30 | 6:30 | 6:30 |
| 7:00 | 7:00 | 7:00 | 7:00 |
| 7:30 | 7:30 | 7:30 | 7:30 |
| 8:00 | 8:00 | 8:00 | 8:00 |
| 8:30 | 8:30 | 8:30 | 8:30 |
| 9:00 | 9:00 | 9:00 | 9:00 |
| 9:30 | 9:30 | 9:30 | 9:30 |
| 10:00 | 10:00 | 10:00 | 10:00 |
| 10:30 | 10:30 | 10:30 | 10:30 |
| 11:00 | 11:00 | 11:00 | 11:00 |
| 11:30 | 11:30 | 11:30 | 11:30 |
| 12:00 p.m. | 12:00 p.m. | 12:00 p.m. | 12:00 p.m. |
| 12:30 | 12:30 | 12:30 | 12:30 |
| 1:00 | 1:00 | 1:00 | 1:00 |
| 1:30 | 1:30 | 1:30 | 1:30 |
| 2:00 | 2:00 | 2:00 | 2:00 |
| 2:30 | 2:30 | 2:30 | 2:30 |
| 3:00 | 3:00 | 3:00 | 3:00 |
| 3:30 | 3:30 | 3:30 | 3:30 |
| 4:00 | 4:00 | 4:00 | 4:00 |
| 4:30 | 4:30 | 4:30 | 4:30 |
| 5:00 | 5:00 | 5:00 | 5:00 |
| 5:30 | 5:30 | 5:30 | 5:30 |
| 6:00 | 6:00 | 6:00 | 6:00 |
| 6:30 | 6:30 | 6:30 | 6:30 |
| 7:00 | 7:00 | 7:00 | 7:00 |
| 7:30 | 7:30 | 7:30 | 7:30 |
| 8:00 | 8:00 | 8:00 | 8:00 |
| 8:30 | 8:30 | 8:30 | 8:30 |
| 9:00 | 9:00 | 9:00 | 9:00 |
| 9:30 | 9:30 | 9:30 | 9:30 |
| 10:00 | 10:00 | 10:00 | 10:00 |

# Prep Your *Week*

## Priorities This Week

- 
- 
- 
- 
- 
- 
- 
- 
- 

## Coaching Cycles

## Classroom Snapshots

## Data Meetings

## Team & PD Meetings

## Feedback Meetings

## Other

# Reflect on Your *Week*

| What goals did you accomplish this week? | What goals did you not accomplish this week? Why? |
|---|---|
| **What can you do to improve next week?** | **Things learned and things to remember:** |

## Goal & Habit Tracker

| Goal or Habit | Day 1 | Day 2 | Day 3 | Day 4 | Day 5 | Day 6 | Day 7 |
|---|---|---|---|---|---|---|---|
| | | | | | | | |
| | | | | | | | |
| | | | | | | | |
| | | | | | | | |

## Notes

Week:

Notes ↗

| Sunday | Monday | Tuesday |
|---|---|---|
| 4:00 a.m. | 4:00 a.m. | 4:00 a.m. |
| 4:30 | 4:30 | 4:30 |
| 5:00 | 5:00 | 5:00 |
| 5:30 | 5:30 | 5:30 |
| 6:00 | 6:00 | 6:00 |
| 6:30 | 6:30 | 6:30 |
| 7:00 | 7:00 | 7:00 |
| 7:30 | 7:30 | 7:30 |
| 8:00 | 8:00 | 8:00 |
| 8:30 | 8:30 | 8:30 |
| 9:00 | 9:00 | 9:00 |
| 9:30 | 9:30 | 9:30 |
| 10:00 | 10:00 | 10:00 |
| 10:30 | 10:30 | 10:30 |
| 11:00 | 11:00 | 11:00 |
| 11:30 | 11:30 | 11:30 |
| 12:00 p.m. | 12:00 p.m. | 12:00 p.m. |
| 12:30 | 12:30 | 12:30 |
| 1:00 | 1:00 | 1:00 |
| 1:30 | 1:30 | 1:30 |
| 2:00 | 2:00 | 2:00 |
| 2:30 | 2:30 | 2:30 |
| 3:00 | 3:00 | 3:00 |
| 3:30 | 3:30 | 3:30 |
| 4:00 | 4:00 | 4:00 |
| 4:30 | 4:30 | 4:30 |
| 5:00 | 5:00 | 5:00 |
| 5:30 | 5:30 | 5:30 |
| 6:00 | 6:00 | 6:00 |
| 6:30 | 6:30 | 6:30 |
| 7:00 | 7:00 | 7:00 |
| 7:30 | 7:30 | 7:30 |
| 8:00 | 8:00 | 8:00 |
| 8:30 | 8:30 | 8:30 |
| 9:00 | 9:00 | 9:00 |
| 9:30 | 9:30 | 9:30 |
| 10:00 | 10:00 | 10:00 |

| Wednesday | Thursday | Friday | Saturday |
|---|---|---|---|
| 4:00 a.m. | 4:00 a.m. | 4:00 a.m. | 4:00 a.m. |
| 4:30 | 4:30 | 4:30 | 4:30 |
| 5:00 | 5:00 | 5:00 | 5:00 |
| 5:30 | 5:30 | 5:30 | 5:30 |
| 6:00 | 6:00 | 6:00 | 6:00 |
| 6:30 | 6:30 | 6:30 | 6:30 |
| 7:00 | 7:00 | 7:00 | 7:00 |
| 7:30 | 7:30 | 7:30 | 7:30 |
| 8:00 | 8:00 | 8:00 | 8:00 |
| 8:30 | 8:30 | 8:30 | 8:30 |
| 9:00 | 9:00 | 9:00 | 9:00 |
| 9:30 | 9:30 | 9:30 | 9:30 |
| 10:00 | 10:00 | 10:00 | 10:00 |
| 10:30 | 10:30 | 10:30 | 10:30 |
| 11:00 | 11:00 | 11:00 | 11:00 |
| 11:30 | 11:30 | 11:30 | 11:30 |
| 12:00 p.m. | 12:00 p.m. | 12:00 p.m. | 12:00 p.m. |
| 12:30 | 12:30 | 12:30 | 12:30 |
| 1:00 | 1:00 | 1:00 | 1:00 |
| 1:30 | 1:30 | 1:30 | 1:30 |
| 2:00 | 2:00 | 2:00 | 2:00 |
| 2:30 | 2:30 | 2:30 | 2:30 |
| 3:00 | 3:00 | 3:00 | 3:00 |
| 3:30 | 3:30 | 3:30 | 3:30 |
| 4:00 | 4:00 | 4:00 | 4:00 |
| 4:30 | 4:30 | 4:30 | 4:30 |
| 5:00 | 5:00 | 5:00 | 5:00 |
| 5:30 | 5:30 | 5:30 | 5:30 |
| 6:00 | 6:00 | 6:00 | 6:00 |
| 6:30 | 6:30 | 6:30 | 6:30 |
| 7:00 | 7:00 | 7:00 | 7:00 |
| 7:30 | 7:30 | 7:30 | 7:30 |
| 8:00 | 8:00 | 8:00 | 8:00 |
| 8:30 | 8:30 | 8:30 | 8:30 |
| 9:00 | 9:00 | 9:00 | 9:00 |
| 9:30 | 9:30 | 9:30 | 9:30 |
| 10:00 | 10:00 | 10:00 | 10:00 |

FEBRUARY

# Prep Your *Week*

## Priorities This Week

- 
- 
- 
- 
- 
- 
- 
- 

## Coaching Cycles

## Classroom Snapshots

## Data Meetings

## Team & PD Meetings

## Feedback Meetings

## Other

# Reflect on Your *Week*

| What goals did you accomplish this week? | What goals did you not accomplish this week? Why? |
|---|---|
| **What can you do to improve next week?** | **Things learned and things to remember:** |

## Goal & Habit Tracker

| Goal or Habit | Day 1 | Day 2 | Day 3 | Day 4 | Day 5 | Day 6 | Day 7 |
|---|---|---|---|---|---|---|---|
| | | | | | | | |
| | | | | | | | |
| | | | | | | | |
| | | | | | | | |

## Notes

Week:

Notes

| Sunday | Monday | Tuesday |
|---|---|---|
| 4:00 a.m. | 4:00 a.m. | 4:00 a.m. |
| 4:30 | 4:30 | 4:30 |
| 5:00 | 5:00 | 5:00 |
| 5:30 | 5:30 | 5:30 |
| 6:00 | 6:00 | 6:00 |
| 6:30 | 6:30 | 6:30 |
| 7:00 | 7:00 | 7:00 |
| 7:30 | 7:30 | 7:30 |
| 8:00 | 8:00 | 8:00 |
| 8:30 | 8:30 | 8:30 |
| 9:00 | 9:00 | 9:00 |
| 9:30 | 9:30 | 9:30 |
| 10:00 | 10:00 | 10:00 |
| 10:30 | 10:30 | 10:30 |
| 11:00 | 11:00 | 11:00 |
| 11:30 | 11:30 | 11:30 |
| 12:00 p.m. | 12:00 p.m. | 12:00 p.m. |
| 12:30 | 12:30 | 12:30 |
| 1:00 | 1:00 | 1:00 |
| 1:30 | 1:30 | 1:30 |
| 2:00 | 2:00 | 2:00 |
| 2:30 | 2:30 | 2:30 |
| 3:00 | 3:00 | 3:00 |
| 3:30 | 3:30 | 3:30 |
| 4:00 | 4:00 | 4:00 |
| 4:30 | 4:30 | 4:30 |
| 5:00 | 5:00 | 5:00 |
| 5:30 | 5:30 | 5:30 |
| 6:00 | 6:00 | 6:00 |
| 6:30 | 6:30 | 6:30 |
| 7:00 | 7:00 | 7:00 |
| 7:30 | 7:30 | 7:30 |
| 8:00 | 8:00 | 8:00 |
| 8:30 | 8:30 | 8:30 |
| 9:00 | 9:00 | 9:00 |
| 9:30 | 9:30 | 9:30 |
| 10:00 | 10:00 | 10:00 |

| Wednesday | Thursday | Friday | Saturday |
|---|---|---|---|
| 4:00 a.m. | 4:00 a.m. | 4:00 a.m. | 4:00 a.m. |
| 4:30 | 4:30 | 4:30 | 4:30 |
| 5:00 | 5:00 | 5:00 | 5:00 |
| 5:30 | 5:30 | 5:30 | 5:30 |
| 6:00 | 6:00 | 6:00 | 6:00 |
| 6:30 | 6:30 | 6:30 | 6:30 |
| 7:00 | 7:00 | 7:00 | 7:00 |
| 7:30 | 7:30 | 7:30 | 7:30 |
| 8:00 | 8:00 | 8:00 | 8:00 |
| 8:30 | 8:30 | 8:30 | 8:30 |
| 9:00 | 9:00 | 9:00 | 9:00 |
| 9:30 | 9:30 | 9:30 | 9:30 |
| 10:00 | 10:00 | 10:00 | 10:00 |
| 10:30 | 10:30 | 10:30 | 10:30 |
| 11:00 | 11:00 | 11:00 | 11:00 |
| 11:30 | 11:30 | 11:30 | 11:30 |
| 12:00 p.m. | 12:00 p.m. | 12:00 p.m. | 12:00 p.m. |
| 12:30 | 12:30 | 12:30 | 12:30 |
| 1:00 | 1:00 | 1:00 | 1:00 |
| 1:30 | 1:30 | 1:30 | 1:30 |
| 2:00 | 2:00 | 2:00 | 2:00 |
| 2:30 | 2:30 | 2:30 | 2:30 |
| 3:00 | 3:00 | 3:00 | 3:00 |
| 3:30 | 3:30 | 3:30 | 3:30 |
| 4:00 | 4:00 | 4:00 | 4:00 |
| 4:30 | 4:30 | 4:30 | 4:30 |
| 5:00 | 5:00 | 5:00 | 5:00 |
| 5:30 | 5:30 | 5:30 | 5:30 |
| 6:00 | 6:00 | 6:00 | 6:00 |
| 6:30 | 6:30 | 6:30 | 6:30 |
| 7:00 | 7:00 | 7:00 | 7:00 |
| 7:30 | 7:30 | 7:30 | 7:30 |
| 8:00 | 8:00 | 8:00 | 8:00 |
| 8:30 | 8:30 | 8:30 | 8:30 |
| 9:00 | 9:00 | 9:00 | 9:00 |
| 9:30 | 9:30 | 9:30 | 9:30 |
| 10:00 | 10:00 | 10:00 | 10:00 |

TO *achieve*
*great things,*
TWO THINGS ARE
NEEDED: A *plan*
AND NOT QUITE
ENOUGH TIME.

—Leonard Bernstein

# Prep Your *Month*

## Personal Goals

| Day | Health & Fitness | Finances | Self-Care & Growth |
|-----|------------------|----------|--------------------|
|     |                  |          |                    |
|     |                  |          |                    |
|     |                  |          |                    |
|     |                  |          |                    |
|     |                  |          |                    |
|     |                  |          |                    |

## Important Reminders

|  |  |
|--|--|
|  |  |
|  |  |
|  |  |
|  |  |
|  |  |
|  |  |
|  |  |

# Prep Your *Month*

| Main Goal | Main Focus | Wins |
|---|---|---|
| | | |

## Monthly Tasks

**Week 1**

**Week 2**

**Week 3**

**Week 4**

**Week 5**

## Must Do This Month

## Save for Next Month

MARCH

# March

Coach. Encourage. Mentor. Praise. Guide. Inspire. Teach.

| Sunday | Monday | Tuesday | Wednesday |
|--------|--------|---------|-----------|
|        |        |         |           |
|        |        |         |           |
|        |        |         |           |
|        |        |         |           |
|        |        |         |           |

## Monthly Focus

| Thursday | Friday | Saturday |
|---|---|---|
| | | |
| | | |
| | | |
| | | |

Notes

MARCH

# Prep Your *Week*

## Priorities This Week

- 
- 
- 
- 
- 
- 
- 
- 

## Coaching Cycles

## Classroom Snapshots

## Data Meetings

## Team & PD Meetings

## Feedback Meetings

## Other

# Reflect on Your *Week*

| | |
|---|---|
| What goals did you accomplish this week? | What goals did you not accomplish this week? Why? |
| What can you do to improve next week? | Things learned and things to remember: |

## Goal & Habit Tracker

| Goal or Habit | Day 1 | Day 2 | Day 3 | Day 4 | Day 5 | Day 6 | Day 7 |
|---|---|---|---|---|---|---|---|
| | | | | | | | |
| | | | | | | | |
| | | | | | | | |
| | | | | | | | |

## Notes

**Week:**

**Notes** ➤

| Sunday | Monday | Tuesday |
|---|---|---|
| 4:00 a.m. | 4:00 a.m. | 4:00 a.m. |
| 4:30 | 4:30 | 4:30 |
| 5:00 | 5:00 | 5:00 |
| 5:30 | 5:30 | 5:30 |
| 6:00 | 6:00 | 6:00 |
| 6:30 | 6:30 | 6:30 |
| 7:00 | 7:00 | 7:00 |
| 7:30 | 7:30 | 7:30 |
| 8:00 | 8:00 | 8:00 |
| 8:30 | 8:30 | 8:30 |
| 9:00 | 9:00 | 9:00 |
| 9:30 | 9:30 | 9:30 |
| 10:00 | 10:00 | 10:00 |
| 10:30 | 10:30 | 10:30 |
| 11:00 | 11:00 | 11:00 |
| 11:30 | 11:30 | 11:30 |
| 12:00 p.m. | 12:00 p.m. | 12:00 p.m. |
| 12:30 | 12:30 | 12:30 |
| 1:00 | 1:00 | 1:00 |
| 1:30 | 1:30 | 1:30 |
| 2:00 | 2:00 | 2:00 |
| 2:30 | 2:30 | 2:30 |
| 3:00 | 3:00 | 3:00 |
| 3:30 | 3:30 | 3:30 |
| 4:00 | 4:00 | 4:00 |
| 4:30 | 4:30 | 4:30 |
| 5:00 | 5:00 | 5:00 |
| 5:30 | 5:30 | 5:30 |
| 6:00 | 6:00 | 6:00 |
| 6:30 | 6:30 | 6:30 |
| 7:00 | 7:00 | 7:00 |
| 7:30 | 7:30 | 7:30 |
| 8:00 | 8:00 | 8:00 |
| 8:30 | 8:30 | 8:30 |
| 9:00 | 9:00 | 9:00 |
| 9:30 | 9:30 | 9:30 |
| 10:00 | 10:00 | 10:00 |

| Wednesday | Thursday | Friday | Saturday |
|---|---|---|---|
| 4:00 a.m. | 4:00 a.m. | 4:00 a.m. | 4:00 a.m. |
| 4:30 | 4:30 | 4:30 | 4:30 |
| 5:00 | 5:00 | 5:00 | 5:00 |
| 5:30 | 5:30 | 5:30 | 5:30 |
| 6:00 | 6:00 | 6:00 | 6:00 |
| 6:30 | 6:30 | 6:30 | 6:30 |
| 7:00 | 7:00 | 7:00 | 7:00 |
| 7:30 | 7:30 | 7:30 | 7:30 |
| 8:00 | 8:00 | 8:00 | 8:00 |
| 8:30 | 8:30 | 8:30 | 8:30 |
| 9:00 | 9:00 | 9:00 | 9:00 |
| 9:30 | 9:30 | 9:30 | 9:30 |
| 10:00 | 10:00 | 10:00 | 10:00 |
| 10:30 | 10:30 | 10:30 | 10:30 |
| 11:00 | 11:00 | 11:00 | 11:00 |
| 11:30 | 11:30 | 11:30 | 11:30 |
| 12:00 p.m. | 12:00 p.m. | 12:00 p.m. | 12:00 p.m. |
| 12:30 | 12:30 | 12:30 | 12:30 |
| 1:00 | 1:00 | 1:00 | 1:00 |
| 1:30 | 1:30 | 1:30 | 1:30 |
| 2:00 | 2:00 | 2:00 | 2:00 |
| 2:30 | 2:30 | 2:30 | 2:30 |
| 3:00 | 3:00 | 3:00 | 3:00 |
| 3:30 | 3:30 | 3:30 | 3:30 |
| 4:00 | 4:00 | 4:00 | 4:00 |
| 4:30 | 4:30 | 4:30 | 4:30 |
| 5:00 | 5:00 | 5:00 | 5:00 |
| 5:30 | 5:30 | 5:30 | 5:30 |
| 6:00 | 6:00 | 6:00 | 6:00 |
| 6:30 | 6:30 | 6:30 | 6:30 |
| 7:00 | 7:00 | 7:00 | 7:00 |
| 7:30 | 7:30 | 7:30 | 7:30 |
| 8:00 | 8:00 | 8:00 | 8:00 |
| 8:30 | 8:30 | 8:30 | 8:30 |
| 9:00 | 9:00 | 9:00 | 9:00 |
| 9:30 | 9:30 | 9:30 | 9:30 |
| 10:00 | 10:00 | 10:00 | 10:00 |

MARCH

# Prep Your *Week*

## Priorities This Week

- 
- 
- 
- 
- 
- 
- 
- 
- 

## Coaching Cycles

## Classroom Snapshots

## Data Meetings

## Team & PD Meetings

## Feedback Meetings

## Other

# Reflect on Your *Week*

| What goals did you accomplish this week? | What goals did you not accomplish this week? Why? |
|---|---|
| What can you do to improve next week? | Things learned and things to remember: |

## Goal & Habit Tracker

| Goal or Habit | Day 1 | Day 2 | Day 3 | Day 4 | Day 5 | Day 6 | Day 7 |
|---|---|---|---|---|---|---|---|
| | | | | | | | |
| | | | | | | | |
| | | | | | | | |
| | | | | | | | |

## Notes

Week:

Notes

| Sunday | Monday | Tuesday |
|---|---|---|
| 4:00 a.m. | 4:00 a.m. | 4:00 a.m. |
| 4:30 | 4:30 | 4:30 |
| 5:00 | 5:00 | 5:00 |
| 5:30 | 5:30 | 5:30 |
| 6:00 | 6:00 | 6:00 |
| 6:30 | 6:30 | 6:30 |
| 7:00 | 7:00 | 7:00 |
| 7:30 | 7:30 | 7:30 |
| 8:00 | 8:00 | 8:00 |
| 8:30 | 8:30 | 8:30 |
| 9:00 | 9:00 | 9:00 |
| 9:30 | 9:30 | 9:30 |
| 10:00 | 10:00 | 10:00 |
| 10:30 | 10:30 | 10:30 |
| 11:00 | 11:00 | 11:00 |
| 11:30 | 11:30 | 11:30 |
| 12:00 p.m. | 12:00 p.m. | 12:00 p.m. |
| 12:30 | 12:30 | 12:30 |
| 1:00 | 1:00 | 1:00 |
| 1:30 | 1:30 | 1:30 |
| 2:00 | 2:00 | 2:00 |
| 2:30 | 2:30 | 2:30 |
| 3:00 | 3:00 | 3:00 |
| 3:30 | 3:30 | 3:30 |
| 4:00 | 4:00 | 4:00 |
| 4:30 | 4:30 | 4:30 |
| 5:00 | 5:00 | 5:00 |
| 5:30 | 5:30 | 5:30 |
| 6:00 | 6:00 | 6:00 |
| 6:30 | 6:30 | 6:30 |
| 7:00 | 7:00 | 7:00 |
| 7:30 | 7:30 | 7:30 |
| 8:00 | 8:00 | 8:00 |
| 8:30 | 8:30 | 8:30 |
| 9:00 | 9:00 | 9:00 |
| 9:30 | 9:30 | 9:30 |
| 10:00 | 10:00 | 10:00 |

| Wednesday | Thursday | Friday | Saturday |
|---|---|---|---|
| 4:00 a.m. | 4:00 a.m. | 4:00 a.m. | 4:00 a.m. |
| 4:30 | 4:30 | 4:30 | 4:30 |
| 5:00 | 5:00 | 5:00 | 5:00 |
| 5:30 | 5:30 | 5:30 | 5:30 |
| 6:00 | 6:00 | 6:00 | 6:00 |
| 6:30 | 6:30 | 6:30 | 6:30 |
| 7:00 | 7:00 | 7:00 | 7:00 |
| 7:30 | 7:30 | 7:30 | 7:30 |
| 8:00 | 8:00 | 8:00 | 8:00 |
| 8:30 | 8:30 | 8:30 | 8:30 |
| 9:00 | 9:00 | 9:00 | 9:00 |
| 9:30 | 9:30 | 9:30 | 9:30 |
| 10:00 | 10:00 | 10:00 | 10:00 |
| 10:30 | 10:30 | 10:30 | 10:30 |
| 11:00 | 11:00 | 11:00 | 11:00 |
| 11:30 | 11:30 | 11:30 | 11:30 |
| 12:00 p.m. | 12:00 p.m. | 12:00 p.m. | 12:00 p.m. |
| 12:30 | 12:30 | 12:30 | 12:30 |
| 1:00 | 1:00 | 1:00 | 1:00 |
| 1:30 | 1:30 | 1:30 | 1:30 |
| 2:00 | 2:00 | 2:00 | 2:00 |
| 2:30 | 2:30 | 2:30 | 2:30 |
| 3:00 | 3:00 | 3:00 | 3:00 |
| 3:30 | 3:30 | 3:30 | 3:30 |
| 4:00 | 4:00 | 4:00 | 4:00 |
| 4:30 | 4:30 | 4:30 | 4:30 |
| 5:00 | 5:00 | 5:00 | 5:00 |
| 5:30 | 5:30 | 5:30 | 5:30 |
| 6:00 | 6:00 | 6:00 | 6:00 |
| 6:30 | 6:30 | 6:30 | 6:30 |
| 7:00 | 7:00 | 7:00 | 7:00 |
| 7:30 | 7:30 | 7:30 | 7:30 |
| 8:00 | 8:00 | 8:00 | 8:00 |
| 8:30 | 8:30 | 8:30 | 8:30 |
| 9:00 | 9:00 | 9:00 | 9:00 |
| 9:30 | 9:30 | 9:30 | 9:30 |
| 10:00 | 10:00 | 10:00 | 10:00 |

MARCH

# Prep Your *Week*

## Priorities This Week

- 
- 
- 
- 
- 
- 
- 
- 
- 

## Coaching Cycles

## Classroom Snapshots

## Data Meetings

## Team & PD Meetings

## Feedback Meetings

## Other

# Reflect on Your Week

| | |
|---|---|
| What goals did you accomplish this week? | What goals did you not accomplish this week? Why? |
| What can you do to improve next week? | Things learned and things to remember: |

## Goal & Habit Tracker

| Goal or Habit | Day 1 | Day 2 | Day 3 | Day 4 | Day 5 | Day 6 | Day 7 |
|---|---|---|---|---|---|---|---|
| | | | | | | | |
| | | | | | | | |
| | | | | | | | |
| | | | | | | | |

## Notes

MARCH

Week:

Notes ➤

| Sunday | Monday | Tuesday |
|---|---|---|
| 4:00 a.m. | 4:00 a.m. | 4:00 a.m. |
| 4:30 | 4:30 | 4:30 |
| 5:00 | 5:00 | 5:00 |
| 5:30 | 5:30 | 5:30 |
| 6:00 | 6:00 | 6:00 |
| 6:30 | 6:30 | 6:30 |
| 7:00 | 7:00 | 7:00 |
| 7:30 | 7:30 | 7:30 |
| 8:00 | 8:00 | 8:00 |
| 8:30 | 8:30 | 8:30 |
| 9:00 | 9:00 | 9:00 |
| 9:30 | 9:30 | 9:30 |
| 10:00 | 10:00 | 10:00 |
| 10:30 | 10:30 | 10:30 |
| 11:00 | 11:00 | 11:00 |
| 11:30 | 11:30 | 11:30 |
| 12:00 p.m. | 12:00 p.m. | 12:00 p.m. |
| 12:30 | 12:30 | 12:30 |
| 1:00 | 1:00 | 1:00 |
| 1:30 | 1:30 | 1:30 |
| 2:00 | 2:00 | 2:00 |
| 2:30 | 2:30 | 2:30 |
| 3:00 | 3:00 | 3:00 |
| 3:30 | 3:30 | 3:30 |
| 4:00 | 4:00 | 4:00 |
| 4:30 | 4:30 | 4:30 |
| 5:00 | 5:00 | 5:00 |
| 5:30 | 5:30 | 5:30 |
| 6:00 | 6:00 | 6:00 |
| 6:30 | 6:30 | 6:30 |
| 7:00 | 7:00 | 7:00 |
| 7:30 | 7:30 | 7:30 |
| 8:00 | 8:00 | 8:00 |
| 8:30 | 8:30 | 8:30 |
| 9:00 | 9:00 | 9:00 |
| 9:30 | 9:30 | 9:30 |
| 10:00 | 10:00 | 10:00 |

| Wednesday | Thursday | Friday | Saturday |
|---|---|---|---|
| 4:00 a.m. | 4:00 a.m. | 4:00 a.m. | 4:00 a.m. |
| 4:30 | 4:30 | 4:30 | 4:30 |
| 5:00 | 5:00 | 5:00 | 5:00 |
| 5:30 | 5:30 | 5:30 | 5:30 |
| 6:00 | 6:00 | 6:00 | 6:00 |
| 6:30 | 6:30 | 6:30 | 6:30 |
| 7:00 | 7:00 | 7:00 | 7:00 |
| 7:30 | 7:30 | 7:30 | 7:30 |
| 8:00 | 8:00 | 8:00 | 8:00 |
| 8:30 | 8:30 | 8:30 | 8:30 |
| 9:00 | 9:00 | 9:00 | 9:00 |
| 9:30 | 9:30 | 9:30 | 9:30 |
| 10:00 | 10:00 | 10:00 | 10:00 |
| 10:30 | 10:30 | 10:30 | 10:30 |
| 11:00 | 11:00 | 11:00 | 11:00 |
| 11:30 | 11:30 | 11:30 | 11:30 |
| 12:00 p.m. | 12:00 p.m. | 12:00 p.m. | 12:00 p.m. |
| 12:30 | 12:30 | 12:30 | 12:30 |
| 1:00 | 1:00 | 1:00 | 1:00 |
| 1:30 | 1:30 | 1:30 | 1:30 |
| 2:00 | 2:00 | 2:00 | 2:00 |
| 2:30 | 2:30 | 2:30 | 2:30 |
| 3:00 | 3:00 | 3:00 | 3:00 |
| 3:30 | 3:30 | 3:30 | 3:30 |
| 4:00 | 4:00 | 4:00 | 4:00 |
| 4:30 | 4:30 | 4:30 | 4:30 |
| 5:00 | 5:00 | 5:00 | 5:00 |
| 5:30 | 5:30 | 5:30 | 5:30 |
| 6:00 | 6:00 | 6:00 | 6:00 |
| 6:30 | 6:30 | 6:30 | 6:30 |
| 7:00 | 7:00 | 7:00 | 7:00 |
| 7:30 | 7:30 | 7:30 | 7:30 |
| 8:00 | 8:00 | 8:00 | 8:00 |
| 8:30 | 8:30 | 8:30 | 8:30 |
| 9:00 | 9:00 | 9:00 | 9:00 |
| 9:30 | 9:30 | 9:30 | 9:30 |
| 10:00 | 10:00 | 10:00 | 10:00 |

MARCH

# Prep Your *Week*

## Priorities This Week

- 
- 
- 
- 
- 
- 
- 
- 

## Coaching Cycles

## Classroom Snapshots

## Data Meetings

## Team & PD Meetings

## Feedback Meetings

## Other

# Reflect on Your *Week*

| What goals did you accomplish this week? | What goals did you not accomplish this week? Why? |
|---|---|
| What can you do to improve next week? | Things learned and things to remember: |

## Goal & Habit Tracker

| Goal or Habit | Day 1 | Day 2 | Day 3 | Day 4 | Day 5 | Day 6 | Day 7 |
|---|---|---|---|---|---|---|---|
|  |  |  |  |  |  |  |  |
|  |  |  |  |  |  |  |  |
|  |  |  |  |  |  |  |  |
|  |  |  |  |  |  |  |  |

## Notes

Week:

Notes ↴

| | Sunday | Monday | Tuesday |
|---|---|---|---|
| | 4:00 a.m. | 4:00 a.m. | 4:00 a.m. |
| | 4:30 | 4:30 | 4:30 |
| | 5:00 | 5:00 | 5:00 |
| | 5:30 | 5:30 | 5:30 |
| | 6:00 | 6:00 | 6:00 |
| | 6:30 | 6:30 | 6:30 |
| | 7:00 | 7:00 | 7:00 |
| | 7:30 | 7:30 | 7:30 |
| | 8:00 | 8:00 | 8:00 |
| | 8:30 | 8:30 | 8:30 |
| | 9:00 | 9:00 | 9:00 |
| | 9:30 | 9:30 | 9:30 |
| | 10:00 | 10:00 | 10:00 |
| | 10:30 | 10:30 | 10:30 |
| | 11:00 | 11:00 | 11:00 |
| | 11:30 | 11:30 | 11:30 |
| | 12:00 p.m. | 12:00 p.m. | 12:00 p.m. |
| | 12:30 | 12:30 | 12:30 |
| | 1:00 | 1:00 | 1:00 |
| | 1:30 | 1:30 | 1:30 |
| | 2:00 | 2:00 | 2:00 |
| | 2:30 | 2:30 | 2:30 |
| | 3:00 | 3:00 | 3:00 |
| | 3:30 | 3:30 | 3:30 |
| | 4:00 | 4:00 | 4:00 |
| | 4:30 | 4:30 | 4:30 |
| | 5:00 | 5:00 | 5:00 |
| | 5:30 | 5:30 | 5:30 |
| | 6:00 | 6:00 | 6:00 |
| | 6:30 | 6:30 | 6:30 |
| | 7:00 | 7:00 | 7:00 |
| | 7:30 | 7:30 | 7:30 |
| | 8:00 | 8:00 | 8:00 |
| | 8:30 | 8:30 | 8:30 |
| | 9:00 | 9:00 | 9:00 |
| | 9:30 | 9:30 | 9:30 |
| | 10:00 | 10:00 | 10:00 |

| Wednesday | Thursday | Friday | Saturday |
|---|---|---|---|
| 4:00 a.m. | 4:00 a.m. | 4:00 a.m. | 4:00 a.m. |
| 4:30 | 4:30 | 4:30 | 4:30 |
| 5:00 | 5:00 | 5:00 | 5:00 |
| 5:30 | 5:30 | 5:30 | 5:30 |
| 6:00 | 6:00 | 6:00 | 6:00 |
| 6:30 | 6:30 | 6:30 | 6:30 |
| 7:00 | 7:00 | 7:00 | 7:00 |
| 7:30 | 7:30 | 7:30 | 7:30 |
| 8:00 | 8:00 | 8:00 | 8:00 |
| 8:30 | 8:30 | 8:30 | 8:30 |
| 9:00 | 9:00 | 9:00 | 9:00 |
| 9:30 | 9:30 | 9:30 | 9:30 |
| 10:00 | 10:00 | 10:00 | 10:00 |
| 10:30 | 10:30 | 10:30 | 10:30 |
| 11:00 | 11:00 | 11:00 | 11:00 |
| 11:30 | 11:30 | 11:30 | 11:30 |
| 12:00 p.m. | 12:00 p.m. | 12:00 p.m. | 12:00 p.m. |
| 12:30 | 12:30 | 12:30 | 12:30 |
| 1:00 | 1:00 | 1:00 | 1:00 |
| 1:30 | 1:30 | 1:30 | 1:30 |
| 2:00 | 2:00 | 2:00 | 2:00 |
| 2:30 | 2:30 | 2:30 | 2:30 |
| 3:00 | 3:00 | 3:00 | 3:00 |
| 3:30 | 3:30 | 3:30 | 3:30 |
| 4:00 | 4:00 | 4:00 | 4:00 |
| 4:30 | 4:30 | 4:30 | 4:30 |
| 5:00 | 5:00 | 5:00 | 5:00 |
| 5:30 | 5:30 | 5:30 | 5:30 |
| 6:00 | 6:00 | 6:00 | 6:00 |
| 6:30 | 6:30 | 6:30 | 6:30 |
| 7:00 | 7:00 | 7:00 | 7:00 |
| 7:30 | 7:30 | 7:30 | 7:30 |
| 8:00 | 8:00 | 8:00 | 8:00 |
| 8:30 | 8:30 | 8:30 | 8:30 |
| 9:00 | 9:00 | 9:00 | 9:00 |
| 9:30 | 9:30 | 9:30 | 9:30 |
| 10:00 | 10:00 | 10:00 | 10:00 |

MARCH

# Prep Your *Week*

## Priorities This Week

- 
- 
- 
- 
- 
- 
- 
- 

## Coaching Cycles

## Classroom Snapshots

## Data Meetings

## Team & PD Meetings

## Feedback Meetings

## Other

# Reflect on Your *Week*

| What goals did you accomplish this week? | What goals did you not accomplish this week? Why? |
|---|---|
| What can you do to improve next week? | Things learned and things to remember: |

## Goal & Habit Tracker

| Goal or Habit | Day 1 | Day 2 | Day 3 | Day 4 | Day 5 | Day 6 | Day 7 |
|---|---|---|---|---|---|---|---|
| | | | | | | | |
| | | | | | | | |
| | | | | | | | |
| | | | | | | | |

## Notes

Week:

Notes

| | Sunday | Monday | Tuesday |
|---|---|---|---|
| | 4:00 a.m. | 4:00 a.m. | 4:00 a.m. |
| | 4:30 | 4:30 | 4:30 |
| | 5:00 | 5:00 | 5:00 |
| | 5:30 | 5:30 | 5:30 |
| | 6:00 | 6:00 | 6:00 |
| | 6:30 | 6:30 | 6:30 |
| | 7:00 | 7:00 | 7:00 |
| | 7:30 | 7:30 | 7:30 |
| | 8:00 | 8:00 | 8:00 |
| | 8:30 | 8:30 | 8:30 |
| | 9:00 | 9:00 | 9:00 |
| | 9:30 | 9:30 | 9:30 |
| | 10:00 | 10:00 | 10:00 |
| | 10:30 | 10:30 | 10:30 |
| | 11:00 | 11:00 | 11:00 |
| | 11:30 | 11:30 | 11:30 |
| | 12:00 p.m. | 12:00 p.m. | 12:00 p.m. |
| | 12:30 | 12:30 | 12:30 |
| | 1:00 | 1:00 | 1:00 |
| | 1:30 | 1:30 | 1:30 |
| | 2:00 | 2:00 | 2:00 |
| | 2:30 | 2:30 | 2:30 |
| | 3:00 | 3:00 | 3:00 |
| | 3:30 | 3:30 | 3:30 |
| | 4:00 | 4:00 | 4:00 |
| | 4:30 | 4:30 | 4:30 |
| | 5:00 | 5:00 | 5:00 |
| | 5:30 | 5:30 | 5:30 |
| | 6:00 | 6:00 | 6:00 |
| | 6:30 | 6:30 | 6:30 |
| | 7:00 | 7:00 | 7:00 |
| | 7:30 | 7:30 | 7:30 |
| | 8:00 | 8:00 | 8:00 |
| | 8:30 | 8:30 | 8:30 |
| | 9:00 | 9:00 | 9:00 |
| | 9:30 | 9:30 | 9:30 |
| | 10:00 | 10:00 | 10:00 |

| Wednesday | Thursday | Friday | Saturday |
|---|---|---|---|
| 4:00 a.m. | 4:00 a.m. | 4:00 a.m. | 4:00 a.m. |
| 4:30 | 4:30 | 4:30 | 4:30 |
| 5:00 | 5:00 | 5:00 | 5:00 |
| 5:30 | 5:30 | 5:30 | 5:30 |
| 6:00 | 6:00 | 6:00 | 6:00 |
| 6:30 | 6:30 | 6:30 | 6:30 |
| 7:00 | 7:00 | 7:00 | 7:00 |
| 7:30 | 7:30 | 7:30 | 7:30 |
| 8:00 | 8:00 | 8:00 | 8:00 |
| 8:30 | 8:30 | 8:30 | 8:30 |
| 9:00 | 9:00 | 9:00 | 9:00 |
| 9:30 | 9:30 | 9:30 | 9:30 |
| 10:00 | 10:00 | 10:00 | 10:00 |
| 10:30 | 10:30 | 10:30 | 10:30 |
| 11:00 | 11:00 | 11:00 | 11:00 |
| 11:30 | 11:30 | 11:30 | 11:30 |
| 12:00 p.m. | 12:00 p.m. | 12:00 p.m. | 12:00 p.m. |
| 12:30 | 12:30 | 12:30 | 12:30 |
| 1:00 | 1:00 | 1:00 | 1:00 |
| 1:30 | 1:30 | 1:30 | 1:30 |
| 2:00 | 2:00 | 2:00 | 2:00 |
| 2:30 | 2:30 | 2:30 | 2:30 |
| 3:00 | 3:00 | 3:00 | 3:00 |
| 3:30 | 3:30 | 3:30 | 3:30 |
| 4:00 | 4:00 | 4:00 | 4:00 |
| 4:30 | 4:30 | 4:30 | 4:30 |
| 5:00 | 5:00 | 5:00 | 5:00 |
| 5:30 | 5:30 | 5:30 | 5:30 |
| 6:00 | 6:00 | 6:00 | 6:00 |
| 6:30 | 6:30 | 6:30 | 6:30 |
| 7:00 | 7:00 | 7:00 | 7:00 |
| 7:30 | 7:30 | 7:30 | 7:30 |
| 8:00 | 8:00 | 8:00 | 8:00 |
| 8:30 | 8:30 | 8:30 | 8:30 |
| 9:00 | 9:00 | 9:00 | 9:00 |
| 9:30 | 9:30 | 9:30 | 9:30 |
| 10:00 | 10:00 | 10:00 | 10:00 |

MARCH

GIVE ME *six hours*
TO CHOP DOWN
A TREE, AND I
WILL SPEND THE
*first four*
SHARPENING THE AXE.

—Abraham Lincoln

# Prep Your *Month*

## Personal Goals

| Day | Health & Fitness | Finances | Self-Care & Growth |
|-----|------------------|----------|--------------------|
|     |                  |          |                    |
|     |                  |          |                    |
|     |                  |          |                    |
|     |                  |          |                    |
|     |                  |          |                    |
|     |                  |          |                    |

## Important Reminders

|  |  |
|--|--|
|  |  |
|  |  |
|  |  |
|  |  |
|  |  |
|  |  |
|  |  |

# Prep Your *Month*

| Main Goal | Main Focus | Wins |
|---|---|---|
|  |  |  |

## Monthly Tasks

Week 1

Week 2

Week 3

Week 4

Week 5

### Must Do This Month

### Save for Next Month

APRIL

# April

"Great leaders don't set out to be a leader . . .
they set out to make a difference. It's never about the role . . .
always about the goal." —Lisa Haisha

| Sunday | Monday | Tuesday | Wednesday |
|--------|--------|---------|-----------|
|        |        |         |           |
|        |        |         |           |
|        |        |         |           |
|        |        |         |           |
|        |        |         |           |

Monthly Focus

| Thursday | Friday | Saturday |
|---|---|---|
|  |  |  |
|  |  |  |
|  |  |  |
|  |  |  |
|  |  |  |

Notes

# Prep Your *Week*

## *Priorities* This Week

- 
- 
- 
- 
- 
- 
- 
- 

## Coaching Cycles

## Classroom Snapshots

## Data Meetings

## Team & PD Meetings

## Feedback Meetings

## Other

# Reflect on Your *Week*

| | |
|---|---|
| **What goals did you accomplish this week?** | **What goals did you not accomplish this week? Why?** |
| **What can you do to improve next week?** | **Things learned and things to remember:** |

## Goal & Habit Tracker

| Goal or Habit | Day 1 | Day 2 | Day 3 | Day 4 | Day 5 | Day 6 | Day 7 |
|---|---|---|---|---|---|---|---|
| | | | | | | | |
| | | | | | | | |
| | | | | | | | |
| | | | | | | | |

## Notes

**Week:**

**Notes**

| Sunday | Monday | Tuesday |
|---|---|---|
| 4:00 a.m. | 4:00 a.m. | 4:00 a.m. |
| 4:30 | 4:30 | 4:30 |
| 5:00 | 5:00 | 5:00 |
| 5:30 | 5:30 | 5:30 |
| 6:00 | 6:00 | 6:00 |
| 6:30 | 6:30 | 6:30 |
| 7:00 | 7:00 | 7:00 |
| 7:30 | 7:30 | 7:30 |
| 8:00 | 8:00 | 8:00 |
| 8:30 | 8:30 | 8:30 |
| 9:00 | 9:00 | 9:00 |
| 9:30 | 9:30 | 9:30 |
| 10:00 | 10:00 | 10:00 |
| 10:30 | 10:30 | 10:30 |
| 11:00 | 11:00 | 11:00 |
| 11:30 | 11:30 | 11:30 |
| 12:00 p.m. | 12:00 p.m. | 12:00 p.m. |
| 12:30 | 12:30 | 12:30 |
| 1:00 | 1:00 | 1:00 |
| 1:30 | 1:30 | 1:30 |
| 2:00 | 2:00 | 2:00 |
| 2:30 | 2:30 | 2:30 |
| 3:00 | 3:00 | 3:00 |
| 3:30 | 3:30 | 3:30 |
| 4:00 | 4:00 | 4:00 |
| 4:30 | 4:30 | 4:30 |
| 5:00 | 5:00 | 5:00 |
| 5:30 | 5:30 | 5:30 |
| 6:00 | 6:00 | 6:00 |
| 6:30 | 6:30 | 6:30 |
| 7:00 | 7:00 | 7:00 |
| 7:30 | 7:30 | 7:30 |
| 8:00 | 8:00 | 8:00 |
| 8:30 | 8:30 | 8:30 |
| 9:00 | 9:00 | 9:00 |
| 9:30 | 9:30 | 9:30 |
| 10:00 | 10:00 | 10:00 |

| Wednesday | Thursday | Friday | Saturday |
|---|---|---|---|
| 4:00 a.m. | 4:00 a.m. | 4:00 a.m. | 4:00 a.m. |
| 4:30 | 4:30 | 4:30 | 4:30 |
| 5:00 | 5:00 | 5:00 | 5:00 |
| 5:30 | 5:30 | 5:30 | 5:30 |
| 6:00 | 6:00 | 6:00 | 6:00 |
| 6:30 | 6:30 | 6:30 | 6:30 |
| 7:00 | 7:00 | 7:00 | 7:00 |
| 7:30 | 7:30 | 7:30 | 7:30 |
| 8:00 | 8:00 | 8:00 | 8:00 |
| 8:30 | 8:30 | 8:30 | 8:30 |
| 9:00 | 9:00 | 9:00 | 9:00 |
| 9:30 | 9:30 | 9:30 | 9:30 |
| 10:00 | 10:00 | 10:00 | 10:00 |
| 10:30 | 10:30 | 10:30 | 10:30 |
| 11:00 | 11:00 | 11:00 | 11:00 |
| 11:30 | 11:30 | 11:30 | 11:30 |
| 12:00 p.m. | 12:00 p.m. | 12:00 p.m. | 12:00 p.m. |
| 12:30 | 12:30 | 12:30 | 12:30 |
| 1:00 | 1:00 | 1:00 | 1:00 |
| 1:30 | 1:30 | 1:30 | 1:30 |
| 2:00 | 2:00 | 2:00 | 2:00 |
| 2:30 | 2:30 | 2:30 | 2:30 |
| 3:00 | 3:00 | 3:00 | 3:00 |
| 3:30 | 3:30 | 3:30 | 3:30 |
| 4:00 | 4:00 | 4:00 | 4:00 |
| 4:30 | 4:30 | 4:30 | 4:30 |
| 5:00 | 5:00 | 5:00 | 5:00 |
| 5:30 | 5:30 | 5:30 | 5:30 |
| 6:00 | 6:00 | 6:00 | 6:00 |
| 6:30 | 6:30 | 6:30 | 6:30 |
| 7:00 | 7:00 | 7:00 | 7:00 |
| 7:30 | 7:30 | 7:30 | 7:30 |
| 8:00 | 8:00 | 8:00 | 8:00 |
| 8:30 | 8:30 | 8:30 | 8:30 |
| 9:00 | 9:00 | 9:00 | 9:00 |
| 9:30 | 9:30 | 9:30 | 9:30 |
| 10:00 | 10:00 | 10:00 | 10:00 |

# Prep Your *Week*

## Priorities This Week

- 
- 
- 
- 
- 
- 
- 
- 

## Coaching Cycles

## Classroom Snapshots

## Data Meetings

## Team & PD Meetings

## Feedback Meetings

## Other

# Reflect on Your *Week*

| What goals did you accomplish this week? | What goals did you not accomplish this week? Why? |
|---|---|
| What can you do to improve next week? | Things learned and things to remember: |

## Goal & Habit Tracker

| Goal or Habit | Day 1 | Day 2 | Day 3 | Day 4 | Day 5 | Day 6 | Day 7 |
|---|---|---|---|---|---|---|---|
| | | | | | | | |
| | | | | | | | |
| | | | | | | | |
| | | | | | | | |

## Notes

APRIL

Notes ➘

| Sunday | Monday | Tuesday |
|---|---|---|
| 4:00 a.m. | 4:00 a.m. | 4:00 a.m. |
| 4:30 | 4:30 | 4:30 |
| 5:00 | 5:00 | 5:00 |
| 5:30 | 5:30 | 5:30 |
| 6:00 | 6:00 | 6:00 |
| 6:30 | 6:30 | 6:30 |
| 7:00 | 7:00 | 7:00 |
| 7:30 | 7:30 | 7:30 |
| 8:00 | 8:00 | 8:00 |
| 8:30 | 8:30 | 8:30 |
| 9:00 | 9:00 | 9:00 |
| 9:30 | 9:30 | 9:30 |
| 10:00 | 10:00 | 10:00 |
| 10:30 | 10:30 | 10:30 |
| 11:00 | 11:00 | 11:00 |
| 11:30 | 11:30 | 11:30 |
| 12:00 p.m. | 12:00 p.m. | 12:00 p.m. |
| 12:30 | 12:30 | 12:30 |
| 1:00 | 1:00 | 1:00 |
| 1:30 | 1:30 | 1:30 |
| 2:00 | 2:00 | 2:00 |
| 2:30 | 2:30 | 2:30 |
| 3:00 | 3:00 | 3:00 |
| 3:30 | 3:30 | 3:30 |
| 4:00 | 4:00 | 4:00 |
| 4:30 | 4:30 | 4:30 |
| 5:00 | 5:00 | 5:00 |
| 5:30 | 5:30 | 5:30 |
| 6:00 | 6:00 | 6:00 |
| 6:30 | 6:30 | 6:30 |
| 7:00 | 7:00 | 7:00 |
| 7:30 | 7:30 | 7:30 |
| 8:00 | 8:00 | 8:00 |
| 8:30 | 8:30 | 8:30 |
| 9:00 | 9:00 | 9:00 |
| 9:30 | 9:30 | 9:30 |
| 10:00 | 10:00 | 10:00 |

| Wednesday | Thursday | Friday | Saturday |
|---|---|---|---|
| 4:00 a.m. | 4:00 a.m. | 4:00 a.m. | 4:00 a.m. |
| 4:30 | 4:30 | 4:30 | 4:30 |
| 5:00 | 5:00 | 5:00 | 5:00 |
| 5:30 | 5:30 | 5:30 | 5:30 |
| 6:00 | 6:00 | 6:00 | 6:00 |
| 6:30 | 6:30 | 6:30 | 6:30 |
| 7:00 | 7:00 | 7:00 | 7:00 |
| 7:30 | 7:30 | 7:30 | 7:30 |
| 8:00 | 8:00 | 8:00 | 8:00 |
| 8:30 | 8:30 | 8:30 | 8:30 |
| 9:00 | 9:00 | 9:00 | 9:00 |
| 9:30 | 9:30 | 9:30 | 9:30 |
| 10:00 | 10:00 | 10:00 | 10:00 |
| 10:30 | 10:30 | 10:30 | 10:30 |
| 11:00 | 11:00 | 11:00 | 11:00 |
| 11:30 | 11:30 | 11:30 | 11:30 |
| 12:00 p.m. | 12:00 p.m. | 12:00 p.m. | 12:00 p.m. |
| 12:30 | 12:30 | 12:30 | 12:30 |
| 1:00 | 1:00 | 1:00 | 1:00 |
| 1:30 | 1:30 | 1:30 | 1:30 |
| 2:00 | 2:00 | 2:00 | 2:00 |
| 2:30 | 2:30 | 2:30 | 2:30 |
| 3:00 | 3:00 | 3:00 | 3:00 |
| 3:30 | 3:30 | 3:30 | 3:30 |
| 4:00 | 4:00 | 4:00 | 4:00 |
| 4:30 | 4:30 | 4:30 | 4:30 |
| 5:00 | 5:00 | 5:00 | 5:00 |
| 5:30 | 5:30 | 5:30 | 5:30 |
| 6:00 | 6:00 | 6:00 | 6:00 |
| 6:30 | 6:30 | 6:30 | 6:30 |
| 7:00 | 7:00 | 7:00 | 7:00 |
| 7:30 | 7:30 | 7:30 | 7:30 |
| 8:00 | 8:00 | 8:00 | 8:00 |
| 8:30 | 8:30 | 8:30 | 8:30 |
| 9:00 | 9:00 | 9:00 | 9:00 |
| 9:30 | 9:30 | 9:30 | 9:30 |
| 10:00 | 10:00 | 10:00 | 10:00 |

APRIL

# Prep Your *Week*

## Priorities This Week

- 
- 
- 
- 
- 
- 
- 
- 

## Coaching Cycles

## Classroom Snapshots

## Data Meetings

## Team & PD Meetings

## Feedback Meetings

## Other

# Reflect on Your *Week*

| What goals did you accomplish this week? | What goals did you not accomplish this week? Why? |
|---|---|
| What can you do to improve next week? | Things learned and things to remember: |

## Goal & Habit Tracker

| Goal or Habit | Day 1 | Day 2 | Day 3 | Day 4 | Day 5 | Day 6 | Day 7 |
|---|---|---|---|---|---|---|---|
| | | | | | | | |
| | | | | | | | |
| | | | | | | | |
| | | | | | | | |

## Notes

Week:

Notes

| Sunday | Monday | Tuesday |
|---|---|---|
| 4:00 a.m. | 4:00 a.m. | 4:00 a.m. |
| 4:30 | 4:30 | 4:30 |
| 5:00 | 5:00 | 5:00 |
| 5:30 | 5:30 | 5:30 |
| 6:00 | 6:00 | 6:00 |
| 6:30 | 6:30 | 6:30 |
| 7:00 | 7:00 | 7:00 |
| 7:30 | 7:30 | 7:30 |
| 8:00 | 8:00 | 8:00 |
| 8:30 | 8:30 | 8:30 |
| 9:00 | 9:00 | 9:00 |
| 9:30 | 9:30 | 9:30 |
| 10:00 | 10:00 | 10:00 |
| 10:30 | 10:30 | 10:30 |
| 11:00 | 11:00 | 11:00 |
| 11:30 | 11:30 | 11:30 |
| 12:00 p.m. | 12:00 p.m. | 12:00 p.m. |
| 12:30 | 12:30 | 12:30 |
| 1:00 | 1:00 | 1:00 |
| 1:30 | 1:30 | 1:30 |
| 2:00 | 2:00 | 2:00 |
| 2:30 | 2:30 | 2:30 |
| 3:00 | 3:00 | 3:00 |
| 3:30 | 3:30 | 3:30 |
| 4:00 | 4:00 | 4:00 |
| 4:30 | 4:30 | 4:30 |
| 5:00 | 5:00 | 5:00 |
| 5:30 | 5:30 | 5:30 |
| 6:00 | 6:00 | 6:00 |
| 6:30 | 6:30 | 6:30 |
| 7:00 | 7:00 | 7:00 |
| 7:30 | 7:30 | 7:30 |
| 8:00 | 8:00 | 8:00 |
| 8:30 | 8:30 | 8:30 |
| 9:00 | 9:00 | 9:00 |
| 9:30 | 9:30 | 9:30 |
| 10:00 | 10:00 | 10:00 |

| Wednesday | Thursday | Friday | Saturday |
|---|---|---|---|
| 4:00 a.m. | 4:00 a.m. | 4:00 a.m. | 4:00 a.m. |
| 4:30 | 4:30 | 4:30 | 4:30 |
| 5:00 | 5:00 | 5:00 | 5:00 |
| 5:30 | 5:30 | 5:30 | 5:30 |
| 6:00 | 6:00 | 6:00 | 6:00 |
| 6:30 | 6:30 | 6:30 | 6:30 |
| 7:00 | 7:00 | 7:00 | 7:00 |
| 7:30 | 7:30 | 7:30 | 7:30 |
| 8:00 | 8:00 | 8:00 | 8:00 |
| 8:30 | 8:30 | 8:30 | 8:30 |
| 9:00 | 9:00 | 9:00 | 9:00 |
| 9:30 | 9:30 | 9:30 | 9:30 |
| 10:00 | 10:00 | 10:00 | 10:00 |
| 10:30 | 10:30 | 10:30 | 10:30 |
| 11:00 | 11:00 | 11:00 | 11:00 |
| 11:30 | 11:30 | 11:30 | 11:30 |
| 12:00 p.m. | 12:00 p.m. | 12:00 p.m. | 12:00 p.m. |
| 12:30 | 12:30 | 12:30 | 12:30 |
| 1:00 | 1:00 | 1:00 | 1:00 |
| 1:30 | 1:30 | 1:30 | 1:30 |
| 2:00 | 2:00 | 2:00 | 2:00 |
| 2:30 | 2:30 | 2:30 | 2:30 |
| 3:00 | 3:00 | 3:00 | 3:00 |
| 3:30 | 3:30 | 3:30 | 3:30 |
| 4:00 | 4:00 | 4:00 | 4:00 |
| 4:30 | 4:30 | 4:30 | 4:30 |
| 5:00 | 5:00 | 5:00 | 5:00 |
| 5:30 | 5:30 | 5:30 | 5:30 |
| 6:00 | 6:00 | 6:00 | 6:00 |
| 6:30 | 6:30 | 6:30 | 6:30 |
| 7:00 | 7:00 | 7:00 | 7:00 |
| 7:30 | 7:30 | 7:30 | 7:30 |
| 8:00 | 8:00 | 8:00 | 8:00 |
| 8:30 | 8:30 | 8:30 | 8:30 |
| 9:00 | 9:00 | 9:00 | 9:00 |
| 9:30 | 9:30 | 9:30 | 9:30 |
| 10:00 | 10:00 | 10:00 | 10:00 |

APRIL

# Prep Your *Week*

| Priorities This Week | Coaching Cycles | Classroom Snapshots |
|---|---|---|
| • | | |
| • | | |
| • | **Data Meetings** | **Team & PD Meetings** |
| • | | |
| • | | |
| • | | |
| • | **Feedback Meetings** | **Other** |
| • | | |
| • | | |

# Reflect on Your *Week*

| | |
|---|---|
| What goals did you accomplish this week? | What goals did you not accomplish this week? Why? |
| What can you do to improve next week? | Things learned and things to remember: |

## Goal & Habit Tracker

| Goal or Habit | Day 1 | Day 2 | Day 3 | Day 4 | Day 5 | Day 6 | Day 7 |
|---|---|---|---|---|---|---|---|
| | | | | | | | |
| | | | | | | | |
| | | | | | | | |
| | | | | | | | |

## Notes

Week:

Notes

| | Sunday | Monday | Tuesday |
|---|---|---|---|
| | 4:00 a.m. | 4:00 a.m. | 4:00 a.m. |
| | 4:30 | 4:30 | 4:30 |
| | 5:00 | 5:00 | 5:00 |
| | 5:30 | 5:30 | 5:30 |
| | 6:00 | 6:00 | 6:00 |
| | 6:30 | 6:30 | 6:30 |
| | 7:00 | 7:00 | 7:00 |
| | 7:30 | 7:30 | 7:30 |
| | 8:00 | 8:00 | 8:00 |
| | 8:30 | 8:30 | 8:30 |
| | 9:00 | 9:00 | 9:00 |
| | 9:30 | 9:30 | 9:30 |
| | 10:00 | 10:00 | 10:00 |
| | 10:30 | 10:30 | 10:30 |
| | 11:00 | 11:00 | 11:00 |
| | 11:30 | 11:30 | 11:30 |
| | 12:00 p.m. | 12:00 p.m. | 12:00 p.m. |
| | 12:30 | 12:30 | 12:30 |
| | 1:00 | 1:00 | 1:00 |
| | 1:30 | 1:30 | 1:30 |
| | 2:00 | 2:00 | 2:00 |
| | 2:30 | 2:30 | 2:30 |
| | 3:00 | 3:00 | 3:00 |
| | 3:30 | 3:30 | 3:30 |
| | 4:00 | 4:00 | 4:00 |
| | 4:30 | 4:30 | 4:30 |
| | 5:00 | 5:00 | 5:00 |
| | 5:30 | 5:30 | 5:30 |
| | 6:00 | 6:00 | 6:00 |
| | 6:30 | 6:30 | 6:30 |
| | 7:00 | 7:00 | 7:00 |
| | 7:30 | 7:30 | 7:30 |
| | 8:00 | 8:00 | 8:00 |
| | 8:30 | 8:30 | 8:30 |
| | 9:00 | 9:00 | 9:00 |
| | 9:30 | 9:30 | 9:30 |
| | 10:00 | 10:00 | 10:00 |

| Wednesday | Thursday | Friday | Saturday |
|---|---|---|---|
| 4:00 a.m. | 4:00 a.m. | 4:00 a.m. | 4:00 a.m. |
| 4:30 | 4:30 | 4:30 | 4:30 |
| 5:00 | 5:00 | 5:00 | 5:00 |
| 5:30 | 5:30 | 5:30 | 5:30 |
| 6:00 | 6:00 | 6:00 | 6:00 |
| 6:30 | 6:30 | 6:30 | 6:30 |
| 7:00 | 7:00 | 7:00 | 7:00 |
| 7:30 | 7:30 | 7:30 | 7:30 |
| 8:00 | 8:00 | 8:00 | 8:00 |
| 8:30 | 8:30 | 8:30 | 8:30 |
| 9:00 | 9:00 | 9:00 | 9:00 |
| 9:30 | 9:30 | 9:30 | 9:30 |
| 10:00 | 10:00 | 10:00 | 10:00 |
| 10:30 | 10:30 | 10:30 | 10:30 |
| 11:00 | 11:00 | 11:00 | 11:00 |
| 11:30 | 11:30 | 11:30 | 11:30 |
| 12:00 p.m. | 12:00 p.m. | 12:00 p.m. | 12:00 p.m. |
| 12:30 | 12:30 | 12:30 | 12:30 |
| 1:00 | 1:00 | 1:00 | 1:00 |
| 1:30 | 1:30 | 1:30 | 1:30 |
| 2:00 | 2:00 | 2:00 | 2:00 |
| 2:30 | 2:30 | 2:30 | 2:30 |
| 3:00 | 3:00 | 3:00 | 3:00 |
| 3:30 | 3:30 | 3:30 | 3:30 |
| 4:00 | 4:00 | 4:00 | 4:00 |
| 4:30 | 4:30 | 4:30 | 4:30 |
| 5:00 | 5:00 | 5:00 | 5:00 |
| 5:30 | 5:30 | 5:30 | 5:30 |
| 6:00 | 6:00 | 6:00 | 6:00 |
| 6:30 | 6:30 | 6:30 | 6:30 |
| 7:00 | 7:00 | 7:00 | 7:00 |
| 7:30 | 7:30 | 7:30 | 7:30 |
| 8:00 | 8:00 | 8:00 | 8:00 |
| 8:30 | 8:30 | 8:30 | 8:30 |
| 9:00 | 9:00 | 9:00 | 9:00 |
| 9:30 | 9:30 | 9:30 | 9:30 |
| 10:00 | 10:00 | 10:00 | 10:00 |

APRIL

# Prep Your *Week*

## Priorities This Week

- 
- 
- 
- 
- 
- 
- 
- 

## Coaching Cycles

## Classroom Snapshots

## Data Meetings

## Team & PD Meetings

## Feedback Meetings

## Other

# Reflect on Your Week

| | |
|---|---|
| What goals did you accomplish this week? | What goals did you not accomplish this week? Why? |
| What can you do to improve next week? | Things learned and things to remember: |

## Goal & Habit Tracker

| Goal or Habit | Day 1 | Day 2 | Day 3 | Day 4 | Day 5 | Day 6 | Day 7 |
|---|---|---|---|---|---|---|---|
| | | | | | | | |
| | | | | | | | |
| | | | | | | | |
| | | | | | | | |

## Notes

Week:

Notes

| Sunday | Monday | Tuesday |
|---|---|---|
| 4:00 a.m. | 4:00 a.m. | 4:00 a.m. |
| 4:30 | 4:30 | 4:30 |
| 5:00 | 5:00 | 5:00 |
| 5:30 | 5:30 | 5:30 |
| 6:00 | 6:00 | 6:00 |
| 6:30 | 6:30 | 6:30 |
| 7:00 | 7:00 | 7:00 |
| 7:30 | 7:30 | 7:30 |
| 8:00 | 8:00 | 8:00 |
| 8:30 | 8:30 | 8:30 |
| 9:00 | 9:00 | 9:00 |
| 9:30 | 9:30 | 9:30 |
| 10:00 | 10:00 | 10:00 |
| 10:30 | 10:30 | 10:30 |
| 11:00 | 11:00 | 11:00 |
| 11:30 | 11:30 | 11:30 |
| 12:00 p.m. | 12:00 p.m. | 12:00 p.m. |
| 12:30 | 12:30 | 12:30 |
| 1:00 | 1:00 | 1:00 |
| 1:30 | 1:30 | 1:30 |
| 2:00 | 2:00 | 2:00 |
| 2:30 | 2:30 | 2:30 |
| 3:00 | 3:00 | 3:00 |
| 3:30 | 3:30 | 3:30 |
| 4:00 | 4:00 | 4:00 |
| 4:30 | 4:30 | 4:30 |
| 5:00 | 5:00 | 5:00 |
| 5:30 | 5:30 | 5:30 |
| 6:00 | 6:00 | 6:00 |
| 6:30 | 6:30 | 6:30 |
| 7:00 | 7:00 | 7:00 |
| 7:30 | 7:30 | 7:30 |
| 8:00 | 8:00 | 8:00 |
| 8:30 | 8:30 | 8:30 |
| 9:00 | 9:00 | 9:00 |
| 9:30 | 9:30 | 9:30 |
| 10:00 | 10:00 | 10:00 |

| Wednesday | Thursday | Friday | Saturday |
|---|---|---|---|
| 4:00 a.m. | 4:00 a.m. | 4:00 a.m. | 4:00 a.m. |
| 4:30 | 4:30 | 4:30 | 4:30 |
| 5:00 | 5:00 | 5:00 | 5:00 |
| 5:30 | 5:30 | 5:30 | 5:30 |
| 6:00 | 6:00 | 6:00 | 6:00 |
| 6:30 | 6:30 | 6:30 | 6:30 |
| 7:00 | 7:00 | 7:00 | 7:00 |
| 7:30 | 7:30 | 7:30 | 7:30 |
| 8:00 | 8:00 | 8:00 | 8:00 |
| 8:30 | 8:30 | 8:30 | 8:30 |
| 9:00 | 9:00 | 9:00 | 9:00 |
| 9:30 | 9:30 | 9:30 | 9:30 |
| 10:00 | 10:00 | 10:00 | 10:00 |
| 10:30 | 10:30 | 10:30 | 10:30 |
| 11:00 | 11:00 | 11:00 | 11:00 |
| 11:30 | 11:30 | 11:30 | 11:30 |
| 12:00 p.m. | 12:00 p.m. | 12:00 p.m. | 12:00 p.m. |
| 12:30 | 12:30 | 12:30 | 12:30 |
| 1:00 | 1:00 | 1:00 | 1:00 |
| 1:30 | 1:30 | 1:30 | 1:30 |
| 2:00 | 2:00 | 2:00 | 2:00 |
| 2:30 | 2:30 | 2:30 | 2:30 |
| 3:00 | 3:00 | 3:00 | 3:00 |
| 3:30 | 3:30 | 3:30 | 3:30 |
| 4:00 | 4:00 | 4:00 | 4:00 |
| 4:30 | 4:30 | 4:30 | 4:30 |
| 5:00 | 5:00 | 5:00 | 5:00 |
| 5:30 | 5:30 | 5:30 | 5:30 |
| 6:00 | 6:00 | 6:00 | 6:00 |
| 6:30 | 6:30 | 6:30 | 6:30 |
| 7:00 | 7:00 | 7:00 | 7:00 |
| 7:30 | 7:30 | 7:30 | 7:30 |
| 8:00 | 8:00 | 8:00 | 8:00 |
| 8:30 | 8:30 | 8:30 | 8:30 |
| 9:00 | 9:00 | 9:00 | 9:00 |
| 9:30 | 9:30 | 9:30 | 9:30 |
| 10:00 | 10:00 | 10:00 | 10:00 |

APRIL

NEVER *begin* THE DAY UNTIL IT IS *finished on paper.*

—Jim Rohn

# Prep Your *Month*

## Personal Goals

| Day | Health & Fitness | Finances | Self-Care & Growth |
|-----|------------------|----------|--------------------|
|     |                  |          |                    |
|     |                  |          |                    |
|     |                  |          |                    |
|     |                  |          |                    |
|     |                  |          |                    |
|     |                  |          |                    |

## Important Reminders

|  |  |
|--|--|
|  |  |
|  |  |
|  |  |
|  |  |
|  |  |
|  |  |
|  |  |

# Prep Your *Month*

| Main Goal | Main Focus | Wins |
|---|---|---|
| | | |

## Monthly Tasks

**Week 1**

**Week 2**

**Week 3**

**Week 4**

**Week 5**

## Must Do This Month

## Save for Next Month

MAY

# May

Potential. Passion. Purpose. Perseverance. *Progress.*

| Sunday | Monday | Tuesday | Wednesday |
|--------|--------|---------|-----------|
|  |  |  |  |
|  |  |  |  |
|  |  |  |  |
|  |  |  |  |
|  |  |  |  |

| Thursday | Friday | Saturday |
|---|---|---|
|  |  |  |
|  |  |  |
|  |  |  |
|  |  |  |
|  |  |  |

Notes

MAY

# Prep Your *Week*

## Priorities This Week

- 
- 
- 
- 
- 
- 
- 
- 

## Coaching Cycles

## Classroom Snapshots

## Data Meetings

## Team & PD Meetings

## Feedback Meetings

## Other

# Reflect on Your *Week*

| What goals did you accomplish this week? | What goals did you not accomplish this week? Why? |
|---|---|
| | |
| What can you do to improve next week? | Things learned and things to remember: |
| | |

## Goal & Habit Tracker

| Goal or Habit | Day 1 | Day 2 | Day 3 | Day 4 | Day 5 | Day 6 | Day 7 |
|---|---|---|---|---|---|---|---|
| | | | | | | | |
| | | | | | | | |
| | | | | | | | |
| | | | | | | | |

## Notes

MAY

Week:

Notes ↴

| | Sunday | Monday | Tuesday |
|---|---|---|---|
| | 4:00 a.m. | 4:00 a.m. | 4:00 a.m. |
| | 4:30 | 4:30 | 4:30 |
| | 5:00 | 5:00 | 5:00 |
| | 5:30 | 5:30 | 5:30 |
| | 6:00 | 6:00 | 6:00 |
| | 6:30 | 6:30 | 6:30 |
| | 7:00 | 7:00 | 7:00 |
| | 7:30 | 7:30 | 7:30 |
| | 8:00 | 8:00 | 8:00 |
| | 8:30 | 8:30 | 8:30 |
| | 9:00 | 9:00 | 9:00 |
| | 9:30 | 9:30 | 9:30 |
| | 10:00 | 10:00 | 10:00 |
| | 10:30 | 10:30 | 10:30 |
| | 11:00 | 11:00 | 11:00 |
| | 11:30 | 11:30 | 11:30 |
| | 12:00 p.m. | 12:00 p.m. | 12:00 p.m. |
| | 12:30 | 12:30 | 12:30 |
| | 1:00 | 1:00 | 1:00 |
| | 1:30 | 1:30 | 1:30 |
| | 2:00 | 2:00 | 2:00 |
| | 2:30 | 2:30 | 2:30 |
| | 3:00 | 3:00 | 3:00 |
| | 3:30 | 3:30 | 3:30 |
| | 4:00 | 4:00 | 4:00 |
| | 4:30 | 4:30 | 4:30 |
| | 5:00 | 5:00 | 5:00 |
| | 5:30 | 5:30 | 5:30 |
| | 6:00 | 6:00 | 6:00 |
| | 6:30 | 6:30 | 6:30 |
| | 7:00 | 7:00 | 7:00 |
| | 7:30 | 7:30 | 7:30 |
| | 8:00 | 8:00 | 8:00 |
| | 8:30 | 8:30 | 8:30 |
| | 9:00 | 9:00 | 9:00 |
| | 9:30 | 9:30 | 9:30 |
| | 10:00 | 10:00 | 10:00 |

| Wednesday | Thursday | Friday | Saturday |
|---|---|---|---|
| 4:00 a.m. | 4:00 a.m. | 4:00 a.m. | 4:00 a.m. |
| 4:30 | 4:30 | 4:30 | 4:30 |
| 5:00 | 5:00 | 5:00 | 5:00 |
| 5:30 | 5:30 | 5:30 | 5:30 |
| 6:00 | 6:00 | 6:00 | 6:00 |
| 6:30 | 6:30 | 6:30 | 6:30 |
| 7:00 | 7:00 | 7:00 | 7:00 |
| 7:30 | 7:30 | 7:30 | 7:30 |
| 8:00 | 8:00 | 8:00 | 8:00 |
| 8:30 | 8:30 | 8:30 | 8:30 |
| 9:00 | 9:00 | 9:00 | 9:00 |
| 9:30 | 9:30 | 9:30 | 9:30 |
| 10:00 | 10:00 | 10:00 | 10:00 |
| 10:30 | 10:30 | 10:30 | 10:30 |
| 11:00 | 11:00 | 11:00 | 11:00 |
| 11:30 | 11:30 | 11:30 | 11:30 |
| 12:00 p.m. | 12:00 p.m. | 12:00 p.m. | 12:00 p.m. |
| 12:30 | 12:30 | 12:30 | 12:30 |
| 1:00 | 1:00 | 1:00 | 1:00 |
| 1:30 | 1:30 | 1:30 | 1:30 |
| 2:00 | 2:00 | 2:00 | 2:00 |
| 2:30 | 2:30 | 2:30 | 2:30 |
| 3:00 | 3:00 | 3:00 | 3:00 |
| 3:30 | 3:30 | 3:30 | 3:30 |
| 4:00 | 4:00 | 4:00 | 4:00 |
| 4:30 | 4:30 | 4:30 | 4:30 |
| 5:00 | 5:00 | 5:00 | 5:00 |
| 5:30 | 5:30 | 5:30 | 5:30 |
| 6:00 | 6:00 | 6:00 | 6:00 |
| 6:30 | 6:30 | 6:30 | 6:30 |
| 7:00 | 7:00 | 7:00 | 7:00 |
| 7:30 | 7:30 | 7:30 | 7:30 |
| 8:00 | 8:00 | 8:00 | 8:00 |
| 8:30 | 8:30 | 8:30 | 8:30 |
| 9:00 | 9:00 | 9:00 | 9:00 |
| 9:30 | 9:30 | 9:30 | 9:30 |
| 10:00 | 10:00 | 10:00 | 10:00 |

MAY

# Prep Your *Week*

## Priorities This Week

- 
- 
- 
- 
- 
- 
- 
- 
- 

## Coaching Cycles

## Classroom Snapshots

## Data Meetings

## Team & PD Meetings

## Feedback Meetings

## Other

# Reflect on Your *Week*

| What goals did you accomplish this week? | What goals did you not accomplish this week? Why? |
|---|---|
| **What can you do to improve next week?** | **Things learned and things to remember:** |

## Goal & Habit Tracker

| Goal or Habit | Day 1 | Day 2 | Day 3 | Day 4 | Day 5 | Day 6 | Day 7 |
|---|---|---|---|---|---|---|---|
| | | | | | | | |
| | | | | | | | |
| | | | | | | | |
| | | | | | | | |

## Notes

MAY

Week:

Notes

| Sunday | Monday | Tuesday |
|---|---|---|
| 4:00 a.m. | 4:00 a.m. | 4:00 a.m. |
| 4:30 | 4:30 | 4:30 |
| 5:00 | 5:00 | 5:00 |
| 5:30 | 5:30 | 5:30 |
| 6:00 | 6:00 | 6:00 |
| 6:30 | 6:30 | 6:30 |
| 7:00 | 7:00 | 7:00 |
| 7:30 | 7:30 | 7:30 |
| 8:00 | 8:00 | 8:00 |
| 8:30 | 8:30 | 8:30 |
| 9:00 | 9:00 | 9:00 |
| 9:30 | 9:30 | 9:30 |
| 10:00 | 10:00 | 10:00 |
| 10:30 | 10:30 | 10:30 |
| 11:00 | 11:00 | 11:00 |
| 11:30 | 11:30 | 11:30 |
| 12:00 p.m. | 12:00 p.m. | 12:00 p.m. |
| 12:30 | 12:30 | 12:30 |
| 1:00 | 1:00 | 1:00 |
| 1:30 | 1:30 | 1:30 |
| 2:00 | 2:00 | 2:00 |
| 2:30 | 2:30 | 2:30 |
| 3:00 | 3:00 | 3:00 |
| 3:30 | 3:30 | 3:30 |
| 4:00 | 4:00 | 4:00 |
| 4:30 | 4:30 | 4:30 |
| 5:00 | 5:00 | 5:00 |
| 5:30 | 5:30 | 5:30 |
| 6:00 | 6:00 | 6:00 |
| 6:30 | 6:30 | 6:30 |
| 7:00 | 7:00 | 7:00 |
| 7:30 | 7:30 | 7:30 |
| 8:00 | 8:00 | 8:00 |
| 8:30 | 8:30 | 8:30 |
| 9:00 | 9:00 | 9:00 |
| 9:30 | 9:30 | 9:30 |
| 10:00 | 10:00 | 10:00 |

| Wednesday | Thursday | Friday | Saturday |
|-----------|----------|--------|----------|
| 4:00 a.m. | 4:00 a.m. | 4:00 a.m. | 4:00 a.m. |
| 4:30 | 4:30 | 4:30 | 4:30 |
| 5:00 | 5:00 | 5:00 | 5:00 |
| 5:30 | 5:30 | 5:30 | 5:30 |
| 6:00 | 6:00 | 6:00 | 6:00 |
| 6:30 | 6:30 | 6:30 | 6:30 |
| 7:00 | 7:00 | 7:00 | 7:00 |
| 7:30 | 7:30 | 7:30 | 7:30 |
| 8:00 | 8:00 | 8:00 | 8:00 |
| 8:30 | 8:30 | 8:30 | 8:30 |
| 9:00 | 9:00 | 9:00 | 9:00 |
| 9:30 | 9:30 | 9:30 | 9:30 |
| 10:00 | 10:00 | 10:00 | 10:00 |
| 10:30 | 10:30 | 10:30 | 10:30 |
| 11:00 | 11:00 | 11:00 | 11:00 |
| 11:30 | 11:30 | 11:30 | 11:30 |
| 12:00 p.m. | 12:00 p.m. | 12:00 p.m. | 12:00 p.m. |
| 12:30 | 12:30 | 12:30 | 12:30 |
| 1:00 | 1:00 | 1:00 | 1:00 |
| 1:30 | 1:30 | 1:30 | 1:30 |
| 2:00 | 2:00 | 2:00 | 2:00 |
| 2:30 | 2:30 | 2:30 | 2:30 |
| 3:00 | 3:00 | 3:00 | 3:00 |
| 3:30 | 3:30 | 3:30 | 3:30 |
| 4:00 | 4:00 | 4:00 | 4:00 |
| 4:30 | 4:30 | 4:30 | 4:30 |
| 5:00 | 5:00 | 5:00 | 5:00 |
| 5:30 | 5:30 | 5:30 | 5:30 |
| 6:00 | 6:00 | 6:00 | 6:00 |
| 6:30 | 6:30 | 6:30 | 6:30 |
| 7:00 | 7:00 | 7:00 | 7:00 |
| 7:30 | 7:30 | 7:30 | 7:30 |
| 8:00 | 8:00 | 8:00 | 8:00 |
| 8:30 | 8:30 | 8:30 | 8:30 |
| 9:00 | 9:00 | 9:00 | 9:00 |
| 9:30 | 9:30 | 9:30 | 9:30 |
| 10:00 | 10:00 | 10:00 | 10:00 |

MAY

# Prep Your *Week*

## *Priorities* This Week

- 
- 
- 
- 
- 
- 
- 
- 

## Coaching Cycles

## Classroom Snapshots

## Data Meetings

## Team & PD Meetings

## Feedback Meetings

## Other

# Reflect on Your *Week*

| What goals did you accomplish this week? | What goals did you not accomplish this week? Why? |
|---|---|
| **What can you do to improve next week?** | **Things learned and things to remember:** |

## Goal & Habit Tracker

| Goal or Habit | Day 1 | Day 2 | Day 3 | Day 4 | Day 5 | Day 6 | Day 7 |
|---|---|---|---|---|---|---|---|
|  |  |  |  |  |  |  |  |
|  |  |  |  |  |  |  |  |
|  |  |  |  |  |  |  |  |
|  |  |  |  |  |  |  |  |

## Notes

MAY

Week:

Notes

| | Sunday | Monday | Tuesday |
|---|---|---|---|
| | 4:00 a.m. | 4:00 a.m. | 4:00 a.m. |
| | 4:30 | 4:30 | 4:30 |
| | 5:00 | 5:00 | 5:00 |
| | 5:30 | 5:30 | 5:30 |
| | 6:00 | 6:00 | 6:00 |
| | 6:30 | 6:30 | 6:30 |
| | 7:00 | 7:00 | 7:00 |
| | 7:30 | 7:30 | 7:30 |
| | 8:00 | 8:00 | 8:00 |
| | 8:30 | 8:30 | 8:30 |
| | 9:00 | 9:00 | 9:00 |
| | 9:30 | 9:30 | 9:30 |
| | 10:00 | 10:00 | 10:00 |
| | 10:30 | 10:30 | 10:30 |
| | 11:00 | 11:00 | 11:00 |
| | 11:30 | 11:30 | 11:30 |
| | 12:00 p.m. | 12:00 p.m. | 12:00 p.m. |
| | 12:30 | 12:30 | 12:30 |
| | 1:00 | 1:00 | 1:00 |
| | 1:30 | 1:30 | 1:30 |
| | 2:00 | 2:00 | 2:00 |
| | 2:30 | 2:30 | 2:30 |
| | 3:00 | 3:00 | 3:00 |
| | 3:30 | 3:30 | 3:30 |
| | 4:00 | 4:00 | 4:00 |
| | 4:30 | 4:30 | 4:30 |
| | 5:00 | 5:00 | 5:00 |
| | 5:30 | 5:30 | 5:30 |
| | 6:00 | 6:00 | 6:00 |
| | 6:30 | 6:30 | 6:30 |
| | 7:00 | 7:00 | 7:00 |
| | 7:30 | 7:30 | 7:30 |
| | 8:00 | 8:00 | 8:00 |
| | 8:30 | 8:30 | 8:30 |
| | 9:00 | 9:00 | 9:00 |
| | 9:30 | 9:30 | 9:30 |
| | 10:00 | 10:00 | 10:00 |

| Wednesday | Thursday | Friday | Saturday |
|---|---|---|---|
| 4:00 a.m. | 4:00 a.m. | 4:00 a.m. | 4:00 a.m. |
| 4:30 | 4:30 | 4:30 | 4:30 |
| 5:00 | 5:00 | 5:00 | 5:00 |
| 5:30 | 5:30 | 5:30 | 5:30 |
| 6:00 | 6:00 | 6:00 | 6:00 |
| 6:30 | 6:30 | 6:30 | 6:30 |
| 7:00 | 7:00 | 7:00 | 7:00 |
| 7:30 | 7:30 | 7:30 | 7:30 |
| 8:00 | 8:00 | 8:00 | 8:00 |
| 8:30 | 8:30 | 8:30 | 8:30 |
| 9:00 | 9:00 | 9:00 | 9:00 |
| 9:30 | 9:30 | 9:30 | 9:30 |
| 10:00 | 10:00 | 10:00 | 10:00 |
| 10:30 | 10:30 | 10:30 | 10:30 |
| 11:00 | 11:00 | 11:00 | 11:00 |
| 11:30 | 11:30 | 11:30 | 11:30 |
| 12:00 p.m. | 12:00 p.m. | 12:00 p.m. | 12:00 p.m. |
| 12:30 | 12:30 | 12:30 | 12:30 |
| 1:00 | 1:00 | 1:00 | 1:00 |
| 1:30 | 1:30 | 1:30 | 1:30 |
| 2:00 | 2:00 | 2:00 | 2:00 |
| 2:30 | 2:30 | 2:30 | 2:30 |
| 3:00 | 3:00 | 3:00 | 3:00 |
| 3:30 | 3:30 | 3:30 | 3:30 |
| 4:00 | 4:00 | 4:00 | 4:00 |
| 4:30 | 4:30 | 4:30 | 4:30 |
| 5:00 | 5:00 | 5:00 | 5:00 |
| 5:30 | 5:30 | 5:30 | 5:30 |
| 6:00 | 6:00 | 6:00 | 6:00 |
| 6:30 | 6:30 | 6:30 | 6:30 |
| 7:00 | 7:00 | 7:00 | 7:00 |
| 7:30 | 7:30 | 7:30 | 7:30 |
| 8:00 | 8:00 | 8:00 | 8:00 |
| 8:30 | 8:30 | 8:30 | 8:30 |
| 9:00 | 9:00 | 9:00 | 9:00 |
| 9:30 | 9:30 | 9:30 | 9:30 |
| 10:00 | 10:00 | 10:00 | 10:00 |

MAY

# Prep Your *Week*

## Priorities This Week

- 
- 
- 
- 
- 
- 
- 
- 

## Coaching Cycles

## Classroom Snapshots

## Data Meetings

## Team & PD Meetings

## Feedback Meetings

## Other

# Reflect on Your Week

| What goals did you accomplish this week? | What goals did you not accomplish this week? Why? |
|---|---|
| What can you do to improve next week? | Things learned and things to remember: |

## Goal & Habit Tracker

| Goal or Habit | Day 1 | Day 2 | Day 3 | Day 4 | Day 5 | Day 6 | Day 7 |
|---|---|---|---|---|---|---|---|
| | | | | | | | |
| | | | | | | | |
| | | | | | | | |
| | | | | | | | |

## Notes

Week:

Notes

| Sunday | Monday | Tuesday |
|---|---|---|
| 4:00 a.m. | 4:00 a.m. | 4:00 a.m. |
| 4:30 | 4:30 | 4:30 |
| 5:00 | 5:00 | 5:00 |
| 5:30 | 5:30 | 5:30 |
| 6:00 | 6:00 | 6:00 |
| 6:30 | 6:30 | 6:30 |
| 7:00 | 7:00 | 7:00 |
| 7:30 | 7:30 | 7:30 |
| 8:00 | 8:00 | 8:00 |
| 8:30 | 8:30 | 8:30 |
| 9:00 | 9:00 | 9:00 |
| 9:30 | 9:30 | 9:30 |
| 10:00 | 10:00 | 10:00 |
| 10:30 | 10:30 | 10:30 |
| 11:00 | 11:00 | 11:00 |
| 11:30 | 11:30 | 11:30 |
| 12:00 p.m. | 12:00 p.m. | 12:00 p.m. |
| 12:30 | 12:30 | 12:30 |
| 1:00 | 1:00 | 1:00 |
| 1:30 | 1:30 | 1:30 |
| 2:00 | 2:00 | 2:00 |
| 2:30 | 2:30 | 2:30 |
| 3:00 | 3:00 | 3:00 |
| 3:30 | 3:30 | 3:30 |
| 4:00 | 4:00 | 4:00 |
| 4:30 | 4:30 | 4:30 |
| 5:00 | 5:00 | 5:00 |
| 5:30 | 5:30 | 5:30 |
| 6:00 | 6:00 | 6:00 |
| 6:30 | 6:30 | 6:30 |
| 7:00 | 7:00 | 7:00 |
| 7:30 | 7:30 | 7:30 |
| 8:00 | 8:00 | 8:00 |
| 8:30 | 8:30 | 8:30 |
| 9:00 | 9:00 | 9:00 |
| 9:30 | 9:30 | 9:30 |
| 10:00 | 10:00 | 10:00 |

| Wednesday | Thursday | Friday | Saturday |
|---|---|---|---|
| 4:00 a.m. | 4:00 a.m. | 4:00 a.m. | 4:00 a.m. |
| 4:30 | 4:30 | 4:30 | 4:30 |
| 5:00 | 5:00 | 5:00 | 5:00 |
| 5:30 | 5:30 | 5:30 | 5:30 |
| 6:00 | 6:00 | 6:00 | 6:00 |
| 6:30 | 6:30 | 6:30 | 6:30 |
| 7:00 | 7:00 | 7:00 | 7:00 |
| 7:30 | 7:30 | 7:30 | 7:30 |
| 8:00 | 8:00 | 8:00 | 8:00 |
| 8:30 | 8:30 | 8:30 | 8:30 |
| 9:00 | 9:00 | 9:00 | 9:00 |
| 9:30 | 9:30 | 9:30 | 9:30 |
| 10:00 | 10:00 | 10:00 | 10:00 |
| 10:30 | 10:30 | 10:30 | 10:30 |
| 11:00 | 11:00 | 11:00 | 11:00 |
| 11:30 | 11:30 | 11:30 | 11:30 |
| 12:00 p.m. | 12:00 p.m. | 12:00 p.m. | 12:00 p.m. |
| 12:30 | 12:30 | 12:30 | 12:30 |
| 1:00 | 1:00 | 1:00 | 1:00 |
| 1:30 | 1:30 | 1:30 | 1:30 |
| 2:00 | 2:00 | 2:00 | 2:00 |
| 2:30 | 2:30 | 2:30 | 2:30 |
| 3:00 | 3:00 | 3:00 | 3:00 |
| 3:30 | 3:30 | 3:30 | 3:30 |
| 4:00 | 4:00 | 4:00 | 4:00 |
| 4:30 | 4:30 | 4:30 | 4:30 |
| 5:00 | 5:00 | 5:00 | 5:00 |
| 5:30 | 5:30 | 5:30 | 5:30 |
| 6:00 | 6:00 | 6:00 | 6:00 |
| 6:30 | 6:30 | 6:30 | 6:30 |
| 7:00 | 7:00 | 7:00 | 7:00 |
| 7:30 | 7:30 | 7:30 | 7:30 |
| 8:00 | 8:00 | 8:00 | 8:00 |
| 8:30 | 8:30 | 8:30 | 8:30 |
| 9:00 | 9:00 | 9:00 | 9:00 |
| 9:30 | 9:30 | 9:30 | 9:30 |
| 10:00 | 10:00 | 10:00 | 10:00 |

MAY

# Prep Your *Week*

## Priorities This Week

- 
- 
- 
- 
- 
- 
- 
- 
- 

## Coaching Cycles

## Classroom Snapshots

## Data Meetings

## Team & PD Meetings

## Feedback Meetings

## Other

# Reflect on Your *Week*

| What goals did you accomplish this week? | What goals did you not accomplish this week? Why? |
|---|---|
| What can you do to improve next week? | Things learned and things to remember: |

## Goal & Habit Tracker

| Goal or Habit | Day 1 | Day 2 | Day 3 | Day 4 | Day 5 | Day 6 | Day 7 |
|---|---|---|---|---|---|---|---|
|  |  |  |  |  |  |  |  |
|  |  |  |  |  |  |  |  |
|  |  |  |  |  |  |  |  |
|  |  |  |  |  |  |  |  |

## Notes

MAY

**Week:**

**Notes** ↴

| Sunday | Monday | Tuesday |
|---|---|---|
| 4:00 a.m. | 4:00 a.m. | 4:00 a.m. |
| 4:30 | 4:30 | 4:30 |
| 5:00 | 5:00 | 5:00 |
| 5:30 | 5:30 | 5:30 |
| 6:00 | 6:00 | 6:00 |
| 6:30 | 6:30 | 6:30 |
| 7:00 | 7:00 | 7:00 |
| 7:30 | 7:30 | 7:30 |
| 8:00 | 8:00 | 8:00 |
| 8:30 | 8:30 | 8:30 |
| 9:00 | 9:00 | 9:00 |
| 9:30 | 9:30 | 9:30 |
| 10:00 | 10:00 | 10:00 |
| 10:30 | 10:30 | 10:30 |
| 11:00 | 11:00 | 11:00 |
| 11:30 | 11:30 | 11:30 |
| 12:00 p.m. | 12:00 p.m. | 12:00 p.m. |
| 12:30 | 12:30 | 12:30 |
| 1:00 | 1:00 | 1:00 |
| 1:30 | 1:30 | 1:30 |
| 2:00 | 2:00 | 2:00 |
| 2:30 | 2:30 | 2:30 |
| 3:00 | 3:00 | 3:00 |
| 3:30 | 3:30 | 3:30 |
| 4:00 | 4:00 | 4:00 |
| 4:30 | 4:30 | 4:30 |
| 5:00 | 5:00 | 5:00 |
| 5:30 | 5:30 | 5:30 |
| 6:00 | 6:00 | 6:00 |
| 6:30 | 6:30 | 6:30 |
| 7:00 | 7:00 | 7:00 |
| 7:30 | 7:30 | 7:30 |
| 8:00 | 8:00 | 8:00 |
| 8:30 | 8:30 | 8:30 |
| 9:00 | 9:00 | 9:00 |
| 9:30 | 9:30 | 9:30 |
| 10:00 | 10:00 | 10:00 |

| Wednesday | Thursday | Friday | Saturday |
|---|---|---|---|
| 4:00 a.m. | 4:00 a.m. | 4:00 a.m. | 4:00 a.m. |
| 4:30 | 4:30 | 4:30 | 4:30 |
| 5:00 | 5:00 | 5:00 | 5:00 |
| 5:30 | 5:30 | 5:30 | 5:30 |
| 6:00 | 6:00 | 6:00 | 6:00 |
| 6:30 | 6:30 | 6:30 | 6:30 |
| 7:00 | 7:00 | 7:00 | 7:00 |
| 7:30 | 7:30 | 7:30 | 7:30 |
| 8:00 | 8:00 | 8:00 | 8:00 |
| 8:30 | 8:30 | 8:30 | 8:30 |
| 9:00 | 9:00 | 9:00 | 9:00 |
| 9:30 | 9:30 | 9:30 | 9:30 |
| 10:00 | 10:00 | 10:00 | 10:00 |
| 10:30 | 10:30 | 10:30 | 10:30 |
| 11:00 | 11:00 | 11:00 | 11:00 |
| 11:30 | 11:30 | 11:30 | 11:30 |
| 12:00 p.m. | 12:00 p.m. | 12:00 p.m. | 12:00 p.m. |
| 12:30 | 12:30 | 12:30 | 12:30 |
| 1:00 | 1:00 | 1:00 | 1:00 |
| 1:30 | 1:30 | 1:30 | 1:30 |
| 2:00 | 2:00 | 2:00 | 2:00 |
| 2:30 | 2:30 | 2:30 | 2:30 |
| 3:00 | 3:00 | 3:00 | 3:00 |
| 3:30 | 3:30 | 3:30 | 3:30 |
| 4:00 | 4:00 | 4:00 | 4:00 |
| 4:30 | 4:30 | 4:30 | 4:30 |
| 5:00 | 5:00 | 5:00 | 5:00 |
| 5:30 | 5:30 | 5:30 | 5:30 |
| 6:00 | 6:00 | 6:00 | 6:00 |
| 6:30 | 6:30 | 6:30 | 6:30 |
| 7:00 | 7:00 | 7:00 | 7:00 |
| 7:30 | 7:30 | 7:30 | 7:30 |
| 8:00 | 8:00 | 8:00 | 8:00 |
| 8:30 | 8:30 | 8:30 | 8:30 |
| 9:00 | 9:00 | 9:00 | 9:00 |
| 9:30 | 9:30 | 9:30 | 9:30 |
| 10:00 | 10:00 | 10:00 | 10:00 |

MAY

IF *Plan A* DOESN'T WORK, THE ALPHABET HAS *25 more* *letters*—204 IF YOU'RE IN JAPAN.

—Claire Cook

# Prep Your *Month*

| | Personal Goals | | |
|---|---|---|---|
| Day | Health & Fitness | Finances | Self-Care & Growth |
| | | | |
| | | | |
| | | | |
| | | | |
| | | | |
| | | | |

| Important Reminders | |
|---|---|
| | |
| | |
| | |
| | |
| | |
| | |
| | |

# Prep Your *Month*

| Main Goal | Main Focus | Wins |
|---|---|---|
| | | |

## Monthly Tasks

**Week 1**

**Week 2**

**Week 3**

**Week 4**

**Week 5**

## Must Do This Month

## Save for Next Month

# June

"If it doesn't *challenge you*, it doesn't *change you*." —Fred DeVito

| Sunday | Monday | Tuesday | Wednesday |
|--------|--------|---------|-----------|
|        |        |         |           |
|        |        |         |           |
|        |        |         |           |
|        |        |         |           |
|        |        |         |           |

## Monthly Focus

| Thursday | Friday | Saturday |
|---|---|---|
|  |  |  |
|  |  |  |
|  |  |  |
|  |  |  |
|  |  |  |

Notes

JUNE

# Prep Your *Week*

## *Priorities* This Week

- 
- 
- 
- 
- 
- 
- 
- 

## Coaching Cycles

## Classroom Snapshots

## Data Meetings

## Team & PD Meetings

## Feedback Meetings

## Other

# Reflect on Your Week

| What goals did you accomplish this week? | What goals did you not accomplish this week? Why? |
|---|---|
| What can you do to improve next week? | Things learned and things to remember: |

## Goal & Habit Tracker

| Goal or Habit | Day 1 | Day 2 | Day 3 | Day 4 | Day 5 | Day 6 | Day 7 |
|---|---|---|---|---|---|---|---|
| | | | | | | | |
| | | | | | | | |
| | | | | | | | |
| | | | | | | | |

## Notes

**Week:**

**Notes**

| | Sunday | Monday | Tuesday |
|---|---|---|---|
| | 4:00 a.m. | 4:00 a.m. | 4:00 a.m. |
| | 4:30 | 4:30 | 4:30 |
| | 5:00 | 5:00 | 5:00 |
| | 5:30 | 5:30 | 5:30 |
| | 6:00 | 6:00 | 6:00 |
| | 6:30 | 6:30 | 6:30 |
| | 7:00 | 7:00 | 7:00 |
| | 7:30 | 7:30 | 7:30 |
| | 8:00 | 8:00 | 8:00 |
| | 8:30 | 8:30 | 8:30 |
| | 9:00 | 9:00 | 9:00 |
| | 9:30 | 9:30 | 9:30 |
| | 10:00 | 10:00 | 10:00 |
| | 10:30 | 10:30 | 10:30 |
| | 11:00 | 11:00 | 11:00 |
| | 11:30 | 11:30 | 11:30 |
| | 12:00 p.m. | 12:00 p.m. | 12:00 p.m. |
| | 12:30 | 12:30 | 12:30 |
| | 1:00 | 1:00 | 1:00 |
| | 1:30 | 1:30 | 1:30 |
| | 2:00 | 2:00 | 2:00 |
| | 2:30 | 2:30 | 2:30 |
| | 3:00 | 3:00 | 3:00 |
| | 3:30 | 3:30 | 3:30 |
| | 4:00 | 4:00 | 4:00 |
| | 4:30 | 4:30 | 4:30 |
| | 5:00 | 5:00 | 5:00 |
| | 5:30 | 5:30 | 5:30 |
| | 6:00 | 6:00 | 6:00 |
| | 6:30 | 6:30 | 6:30 |
| | 7:00 | 7:00 | 7:00 |
| | 7:30 | 7:30 | 7:30 |
| | 8:00 | 8:00 | 8:00 |
| | 8:30 | 8:30 | 8:30 |
| | 9:00 | 9:00 | 9:00 |
| | 9:30 | 9:30 | 9:30 |
| | 10:00 | 10:00 | 10:00 |

| Wednesday | Thursday | Friday | Saturday |
|---|---|---|---|
| 4:00 a.m. | 4:00 a.m. | 4:00 a.m. | 4:00 a.m. |
| 4:30 | 4:30 | 4:30 | 4:30 |
| 5:00 | 5:00 | 5:00 | 5:00 |
| 5:30 | 5:30 | 5:30 | 5:30 |
| 6:00 | 6:00 | 6:00 | 6:00 |
| 6:30 | 6:30 | 6:30 | 6:30 |
| 7:00 | 7:00 | 7:00 | 7:00 |
| 7:30 | 7:30 | 7:30 | 7:30 |
| 8:00 | 8:00 | 8:00 | 8:00 |
| 8:30 | 8:30 | 8:30 | 8:30 |
| 9:00 | 9:00 | 9:00 | 9:00 |
| 9:30 | 9:30 | 9:30 | 9:30 |
| 10:00 | 10:00 | 10:00 | 10:00 |
| 10:30 | 10:30 | 10:30 | 10:30 |
| 11:00 | 11:00 | 11:00 | 11:00 |
| 11:30 | 11:30 | 11:30 | 11:30 |
| 12:00 p.m. | 12:00 p.m. | 12:00 p.m. | 12:00 p.m. |
| 12:30 | 12:30 | 12:30 | 12:30 |
| 1:00 | 1:00 | 1:00 | 1:00 |
| 1:30 | 1:30 | 1:30 | 1:30 |
| 2:00 | 2:00 | 2:00 | 2:00 |
| 2:30 | 2:30 | 2:30 | 2:30 |
| 3:00 | 3:00 | 3:00 | 3:00 |
| 3:30 | 3:30 | 3:30 | 3:30 |
| 4:00 | 4:00 | 4:00 | 4:00 |
| 4:30 | 4:30 | 4:30 | 4:30 |
| 5:00 | 5:00 | 5:00 | 5:00 |
| 5:30 | 5:30 | 5:30 | 5:30 |
| 6:00 | 6:00 | 6:00 | 6:00 |
| 6:30 | 6:30 | 6:30 | 6:30 |
| 7:00 | 7:00 | 7:00 | 7:00 |
| 7:30 | 7:30 | 7:30 | 7:30 |
| 8:00 | 8:00 | 8:00 | 8:00 |
| 8:30 | 8:30 | 8:30 | 8:30 |
| 9:00 | 9:00 | 9:00 | 9:00 |
| 9:30 | 9:30 | 9:30 | 9:30 |
| 10:00 | 10:00 | 10:00 | 10:00 |

# Prep Your *Week*

## Priorities This Week

- 
- 
- 
- 
- 
- 
- 
- 

## Coaching Cycles

## Classroom Snapshots

## Data Meetings

## Team & PD Meetings

## Feedback Meetings

## Other

# Reflect on Your *Week*

| What goals did you accomplish this week? | What goals did you not accomplish this week? Why? |
|---|---|
| What can you do to improve next week? | Things learned and things to remember: |

## Goal & Habit Tracker

| Goal or Habit | Day 1 | Day 2 | Day 3 | Day 4 | Day 5 | Day 6 | Day 7 |
|---|---|---|---|---|---|---|---|
| | | | | | | | |
| | | | | | | | |
| | | | | | | | |
| | | | | | | | |

## Notes

Week:

Notes ↗

| | Sunday | Monday | Tuesday |
|---|---|---|---|
| | 4:00 a.m. | 4:00 a.m. | 4:00 a.m. |
| | 4:30 | 4:30 | 4:30 |
| | 5:00 | 5:00 | 5:00 |
| | 5:30 | 5:30 | 5:30 |
| | 6:00 | 6:00 | 6:00 |
| | 6:30 | 6:30 | 6:30 |
| | 7:00 | 7:00 | 7:00 |
| | 7:30 | 7:30 | 7:30 |
| | 8:00 | 8:00 | 8:00 |
| | 8:30 | 8:30 | 8:30 |
| | 9:00 | 9:00 | 9:00 |
| | 9:30 | 9:30 | 9:30 |
| | 10:00 | 10:00 | 10:00 |
| | 10:30 | 10:30 | 10:30 |
| | 11:00 | 11:00 | 11:00 |
| | 11:30 | 11:30 | 11:30 |
| | 12:00 p.m. | 12:00 p.m. | 12:00 p.m. |
| | 12:30 | 12:30 | 12:30 |
| | 1:00 | 1:00 | 1:00 |
| | 1:30 | 1:30 | 1:30 |
| | 2:00 | 2:00 | 2:00 |
| | 2:30 | 2:30 | 2:30 |
| | 3:00 | 3:00 | 3:00 |
| | 3:30 | 3:30 | 3:30 |
| | 4:00 | 4:00 | 4:00 |
| | 4:30 | 4:30 | 4:30 |
| | 5:00 | 5:00 | 5:00 |
| | 5:30 | 5:30 | 5:30 |
| | 6:00 | 6:00 | 6:00 |
| | 6:30 | 6:30 | 6:30 |
| | 7:00 | 7:00 | 7:00 |
| | 7:30 | 7:30 | 7:30 |
| | 8:00 | 8:00 | 8:00 |
| | 8:30 | 8:30 | 8:30 |
| | 9:00 | 9:00 | 9:00 |
| | 9:30 | 9:30 | 9:30 |
| | 10:00 | 10:00 | 10:00 |

| Wednesday | Thursday | Friday | Saturday |
|---|---|---|---|
| 4:00 a.m. | 4:00 a.m. | 4:00 a.m. | 4:00 a.m. |
| 4:30 | 4:30 | 4:30 | 4:30 |
| 5:00 | 5:00 | 5:00 | 5:00 |
| 5:30 | 5:30 | 5:30 | 5:30 |
| 6:00 | 6:00 | 6:00 | 6:00 |
| 6:30 | 6:30 | 6:30 | 6:30 |
| 7:00 | 7:00 | 7:00 | 7:00 |
| 7:30 | 7:30 | 7:30 | 7:30 |
| 8:00 | 8:00 | 8:00 | 8:00 |
| 8:30 | 8:30 | 8:30 | 8:30 |
| 9:00 | 9:00 | 9:00 | 9:00 |
| 9:30 | 9:30 | 9:30 | 9:30 |
| 10:00 | 10:00 | 10:00 | 10:00 |
| 10:30 | 10:30 | 10:30 | 10:30 |
| 11:00 | 11:00 | 11:00 | 11:00 |
| 11:30 | 11:30 | 11:30 | 11:30 |
| 12:00 p.m. | 12:00 p.m. | 12:00 p.m. | 12:00 p.m. |
| 12:30 | 12:30 | 12:30 | 12:30 |
| 1:00 | 1:00 | 1:00 | 1:00 |
| 1:30 | 1:30 | 1:30 | 1:30 |
| 2:00 | 2:00 | 2:00 | 2:00 |
| 2:30 | 2:30 | 2:30 | 2:30 |
| 3:00 | 3:00 | 3:00 | 3:00 |
| 3:30 | 3:30 | 3:30 | 3:30 |
| 4:00 | 4:00 | 4:00 | 4:00 |
| 4:30 | 4:30 | 4:30 | 4:30 |
| 5:00 | 5:00 | 5:00 | 5:00 |
| 5:30 | 5:30 | 5:30 | 5:30 |
| 6:00 | 6:00 | 6:00 | 6:00 |
| 6:30 | 6:30 | 6:30 | 6:30 |
| 7:00 | 7:00 | 7:00 | 7:00 |
| 7:30 | 7:30 | 7:30 | 7:30 |
| 8:00 | 8:00 | 8:00 | 8:00 |
| 8:30 | 8:30 | 8:30 | 8:30 |
| 9:00 | 9:00 | 9:00 | 9:00 |
| 9:30 | 9:30 | 9:30 | 9:30 |
| 10:00 | 10:00 | 10:00 | 10:00 |

JUNE

# Prep Your *Week*

## Priorities This Week

- 
- 
- 
- 
- 
- 
- 
- 

## Coaching Cycles

## Classroom Snapshots

## Data Meetings

## Team & PD Meetings

## Feedback Meetings

## Other

# Reflect on Your Week

| What goals did you accomplish this week? | What goals did you not accomplish this week? Why? |
|---|---|
| What can you do to improve next week? | Things learned and things to remember: |

## Goal & Habit Tracker

| Goal or Habit | Day 1 | Day 2 | Day 3 | Day 4 | Day 5 | Day 6 | Day 7 |
|---|---|---|---|---|---|---|---|
| | | | | | | | |
| | | | | | | | |
| | | | | | | | |
| | | | | | | | |

## Notes

Week:

Notes ↴

| Sunday | Monday | Tuesday |
|---|---|---|
| 4:00 a.m. | 4:00 a.m. | 4:00 a.m. |
| 4:30 | 4:30 | 4:30 |
| 5:00 | 5:00 | 5:00 |
| 5:30 | 5:30 | 5:30 |
| 6:00 | 6:00 | 6:00 |
| 6:30 | 6:30 | 6:30 |
| 7:00 | 7:00 | 7:00 |
| 7:30 | 7:30 | 7:30 |
| 8:00 | 8:00 | 8:00 |
| 8:30 | 8:30 | 8:30 |
| 9:00 | 9:00 | 9:00 |
| 9:30 | 9:30 | 9:30 |
| 10:00 | 10:00 | 10:00 |
| 10:30 | 10:30 | 10:30 |
| 11:00 | 11:00 | 11:00 |
| 11:30 | 11:30 | 11:30 |
| 12:00 p.m. | 12:00 p.m. | 12:00 p.m. |
| 12:30 | 12:30 | 12:30 |
| 1:00 | 1:00 | 1:00 |
| 1:30 | 1:30 | 1:30 |
| 2:00 | 2:00 | 2:00 |
| 2:30 | 2:30 | 2:30 |
| 3:00 | 3:00 | 3:00 |
| 3:30 | 3:30 | 3:30 |
| 4:00 | 4:00 | 4:00 |
| 4:30 | 4:30 | 4:30 |
| 5:00 | 5:00 | 5:00 |
| 5:30 | 5:30 | 5:30 |
| 6:00 | 6:00 | 6:00 |
| 6:30 | 6:30 | 6:30 |
| 7:00 | 7:00 | 7:00 |
| 7:30 | 7:30 | 7:30 |
| 8:00 | 8:00 | 8:00 |
| 8:30 | 8:30 | 8:30 |
| 9:00 | 9:00 | 9:00 |
| 9:30 | 9:30 | 9:30 |
| 10:00 | 10:00 | 10:00 |

| Wednesday | Thursday | Friday | Saturday |
|---|---|---|---|
| 4:00 a.m. | 4:00 a.m. | 4:00 a.m. | 4:00 a.m. |
| 4:30 | 4:30 | 4:30 | 4:30 |
| 5:00 | 5:00 | 5:00 | 5:00 |
| 5:30 | 5:30 | 5:30 | 5:30 |
| 6:00 | 6:00 | 6:00 | 6:00 |
| 6:30 | 6:30 | 6:30 | 6:30 |
| 7:00 | 7:00 | 7:00 | 7:00 |
| 7:30 | 7:30 | 7:30 | 7:30 |
| 8:00 | 8:00 | 8:00 | 8:00 |
| 8:30 | 8:30 | 8:30 | 8:30 |
| 9:00 | 9:00 | 9:00 | 9:00 |
| 9:30 | 9:30 | 9:30 | 9:30 |
| 10:00 | 10:00 | 10:00 | 10:00 |
| 10:30 | 10:30 | 10:30 | 10:30 |
| 11:00 | 11:00 | 11:00 | 11:00 |
| 11:30 | 11:30 | 11:30 | 11:30 |
| 12:00 p.m. | 12:00 p.m. | 12:00 p.m. | 12:00 p.m. |
| 12:30 | 12:30 | 12:30 | 12:30 |
| 1:00 | 1:00 | 1:00 | 1:00 |
| 1:30 | 1:30 | 1:30 | 1:30 |
| 2:00 | 2:00 | 2:00 | 2:00 |
| 2:30 | 2:30 | 2:30 | 2:30 |
| 3:00 | 3:00 | 3:00 | 3:00 |
| 3:30 | 3:30 | 3:30 | 3:30 |
| 4:00 | 4:00 | 4:00 | 4:00 |
| 4:30 | 4:30 | 4:30 | 4:30 |
| 5:00 | 5:00 | 5:00 | 5:00 |
| 5:30 | 5:30 | 5:30 | 5:30 |
| 6:00 | 6:00 | 6:00 | 6:00 |
| 6:30 | 6:30 | 6:30 | 6:30 |
| 7:00 | 7:00 | 7:00 | 7:00 |
| 7:30 | 7:30 | 7:30 | 7:30 |
| 8:00 | 8:00 | 8:00 | 8:00 |
| 8:30 | 8:30 | 8:30 | 8:30 |
| 9:00 | 9:00 | 9:00 | 9:00 |
| 9:30 | 9:30 | 9:30 | 9:30 |
| 10:00 | 10:00 | 10:00 | 10:00 |

# Prep Your *Week*

## Priorities This Week

- 
- 
- 
- 
- 
- 
- 
- 

## Coaching Cycles

## Classroom Snapshots

## Data Meetings

## Team & PD Meetings

## Feedback Meetings

## Other

# Reflect on Your Week

| What goals did you accomplish this week? | What goals did you not accomplish this week? Why? |
|---|---|
| What can you do to improve next week? | Things learned and things to remember: |

## Goal & Habit Tracker

| Goal or Habit | Day 1 | Day 2 | Day 3 | Day 4 | Day 5 | Day 6 | Day 7 |
|---|---|---|---|---|---|---|---|
|  |  |  |  |  |  |  |  |
|  |  |  |  |  |  |  |  |
|  |  |  |  |  |  |  |  |
|  |  |  |  |  |  |  |  |

## Notes

Notes

| Sunday | Monday | Tuesday |
|---|---|---|
| 4:00 a.m. | 4:00 a.m. | 4:00 a.m. |
| 4:30 | 4:30 | 4:30 |
| 5:00 | 5:00 | 5:00 |
| 5:30 | 5:30 | 5:30 |
| 6:00 | 6:00 | 6:00 |
| 6:30 | 6:30 | 6:30 |
| 7:00 | 7:00 | 7:00 |
| 7:30 | 7:30 | 7:30 |
| 8:00 | 8:00 | 8:00 |
| 8:30 | 8:30 | 8:30 |
| 9:00 | 9:00 | 9:00 |
| 9:30 | 9:30 | 9:30 |
| 10:00 | 10:00 | 10:00 |
| 10:30 | 10:30 | 10:30 |
| 11:00 | 11:00 | 11:00 |
| 11:30 | 11:30 | 11:30 |
| 12:00 p.m. | 12:00 p.m. | 12:00 p.m. |
| 12:30 | 12:30 | 12:30 |
| 1:00 | 1:00 | 1:00 |
| 1:30 | 1:30 | 1:30 |
| 2:00 | 2:00 | 2:00 |
| 2:30 | 2:30 | 2:30 |
| 3:00 | 3:00 | 3:00 |
| 3:30 | 3:30 | 3:30 |
| 4:00 | 4:00 | 4:00 |
| 4:30 | 4:30 | 4:30 |
| 5:00 | 5:00 | 5:00 |
| 5:30 | 5:30 | 5:30 |
| 6:00 | 6:00 | 6:00 |
| 6:30 | 6:30 | 6:30 |
| 7:00 | 7:00 | 7:00 |
| 7:30 | 7:30 | 7:30 |
| 8:00 | 8:00 | 8:00 |
| 8:30 | 8:30 | 8:30 |
| 9:00 | 9:00 | 9:00 |
| 9:30 | 9:30 | 9:30 |
| 10:00 | 10:00 | 10:00 |

| Wednesday | Thursday | Friday | Saturday |
|---|---|---|---|
| 4:00 a.m. | 4:00 a.m. | 4:00 a.m. | 4:00 a.m. |
| 4:30 | 4:30 | 4:30 | 4:30 |
| 5:00 | 5:00 | 5:00 | 5:00 |
| 5:30 | 5:30 | 5:30 | 5:30 |
| 6:00 | 6:00 | 6:00 | 6:00 |
| 6:30 | 6:30 | 6:30 | 6:30 |
| 7:00 | 7:00 | 7:00 | 7:00 |
| 7:30 | 7:30 | 7:30 | 7:30 |
| 8:00 | 8:00 | 8:00 | 8:00 |
| 8:30 | 8:30 | 8:30 | 8:30 |
| 9:00 | 9:00 | 9:00 | 9:00 |
| 9:30 | 9:30 | 9:30 | 9:30 |
| 10:00 | 10:00 | 10:00 | 10:00 |
| 10:30 | 10:30 | 10:30 | 10:30 |
| 11:00 | 11:00 | 11:00 | 11:00 |
| 11:30 | 11:30 | 11:30 | 11:30 |
| 12:00 p.m. | 12:00 p.m. | 12:00 p.m. | 12:00 p.m. |
| 12:30 | 12:30 | 12:30 | 12:30 |
| 1:00 | 1:00 | 1:00 | 1:00 |
| 1:30 | 1:30 | 1:30 | 1:30 |
| 2:00 | 2:00 | 2:00 | 2:00 |
| 2:30 | 2:30 | 2:30 | 2:30 |
| 3:00 | 3:00 | 3:00 | 3:00 |
| 3:30 | 3:30 | 3:30 | 3:30 |
| 4:00 | 4:00 | 4:00 | 4:00 |
| 4:30 | 4:30 | 4:30 | 4:30 |
| 5:00 | 5:00 | 5:00 | 5:00 |
| 5:30 | 5:30 | 5:30 | 5:30 |
| 6:00 | 6:00 | 6:00 | 6:00 |
| 6:30 | 6:30 | 6:30 | 6:30 |
| 7:00 | 7:00 | 7:00 | 7:00 |
| 7:30 | 7:30 | 7:30 | 7:30 |
| 8:00 | 8:00 | 8:00 | 8:00 |
| 8:30 | 8:30 | 8:30 | 8:30 |
| 9:00 | 9:00 | 9:00 | 9:00 |
| 9:30 | 9:30 | 9:30 | 9:30 |
| 10:00 | 10:00 | 10:00 | 10:00 |

JUNE

# Prep Your *Week*

## Priorities This Week

- 
- 
- 
- 
- 
- 
- 
- 

## Coaching Cycles

## Classroom Snapshots

## Data Meetings

## Team & PD Meetings

## Feedback Meetings

## Other

# Reflect on Your Week

| | |
|---|---|
| What goals did you accomplish this week? | What goals did you not accomplish this week? Why? |
| What can you do to improve next week? | Things learned and things to remember: |

## Goal & Habit Tracker

| Goal or Habit | Day 1 | Day 2 | Day 3 | Day 4 | Day 5 | Day 6 | Day 7 |
|---|---|---|---|---|---|---|---|
| | | | | | | | |
| | | | | | | | |
| | | | | | | | |
| | | | | | | | |

## Notes

Week:

Notes

| | Sunday | Monday | Tuesday |
|---|---|---|---|
| | 4:00 a.m. | 4:00 a.m. | 4:00 a.m. |
| | 4:30 | 4:30 | 4:30 |
| | 5:00 | 5:00 | 5:00 |
| | 5:30 | 5:30 | 5:30 |
| | 6:00 | 6:00 | 6:00 |
| | 6:30 | 6:30 | 6:30 |
| | 7:00 | 7:00 | 7:00 |
| | 7:30 | 7:30 | 7:30 |
| | 8:00 | 8:00 | 8:00 |
| | 8:30 | 8:30 | 8:30 |
| | 9:00 | 9:00 | 9:00 |
| | 9:30 | 9:30 | 9:30 |
| | 10:00 | 10:00 | 10:00 |
| | 10:30 | 10:30 | 10:30 |
| | 11:00 | 11:00 | 11:00 |
| | 11:30 | 11:30 | 11:30 |
| | 12:00 p.m. | 12:00 p.m. | 12:00 p.m. |
| | 12:30 | 12:30 | 12:30 |
| | 1:00 | 1:00 | 1:00 |
| | 1:30 | 1:30 | 1:30 |
| | 2:00 | 2:00 | 2:00 |
| | 2:30 | 2:30 | 2:30 |
| | 3:00 | 3:00 | 3:00 |
| | 3:30 | 3:30 | 3:30 |
| | 4:00 | 4:00 | 4:00 |
| | 4:30 | 4:30 | 4:30 |
| | 5:00 | 5:00 | 5:00 |
| | 5:30 | 5:30 | 5:30 |
| | 6:00 | 6:00 | 6:00 |
| | 6:30 | 6:30 | 6:30 |
| | 7:00 | 7:00 | 7:00 |
| | 7:30 | 7:30 | 7:30 |
| | 8:00 | 8:00 | 8:00 |
| | 8:30 | 8:30 | 8:30 |
| | 9:00 | 9:00 | 9:00 |
| | 9:30 | 9:30 | 9:30 |
| | 10:00 | 10:00 | 10:00 |

| Wednesday | Thursday | Friday | Saturday |
|---|---|---|---|
| 4:00 a.m. | 4:00 a.m. | 4:00 a.m. | 4:00 a.m. |
| 4:30 | 4:30 | 4:30 | 4:30 |
| 5:00 | 5:00 | 5:00 | 5:00 |
| 5:30 | 5:30 | 5:30 | 5:30 |
| 6:00 | 6:00 | 6:00 | 6:00 |
| 6:30 | 6:30 | 6:30 | 6:30 |
| 7:00 | 7:00 | 7:00 | 7:00 |
| 7:30 | 7:30 | 7:30 | 7:30 |
| 8:00 | 8:00 | 8:00 | 8:00 |
| 8:30 | 8:30 | 8:30 | 8:30 |
| 9:00 | 9:00 | 9:00 | 9:00 |
| 9:30 | 9:30 | 9:30 | 9:30 |
| 10:00 | 10:00 | 10:00 | 10:00 |
| 10:30 | 10:30 | 10:30 | 10:30 |
| 11:00 | 11:00 | 11:00 | 11:00 |
| 11:30 | 11:30 | 11:30 | 11:30 |
| 12:00 p.m. | 12:00 p.m. | 12:00 p.m. | 12:00 p.m. |
| 12:30 | 12:30 | 12:30 | 12:30 |
| 1:00 | 1:00 | 1:00 | 1:00 |
| 1:30 | 1:30 | 1:30 | 1:30 |
| 2:00 | 2:00 | 2:00 | 2:00 |
| 2:30 | 2:30 | 2:30 | 2:30 |
| 3:00 | 3:00 | 3:00 | 3:00 |
| 3:30 | 3:30 | 3:30 | 3:30 |
| 4:00 | 4:00 | 4:00 | 4:00 |
| 4:30 | 4:30 | 4:30 | 4:30 |
| 5:00 | 5:00 | 5:00 | 5:00 |
| 5:30 | 5:30 | 5:30 | 5:30 |
| 6:00 | 6:00 | 6:00 | 6:00 |
| 6:30 | 6:30 | 6:30 | 6:30 |
| 7:00 | 7:00 | 7:00 | 7:00 |
| 7:30 | 7:30 | 7:30 | 7:30 |
| 8:00 | 8:00 | 8:00 | 8:00 |
| 8:30 | 8:30 | 8:30 | 8:30 |
| 9:00 | 9:00 | 9:00 | 9:00 |
| 9:30 | 9:30 | 9:30 | 9:30 |
| 10:00 | 10:00 | 10:00 | 10:00 |

JUNE

### Simply Instructional Coaching
*Nicole S. Turner*
Get real talk about the trials and joys of being an instructional coach. Drawing from the latest research and personal experience, author Nicole S. Turner offers foundational advice, a practical coaching framework, and reflection opportunities to help you level up your career.
**BKG108**

### 180 Days of Self-Care for Busy Educators
*Tina H. Boogren*
Rely on *180 Days of Self-Care for Busy Educators* to help you lead a happier, healthier more fulfilled life inside and outside of the classroom. With Tina H. Boogren's guidance, you will work through 36 weeks of self-care strategies during the school year.
**BKF920**

### Everyday Instructional Coaching
*Nathan D. Lang-Raad*
Discover seven drivers you can use to improve your daily coaching practices: collaboration, transparency, inquiry, discourse, reverberation, sincerity, and influence. Each of the book's chapters defines, describes, and offers tips for implementing one of the seven drivers.
**BKF802**

### Coaching for Significant and Sustained Change in the Classroom
*Tom Roy*
Keeping educators' skills sharp in a constantly changing world can be a challenge. But coaching provides a focused, one-on-one plan for improvement. Designed for coaches and administrators, this practical guide details how to build a strong coaching program that drives significant schoolwide change.
**BKL038**

## Solution Tree | Press
a division of
Solution Tree

Visit SolutionTree.com or call 800.733.6786 to order.

## Wait! Your professional development journey doesn't have to end with the last pages of this book.

We realize improving student learning doesn't happen overnight. And your school or district shouldn't be left to puzzle out all the details of this process alone.

**No matter where you are on the journey, we're committed to helping you get to the next stage.**

Take advantage of everything from **custom workshops** to **keynote presentations** and **interactive web and video conferencing**. We can even help you develop an action plan tailored to fit your specific needs.

*Let's get the conversation started.*

Call 888.763.9045 today.

SolutionTree.com